LEGENDARY LOCALS

OF

CONCORD

NORTH CAROLINA

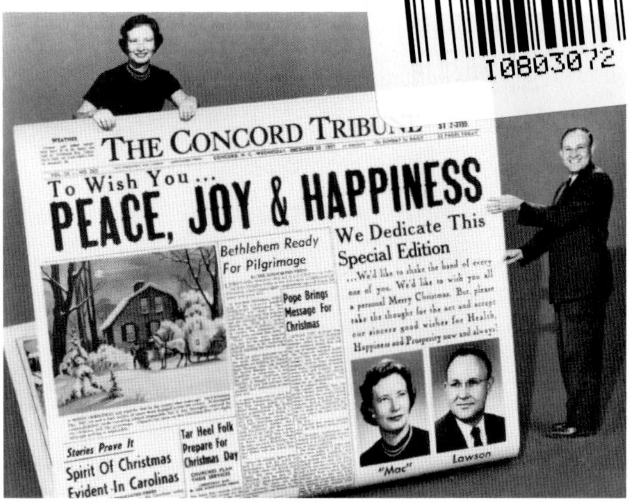

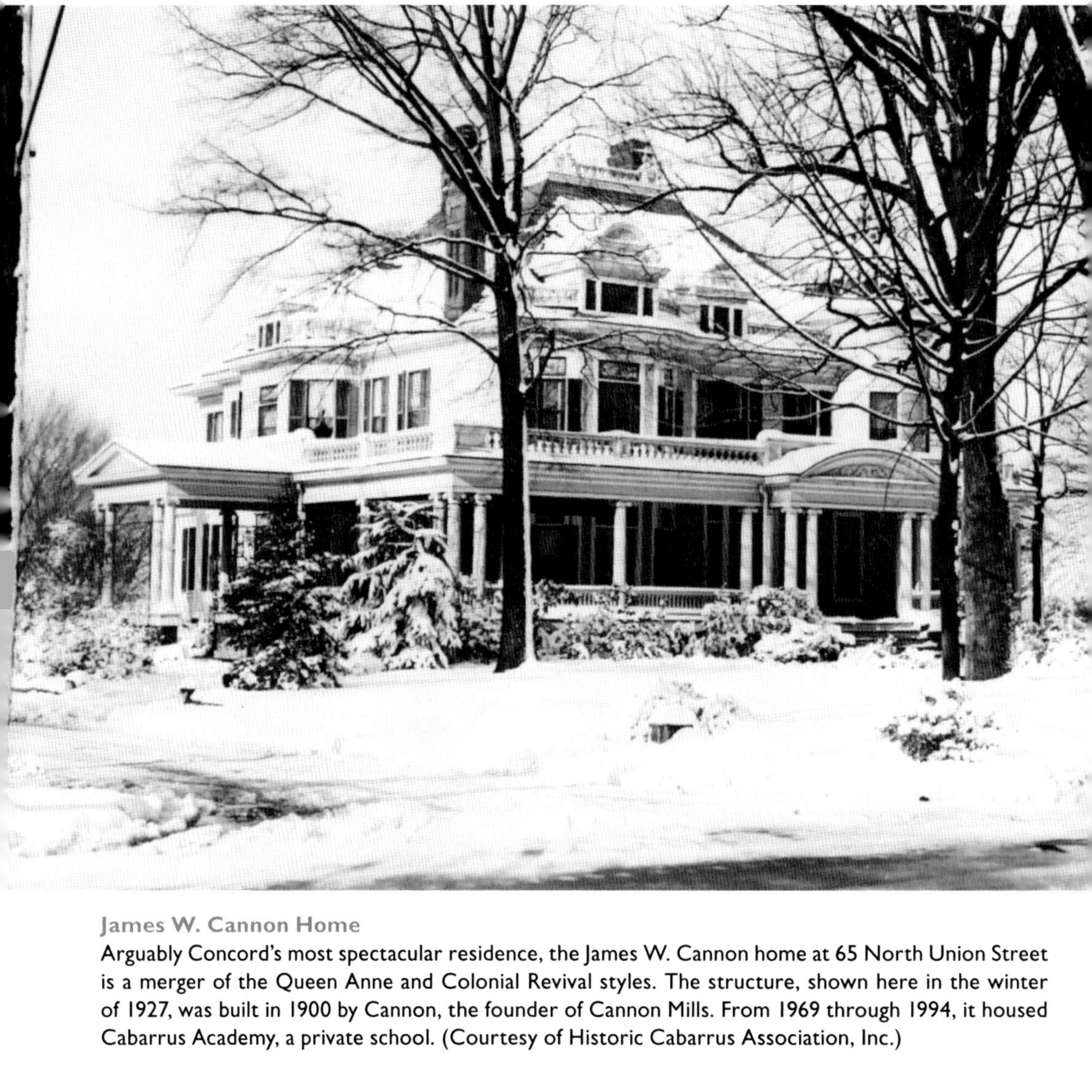

James W. Cannon Home

Arguably Concord's most spectacular residence, the James W. Cannon home at 65 North Union Street is a merger of the Queen Anne and Colonial Revival styles. The structure, shown here in the winter of 1927, was built in 1900 by Cannon, the founder of Cannon Mills. From 1969 through 1994, it housed Cabarrus Academy, a private school. (Courtesy of Historic Cabarrus Association, Inc.)

Page 1: Lawson Bonds

From twitching toddlers to beautiful brides, hundreds of baby boomers grinned "cheese" before Bonds (the Olan Mills of Concord) and his wife, Maxine "Mac." When he was not snapping smiles in his downtown portrait studio, located upstairs at 38 Union Street South, Bonds was a photographer for the *Concord Tribune*. His studio was in operation from the mid-1950s until 1988. Bonds died in 2010. (Courtesy of Concord Public Library.)

LEGENDARY LOCALS

OF

CONCORD

NORTH CAROLINA

MICHAEL EURY

LEGENDARY LOCALS

ISBN 978-1-4671-0101-1

Legendary Locals is an imprint of Arcadia Publishing
Charleston, South Carolina

Printed in the United States of America

Library of Congress Control Number: 2013936166

For all general information, please contact Arcadia Publishing:
Telephone 843-853-2070
Fax 843-853-0044
E-mail sales@arcadiapublishing.com
For customer service and orders:
Toll-Free 1-888-313-2665

Visit us on the Internet at www.arcadiapublishing.com

Dedication
To Concord's community and business leaders: may your actions of today make you the legends of tomorrow.

On the Front Cover: Clockwise from top left:
Charles A. Cannon, businessman and philanthropist (Courtesy of Kannapolis History Associates; see page 28), Daniel Truhitte, entertainer (Courtesy of Bella Zu Photography; see page 119), Warren C. Coleman, businessman (Courtesy of the Library of Congress; see page 14), Mable Parker McLean, educator (Courtesy of Historic Cabarrus Association, Inc.; see page 99), Ruth Coltrane Cannon, cultural patron (Courtesy of Historic Cabarrus Association, Inc.; see page 30); Daniel Branson Coltrane, banker (Courtesy of Concord Public Library; see page 24), Tracy N. Spencer, veterinarian (Courtesy of the Boys and Girls Club; see page 92), Robert L. Burrage Jr., businessman (Courtesy of Robert E. Burrage Sr.; see page 62), William "Billy" Goodman, baseball player (Courtesy of Cloetta; see page 108).

On the Back Cover: From left to right:
The Avett Brothers, entertainers (Courtesy of Ramseur Records; see page 122), Lester D. Coltrane Sr., businessman (Courtesy of Historic Cabarrus Association, Inc.; see page 26).

CONTENTS

ACKNOWLEDGMENTS

When researching the community's history for my previous book with Arcadia Publishing, Images of America: *Concord* (2011), I became captivated by the personal stories of Concord's founders, movers and shakers, and everyday Joes. And thus, it is a great honor to share many of those stories in this book. (I only wish that space allowed me to include everyone I consider legendary.)

This volume would not be possible without the foundation of decades of research by Concord's historians, newspaper reporters, and photographers. I am indebted to Patricia Curl of the Lore History Room at the Cabarrus County Public Library, Concord Branch (herewith Concord Public Library), for assisting with my research, providing images, and reviewing my manuscript for accuracy. Trish is one of Concord's living legends.

I wish to thank Helen Arthur-Cornett, my mentor and friend, for her input and manuscript review. Helen has forgotten more about Concord's heritage than I will ever know, and her assistance has been invaluable.

My brother, librarian John S. Eury, was also vital to my research.

I also gratefully acknowledge Historic Cabarrus Association, Inc., upon whose board of directors I am privileged to serve, for allowing me access to its archive of images from its Concord Museum and Confederate Memorial Hall collections. Unless otherwise noted, all images appear courtesy of Historic Cabarrus Association, Inc.

The following people and organizations provided information, access to special collections, permissions, or helped in some fashion: Mona Barnhardt, Frances Brown, Lee Buchanan, Allen Craven, Ford Craven, Bernard Davis Jr., Aggie Eury, Sue Byrd Eury, Joanne Gonnerman, Gail Honeycutt, the *Independent Tribune*, Debra Johnson, Kannapolis History Associates, Gail Moon Kiser, Michael Knox, Rev. Andy Langford, Lisa Linker, Lois Marlow, Geraldine Mills, Peg Morrison, James Nix, Alex Patterson, George M. Patterson, Jim Ramseur, Cindy Little Ritchie, John Robinson of Sideshow World, Jim Summers, Mary Wilder, and Anne Wilson. My sincere thanks go to each of you.

Finally, my deepest gratitude goes to my wife, Rose Rummel-Eury, who adopted my hometown as hers, and who listens to my ramblings about local stories and loves me enough to feign interest when her mind might be elsewhere.

INTRODUCTION

Concord's premier legendary local never resided in this city. Emigrating from France to coastal North Carolina in 1776, Stephen Cabarrus earnestly devoted himself to the common good, working his way through local government toward an eventual role as speaker of the North Carolina House of Commons.

Shortly before Cabarrus's arrival in the Tar Heel State, the region that would soon take his name began to take shape. In the mid-1700s Scotch-Irish and German pioneers settled in Mecklenburg County in what would become the Concord area, its fertile countryside ripe for homes and farming. These were devout, indomitable, and often stubborn people. Nine of them, young men in their late teens and early 20s, would become renowned as the Cabarrus Black Boys, after initiating what could very well be the colonies' first strike for independence in May 1771.

In 1792, determined locals splintered from Mecklenburg, creating a new county that the state legislature named after Cabarrus. The most obstinate among them squabbled over the site of the county seat, prompting Speaker Cabarrus to pen a rousing 1794 letter to the county's founders beseeching a "concord" that not only inspired the city's name but also that of its main street, Union.

In an April 1796 county court session, plots within a 26-acre tract between Three Mile Branch and the Indian Trading Path were auctioned to the first landowners of Concord. Just a stone's throw from town in the Midland area of Cabarrus County, the United States' first documented gold discovery occurred in 1799 on John Reed's farm, today known as the historical site Reed Gold Mine. A regional gold boom followed. Concord incorporated in 1806, and organized city government began in 1837 with a small group of commissioners functioning under Mayor J.L. Beard (then magistrate of police).

Mother Nature played an important role in helping the nascent city cultivate its original industry. Western Cabarrus County's "black jack" soil sprouted abundant cotton, which savvy businessmen were keen to exploit. Concord's first textile mill, the Concord Steam Cotton Factory, opened shop in 1839 just north of the city limits in what became known as the Forest Hill township. Originally, the Methodists in Forest Hill preferred to keep their distance from grubby downtown Concord, whose citizens they regarded as disorderly, but in the late 1880s, the township officially incorporated into the city.

The Concord Steam Cotton Factory, now known as Locke Mill Plaza, fast-tracked a succession of mills, earning fortunes for investors such as Paul Barringer, John M. Odell, and James W. Cannon. From this prosperity flourished the august Victorian homes of North Union Street, their imposing architecture muted today only by the shadow of towering elm and oak trees. Similar residential development began south of downtown on South Union Street.

In the early 1850s, a railroad—a gateway for the export of cotton and cloth products—was constructed on Concord's west side on Depot Street (now Cabarrus Avenue). Concord was then unmistakably a mill town, providing opportunities for ambitious investors and factory workers while slaves performed the backbreaking labor of picking cotton.

The Civil War negatively impacted the city's textile business, robbing its workforce for combat and requiring those left behind to manufacture material for uniforms for Confederate soldiers. Reconstruction was economically cruel to Concord as well, but after a brief occupation by US forces, Concord's textile business prospered anew.

Toward the end of the 19th century, Concord began a metamorphosis, its dense cluster of bustling businesses illuminated in 1888 by an electrical system. Warren C. Coleman broke racial barriers as the state's wealthiest African American (his mercantile and real estate ventures were highly successful), and he made history when he staffed his cotton mill exclusively with black workers. Confederate veteran Daniel Branson Coltrane opened the town's first financial institution, the Concord National Bank, and his son Lester D. Coltrane Sr. started the Concord Telephone Company.

Concord's streets in the late 1800s and early 1900s were unpaved and jammed with horses, mules, buggies, and pedestrians. A steam-powered trolley chugged along Union Street, choking the air with its billows. Soon, however, the affluence of the city's textile mills buoyed a movement to gentrify the downtown: streets were paved, elegant streetlights were added, and stately municipal buildings, banks, businesses, and churches developed. Automobiles and buses supplanted horses and wagons. Concord's dual role as the seat of Cabarrus County and as the business and entertainment nerve net of the region attracted people in nearby communities to "come in to town." Drugstores, snack bars, movie theaters, furniture stores, department stores, jewelers, a shoe fix-it shop, dime stores, gas stations, grocers, and music marts—you name it, downtown Concord offered it.

Concord's population steadily increased throughout the 1900s, settling by the mid-20th century at approximately 18,000, a comfortable figure that remained for several decades. During the past 30-plus years, the recruitment of midsized and large employers, land annexation, and the high-octane evolution of the motorsports and tourism businesses have recreated Concord into a dynamic city of 60 square miles and 81,000 residents.

Some old-timers might grouse that Concord has grown "too big for its britches," but this city has never lost sight of its past as it has raced into the future. In early 2013, Union Street was named People's Choice for Great Main Street in a statewide initiative sponsored by the American Planning Association. This alluring avenue bridges the community with a history that was forged by those who leapt bravely into uncertainty, breached insurmountable barriers, made their families proud, and tickled our funny bones. These are the legendary locals of Concord, our friends and neighbors whose stories we cherish.

CHAPTER ONE

Piedmont Pioneers

Imagine stepping into the unknown—a frightening proposition that might intimidate even the heartiest of souls.

For the most industrious of Concord's earliest citizens, their achievements, which have been viewed through the lens of history and have, perhaps, been taken for granted, must have given them pause. The first textile businessmen had no guarantee that Concord's cotton boom would last, and some, like John M. Odell and Warren C. Coleman, ultimately failed in their enterprises. Empire builders such as textile baron James W. Cannon, and more recently, motorsports mogul Bruton Smith, were at one time untried but motivated, and they only achieved their successes through hard work, good instincts, and perseverance.

Consider the unbearable pressure that weighed upon Frederick H. Watkins, Concord's first doctor of color, or Leland S. Cozart, the first African American president of Barber-Scotia College, as they shattered ethnic barriers to establish themselves within their professions. The same can be said of Lawrence Evans, Concord's first black cop, who stared down not only criminals but also racists. Mary Snead Boger stonewalled adversity of a different type to preserve a landmark and create a cultural institution.

Others among these Piedmont pioneers were simply living their lives and supporting their families when chance nudged them into the role of trailblazer. John Reed's farm occupied his attention, and he gave little regard to the large stone his son Conrad found in a creek on the family's property, at first unaware that he had literally struck gold. Chris Measmer, the youngest North Carolinian to be elected a county commissioner, would not regard himself as a pioneer, but nevertheless proved that politics does not have to remain the domain of elders.

Regardless of their circumstances, these legendary locals opened doors through which a future of hope and harmony would emerge.

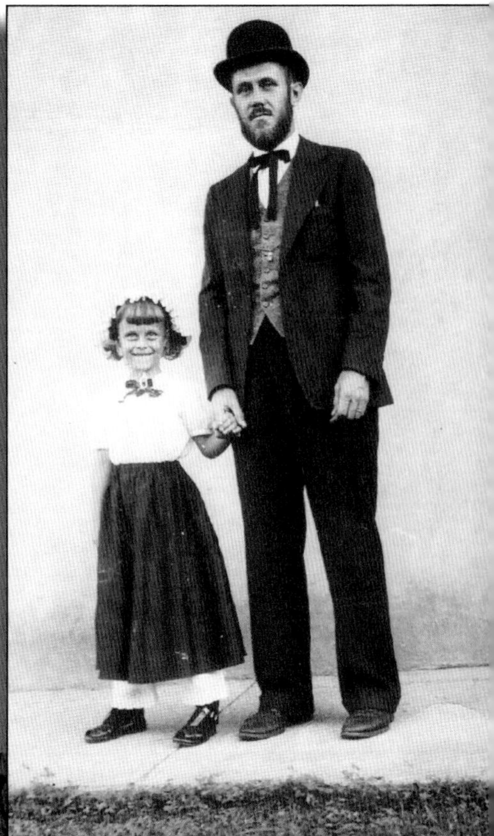

John Reed

In 1799, this German immigrant's 12-year-old son Conrad unearthed a 17-pound stone in Little Meadow Creek that the family used as a doorstop for three years. Once the rock was documented as the nation's first gold find, a regional mining rush followed. At the discovery's sesquicentennial in 1949, Concord men were "required" to grow a beard befitting of the mining era, as did John A. Fisher, shown here with daughter Rosemary. Clean-shaven men who refused to comply with this directive were comically sentenced to "jail." A beard-growing contest and other festivities commemorated this anniversary. Reed's former farmland, just outside of Concord near Midland, is now Reed Gold Mine, a state historic site. The 1980s photograph below shows a group about to begin a mine tour. (Right, courtesy of Rosemary Goodman; below, courtesy of Kannapolis History Associates.)

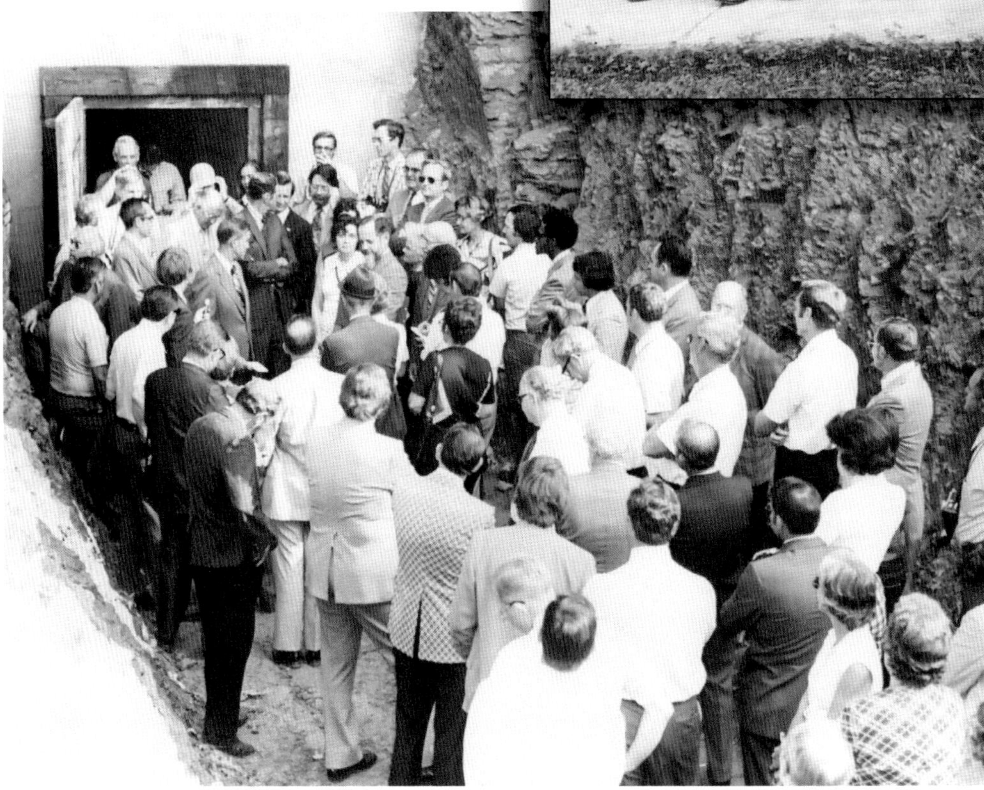

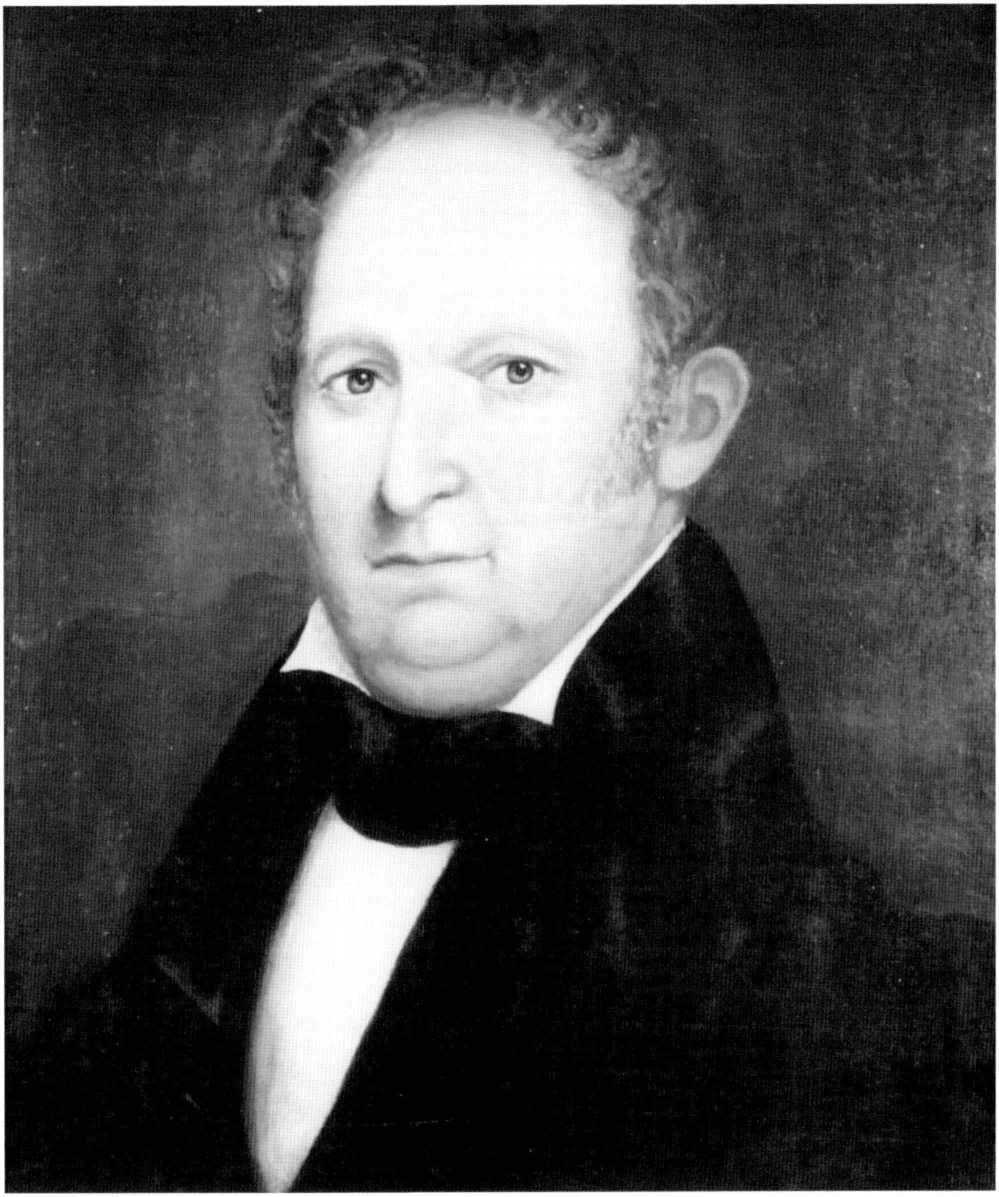

Paul Barringer

The son of John Paul Barringer, a pugnacious patriot whose gravestone was defiled by bitter British troops, General Barringer distinguished himself as a military leader during the War of 1812. In civilian life, he served as president of Concord's first textile mill, the Concord Steam Cotton Factory, established in 1839. Of his eight children, his son Rufus Barringer was a Confederate general, son David was the ambassador to Spain and served in Congress with Abraham Lincoln, and youngest son Victor was a prominent Concord judge. One of the city's most famous historical events occurred in Victor Barringer's home on North Union Street. On April 18, 1865, fifteen days after the fall of Richmond to Union forces during the waning days of the Civil War, Barringer offered a night's lodging to Confederate president Jefferson Davis, who was en route to Atlanta. The home was razed in 1971 to make way for the Concord branch of the Cabarrus County Public Library.

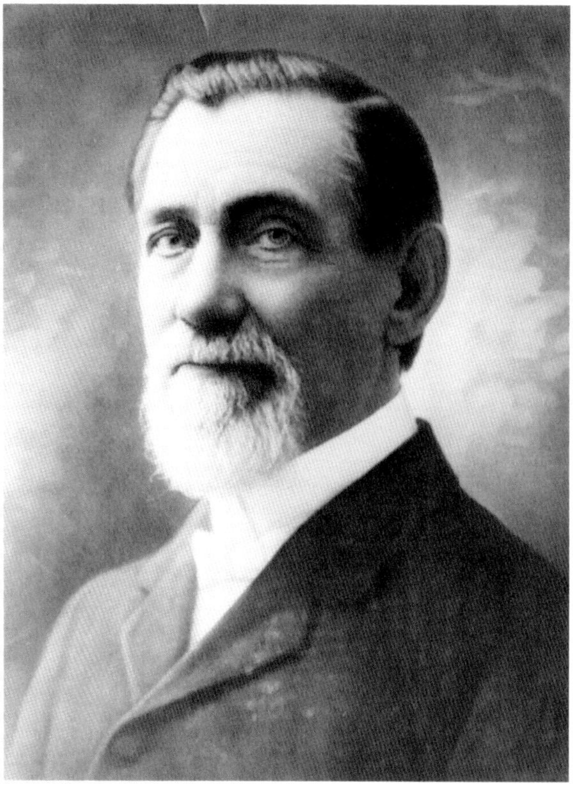

John M. Odell

In 1877, Odell, a former Confederate army captain and a teacher, purchased the Concord Steam Cotton Factory, defunct since the 1873 financial panic. The revitalization of the plant (renamed Odell Mills) that followed stimulated the growth of its surrounding community, Forest Hill, including the establishment of Forest Hill Methodist Church, originally adjacent to the mill. Odell's mansion, overlooking his mill at North Union and Buffalo Streets, remains one of Concord's most celebrated homes today. In the yard of the home is a boulder behind which Odell purportedly ducked for cover during a Civil War battle in Virginia; postwar, he had the stone transported to Concord as a memento.

Odell's empire unfortunately went up in flames in August 1908 when his plant, shown in the photograph below, burned to the ground, bankrupting its owner. (Below, courtesy of Concord Public Library.)

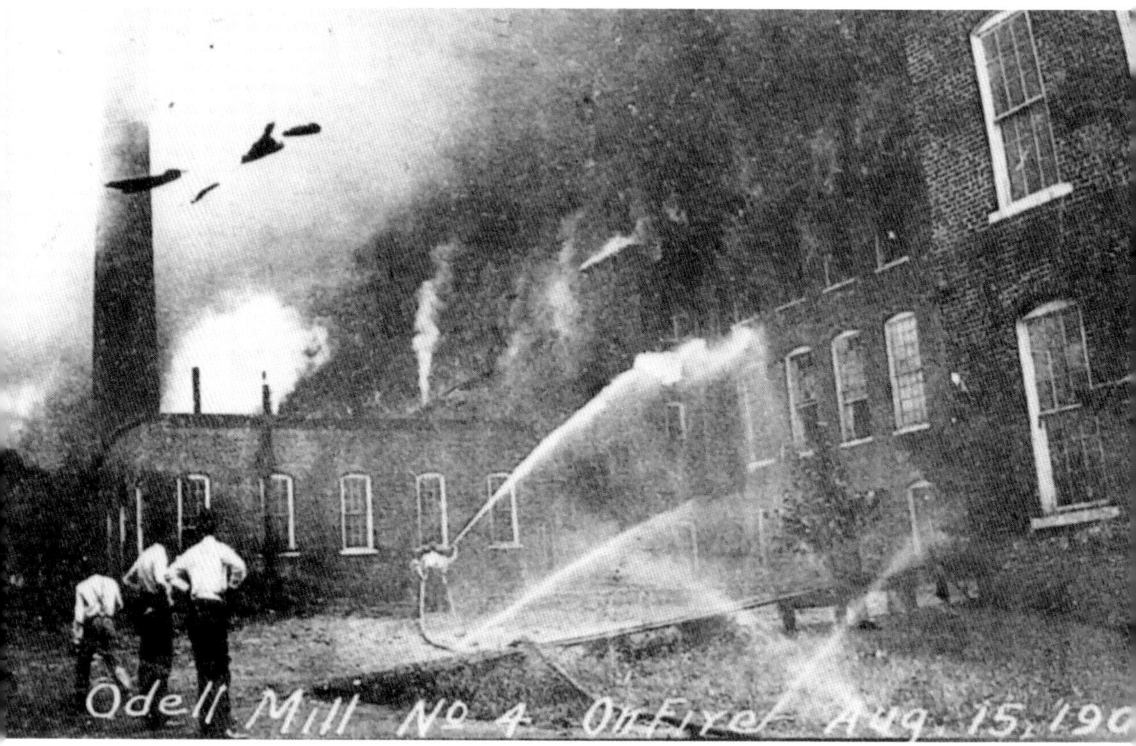

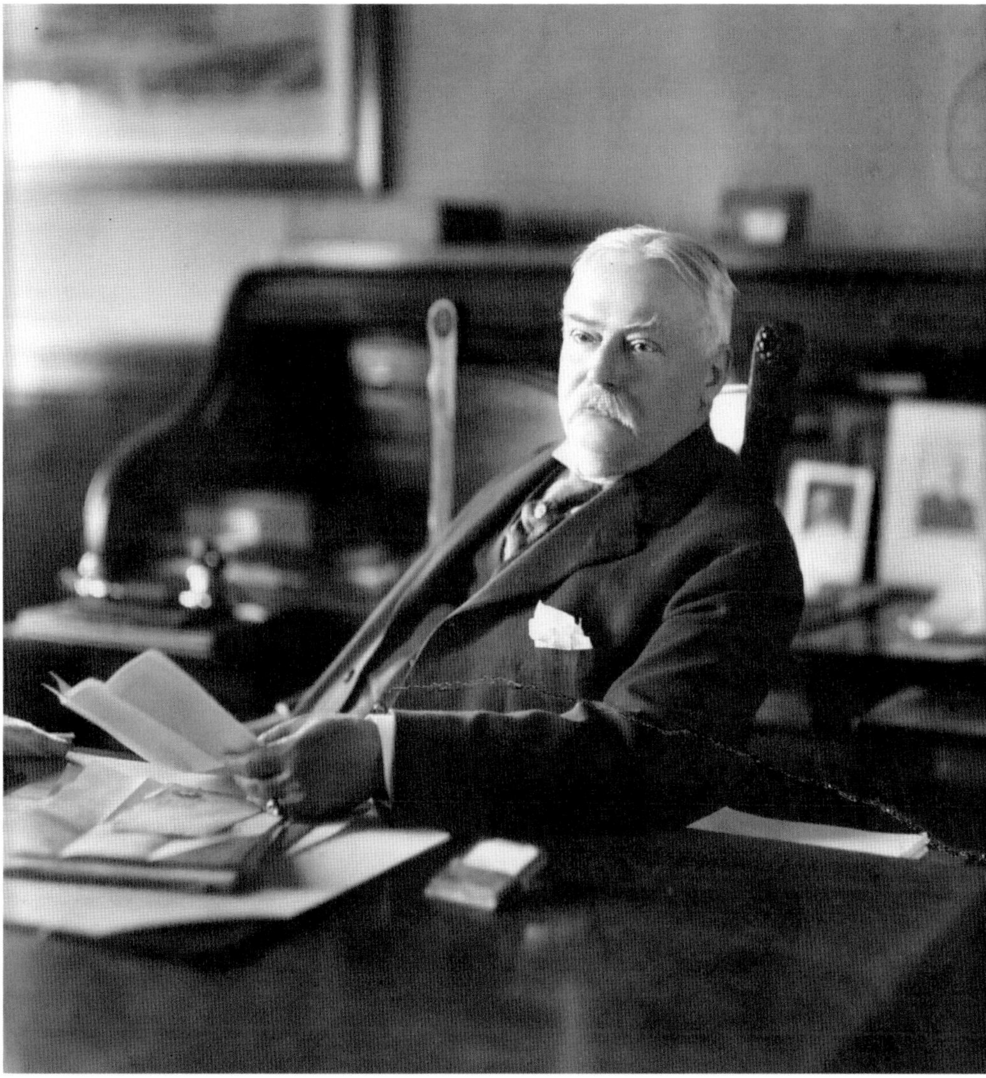

James W. Cannon

The patriarch of Concord's foremost dynasty, Cannon built his company from the bottom up. As a teenager, he toiled as a store clerk for his brother David Franklin Cannon, keenly observing the region's mushrooming textile industry. While operating local businesses with merchants John W. Wadsworth and P.B. Fetzer, Cannon established a reputation as a cotton buyer and cultivated a demand for his "Cannon Cloth." By the late 1880s, he had opened his first plant, the Cabarrus Cotton Mill. His empire grew with his own business, the Cannon Manufacturing Company, and a host of other plants he acquired, including Gibson Mills, Franklin Mills, and Tuscarora Mills.

Whereas most of Concord's other mills produced yarn or cloth that was shipped elsewhere for production, Cannon's plants were primed to manufacture a principal product, Cannon Towels, which became a widely distributed brand. Cannon purchased 600 acres near Concord in 1905 and on that site constructed a village, which is today the city of Kannapolis. Cannon Mills Plant No. 1 was the city's nucleus, and surrounding small mill houses were erected for workers to rent. Cannon's philanthropy included endowments to establish an elaborate YMCA and improve the county's infrastructure. (Courtesy of Kannapolis History Associates.)

Warren C. Coleman

The second of two illegitimate sons born of Rufus Barringer, a white man who later became a Confederate general, and Roxanna Coleman, a black slave owned by Daniel Coleman Sr., Coleman, born in 1849, refused to be defined by the mundane farm tasks required of him during his childhood as a slave. During the Civil War, his production of footwear for the Confederacy predestined his future as a merchant. After emancipation, the ambitious young man was mentored and educated by William M. Coleman, who later became North Carolina's attorney general. By the 1890s, Coleman had become North Carolina's wealthiest African American entrepreneur, thanks to his successful general store and barbershop in downtown Concord and his real estate dealings.

Witnessing Concord's textile expansion, Coleman envisioned a cotton mill that afforded employment opportunities for "colored" workers and managers. With the assistance of his board of directors (below) as well as progressive white businessmen, Coleman (front row, right) opened the Coleman Manufacturing Company in 1901. Financial reversals eventually crippled the mill, and it became insolvent with Coleman's death in 1904.

The 1988 dedication of the Coleman historical marker on Highway 601 took place in a ceremony officiated by Concord mayor Bernie Edwards (opposite, below, standing directly under the marker). At the recommendation of city councilman Jim Ramseur, on March 28, 2001, that stretch of highway was renamed Warren C. Coleman Boulevard. (Below, courtesy of the Library of Congress, Prints and Photographs Division; opposite, top, Historic Cabarrus Association, Inc.; opposite, bottom, Kannapolis History Associates.)

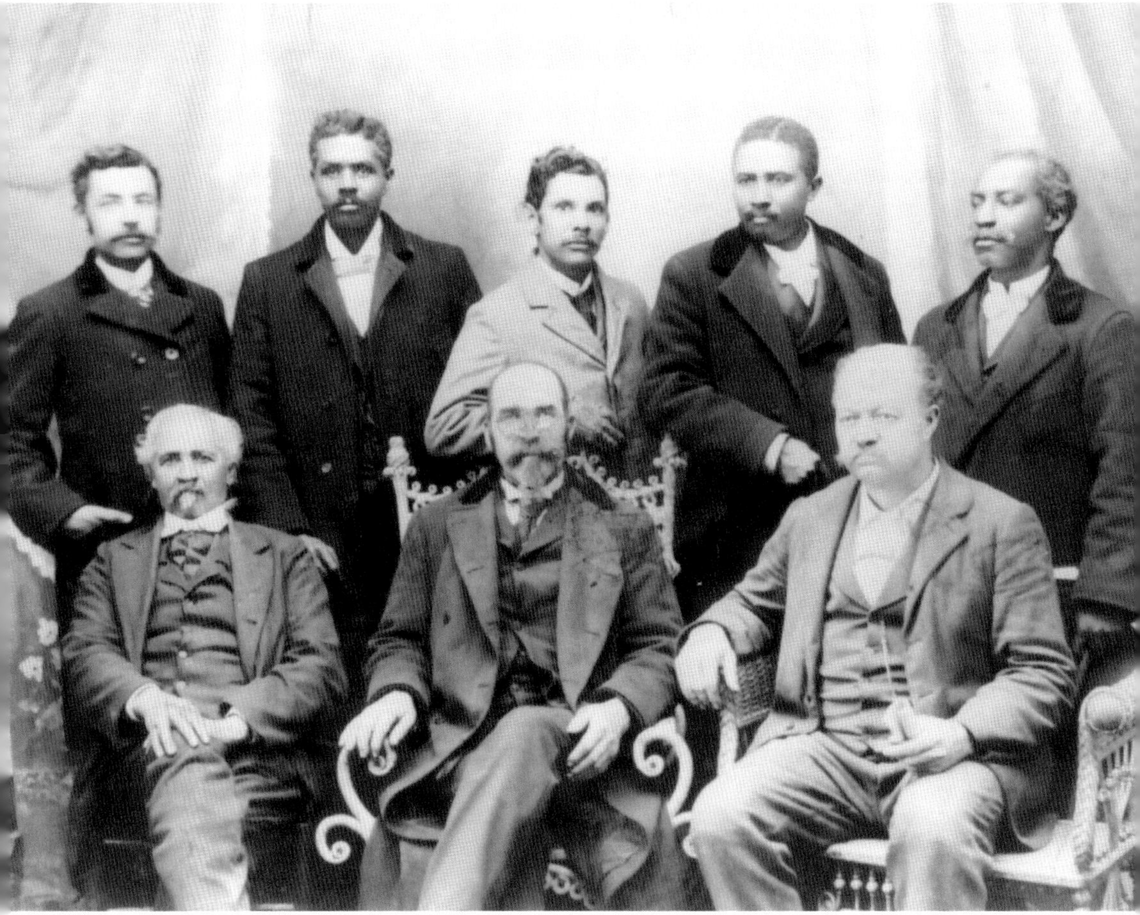

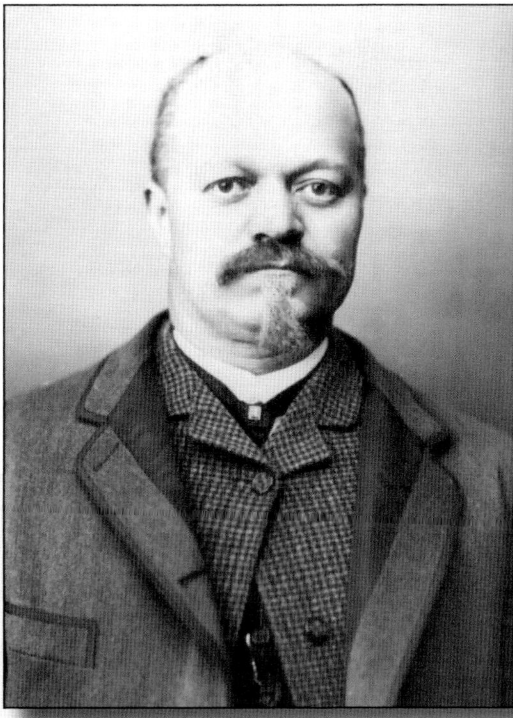

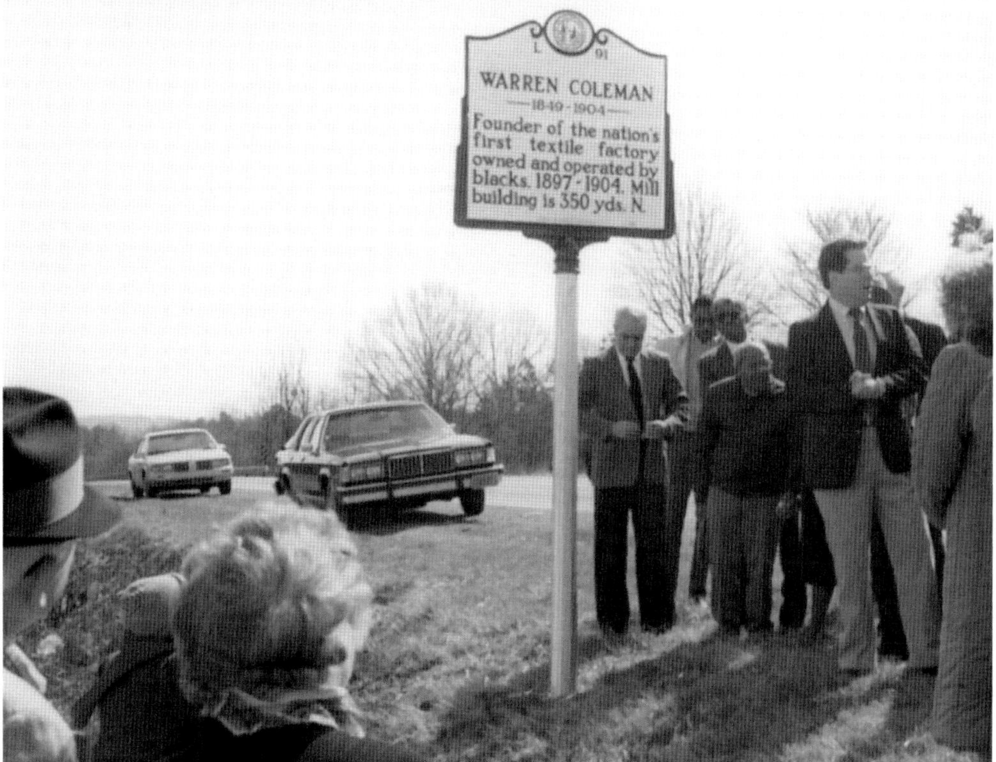
L 91
WARREN COLEMAN
1849 - 1904
Founder of the nation's first textile factory owned and operated by blacks. 1897 - 1904. Mill building is 350 yds. N.

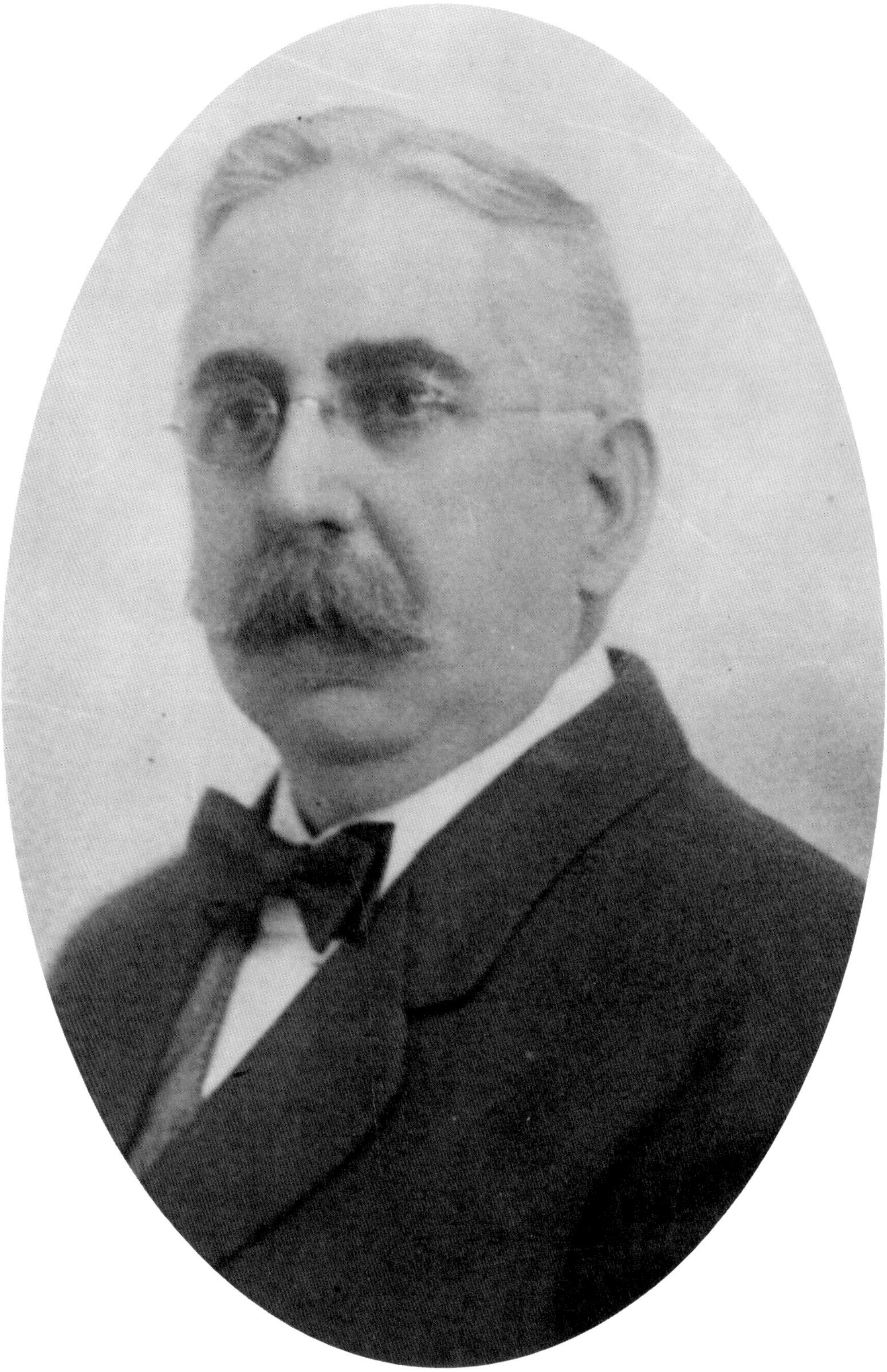

James P. Cook (BELOW AND OPPOSITE PAGE)
Simultaneously serving as county school superintendent and editor of Concord's *Daily Standard* in the 1890s, Cook became passionate about the humane treatment of juvenile offenders. He oversaw a campaign to build North Carolina's first correctional institution for boys, Stonewall Jackson Manual Training and Industrial School (now Stonewall Jackson Training School), founded in 1909. This 1930s aerial photograph shows Stonewall Jackson Training School in its heyday, during which time it was a self-sufficient "city" unto itself, boasting 15 cottages, acres of farmland, and vocational training centers for textiles, printing, and other trades. Today, much of this acreage is the recreational facility Frank Liske Park. (Left, courtesy of Concord Public Library.)

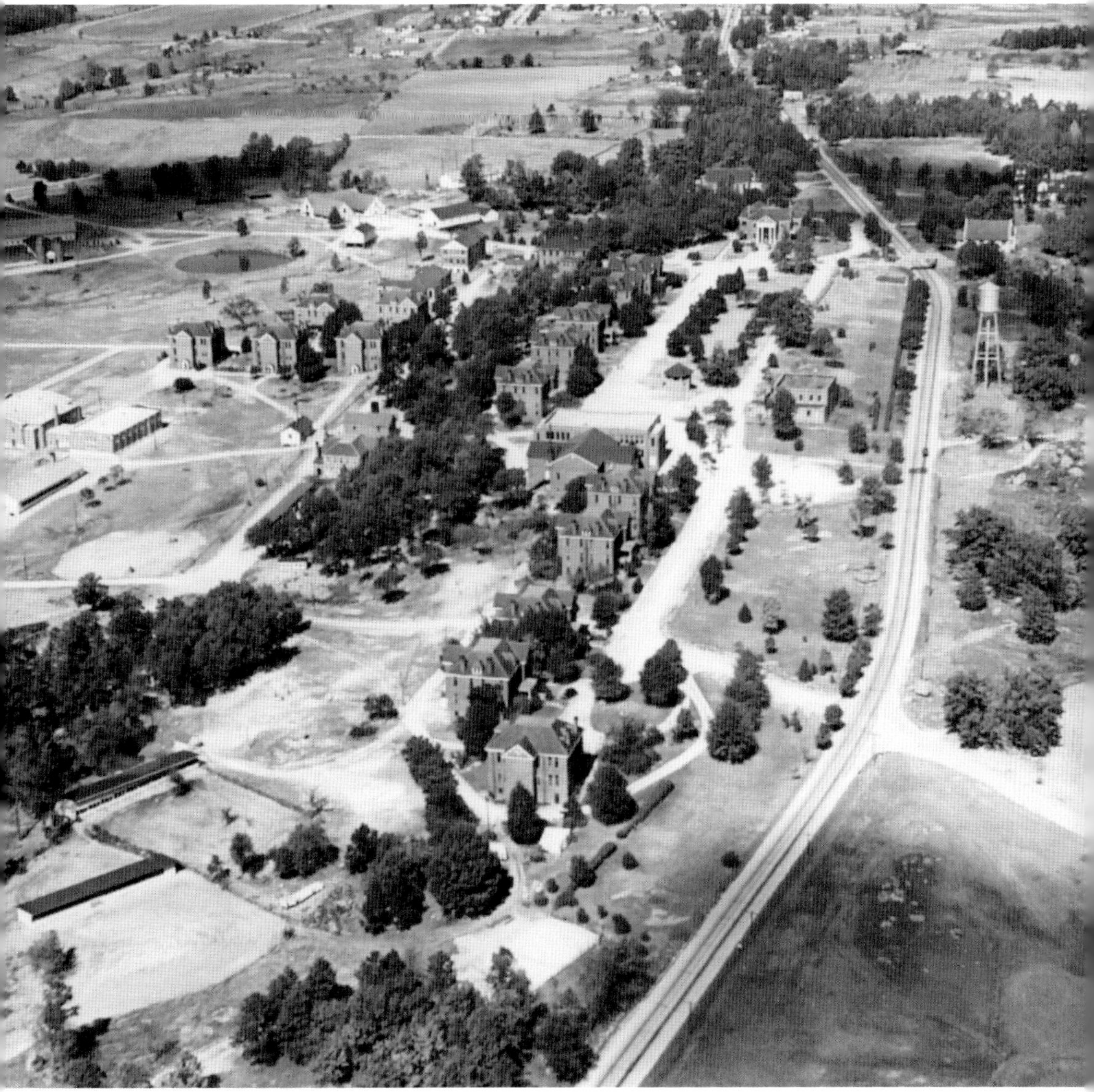

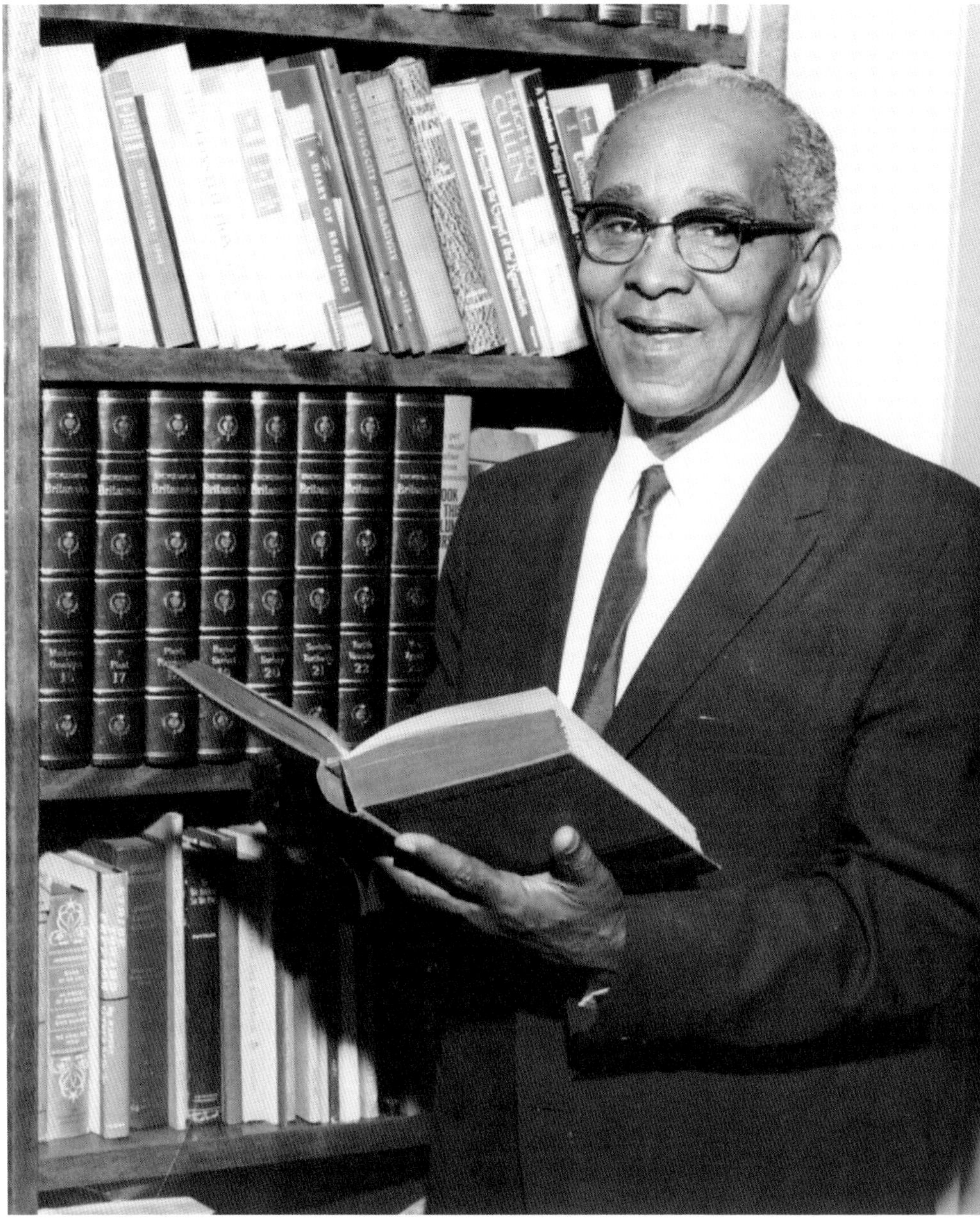

Leland S. Cozart

The mission of Concord's Barber-Scotia College, founded in 1867 as Scotia Seminary by Presbyterian minister Rev. Luke Dorland, was to educate the daughters of newly freed slaves to become teachers and social workers. In 1932, Doctor Cozart ushered in a new era for the school as its first black president; his five predecessors, as well as the majority of the previous teaching staffs, were Caucasian. This cultural distinction aside, Cozart presided over the college for an unprecedented 32 years, taking the position during the same year that Scotia Women's College (the school's second name) merged with Alabama's Barber Memorial College, achieving the name by which it has since been known. During Cozart's presidency, the college became a four-year institution, began offering a bachelor's degree, and opened to students regardless of gender or race. (Photograph by Frankie Furr.)

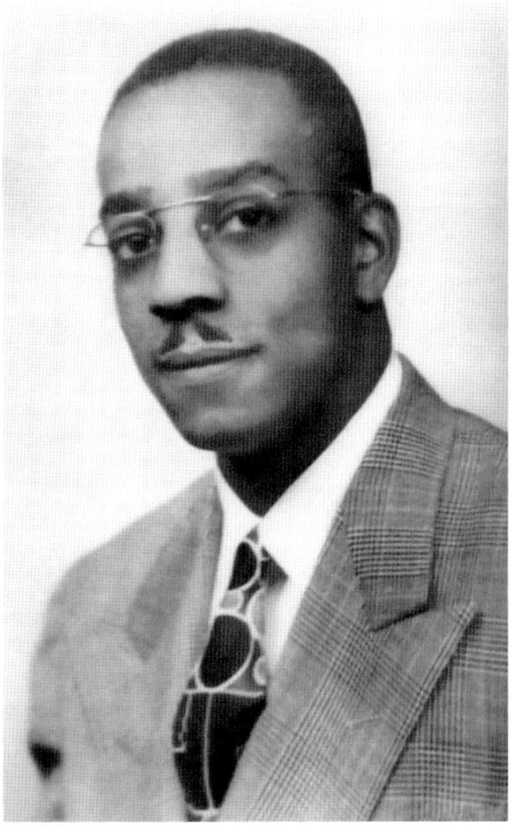

Frederick H. Watkins
Born in 1860 in Rockingham, North Carolina, Dr. Watkins, a general practitioner, was Concord's first African American physician and the city's first black surgeon. He operated his private medical practice in the late 19th and early 20th centuries and died in 1925. (Courtesy of Bernard Davis Jr.)

Lawrence Evans
While Jim Crow laws maintained the racial divide in schools and neighborhoods, in 1952, the Concord Police Department broke color barriers by installing Evans (left) as its first African American officer. Other black policemen soon followed, but few remained on the force during this tumultuous time; those who did often weathered racism and hostility from the community. Both Evans and David "Chalk" Steele Sr., shown here in the early 1960s, became sergeants.

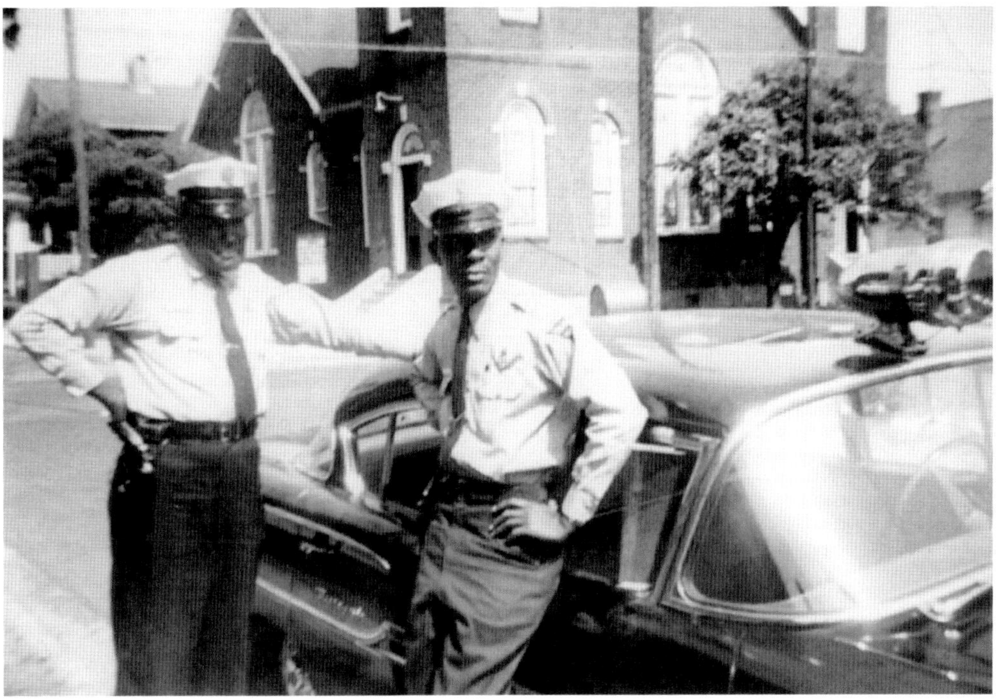

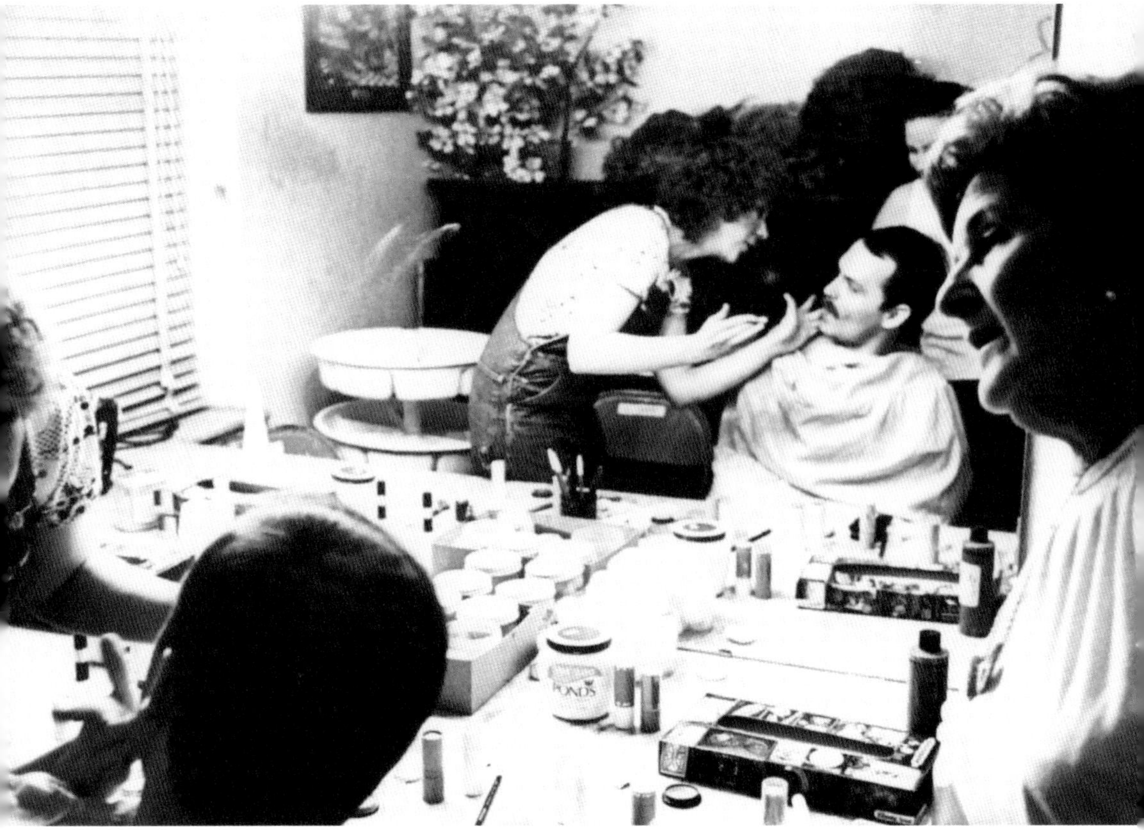

Mary Snead Boger

Boger was the heart and soul of Concord's cultural and literary arenas for decades. Born in 1920 and raised in the South, as a teen she moved to Concord with her parents. A 1936 graduate of Concord High School, after college she spent two summers as an actor at the Phidelah Rice School of Theatre on Martha's Vineyard. She declined a scholarship from the Pasadena Playhouse in 1940 so that she might return to Concord to marry Charles E. Boger Jr. (The scholarship then went to Eleanor Parker, who became a screen star.) Boger was a writer for the *Concord Tribune* during World War II and a drama and speech teacher. After a professional hiatus, during which time she raised her four sons, Boger returned to the community limelight in 1964 as a book reviewer, public speaker, and author. In 1973, she was part of a public campaign to preserve Cabarrus County's magnificent 1876 Victorian courthouse, defiantly staring down a wrecking ball that was slated to raze the building for a parking lot. Thanks to the impassioned Boger and others, funds were procured to remodel the "Old Courthouse" into a showplace for amateur community stage productions, giving birth to Concord's Old Courthouse Theatre (OCT), which today operates from the former First Baptist Church on Spring Street. After a trial production in the summer of 1976, the OCT launched its first season later that year, with Boger serving as artistic director. With an unquenchable thirst for excellence, Boger nurtured local talent and cultivated the OCT's reputation throughout the region. She retired in 1987, but her spirit and reputation continue to inspire the theater's actors and volunteers today, with the Mary Snead Boger Lifetime Achievement Award presented annually. Boger died in 2011 at age 90. Boger (right) supervises while Becky Porter applies makeup to John Kearns for *Jesus Christ Superstar* during the OCT's 1979–1980 season. (Photograph by Frankie Furr.)

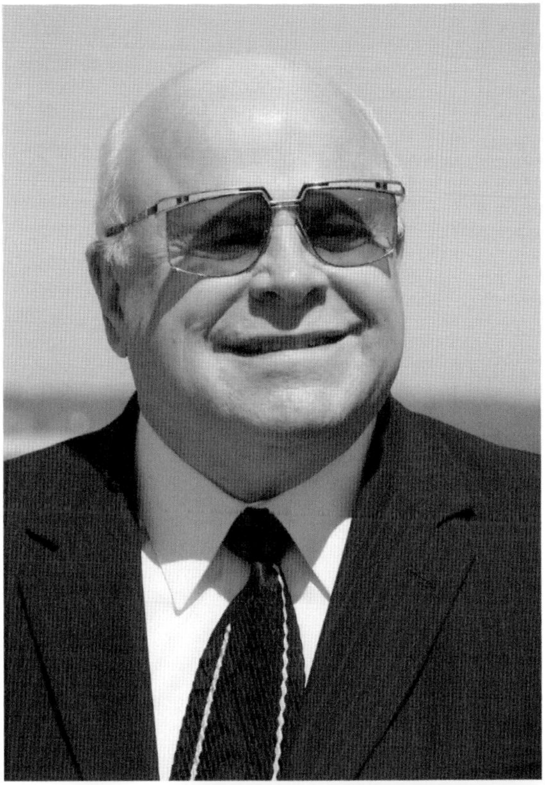

Bruton Smith

By his late teens, Smith, now chief executive officer of Speedway Motorsports, Inc., was promoting short-track races at the Concord Motor Speedway. In 1959, he partnered with stock-car driver Chris Turner to build the Charlotte Motor Speedway on Highway 29 in Concord. Smith departed the venture in 1962 but returned in 1975 as its major shareholder, hiring H.A. "Humpy" Wheeler Jr. as general manager. Smith steered what was originally a 1.5-mile racetrack toward unparalleled improvements, including grandstand expansions and the construction of luxury suites, adjacent condos, a dirt track, and a drag strip. The Speedway's growth has spawned a multimillion-dollar network of hotels, restaurants, malls, and housing developments, connected by a thoroughfare aptly named Bruton Smith Boulevard. The 1986 photograph below shows Smith (right) with Kannapolis-born racing legend Dale Earnhardt. (Both, courtesy of CMS Archives/HHP Photo.)

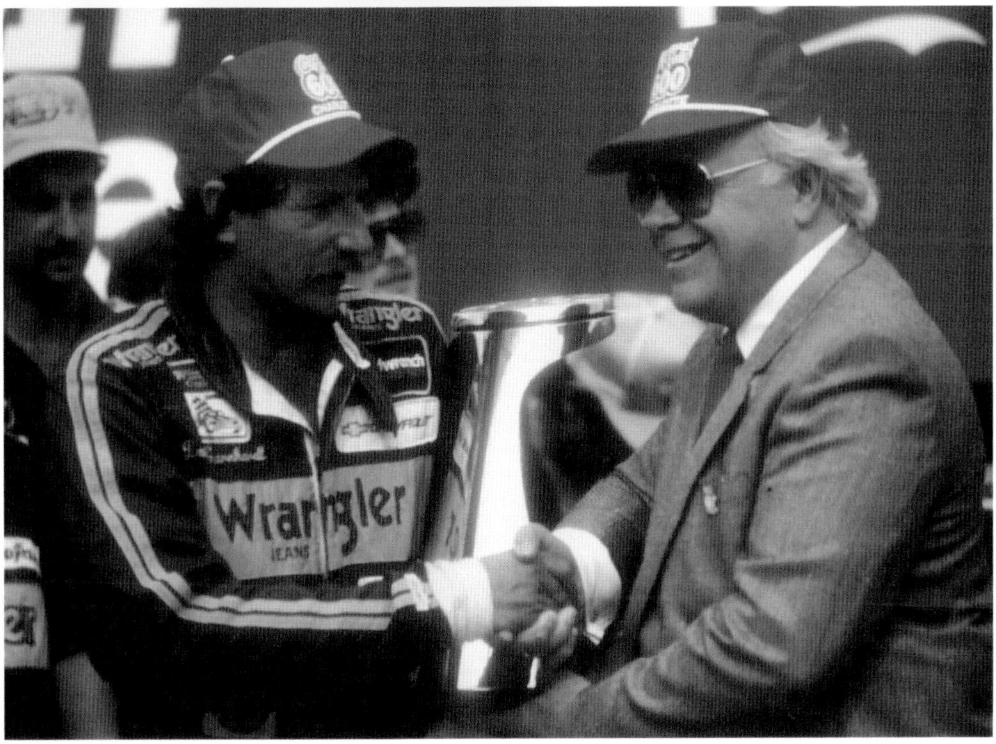

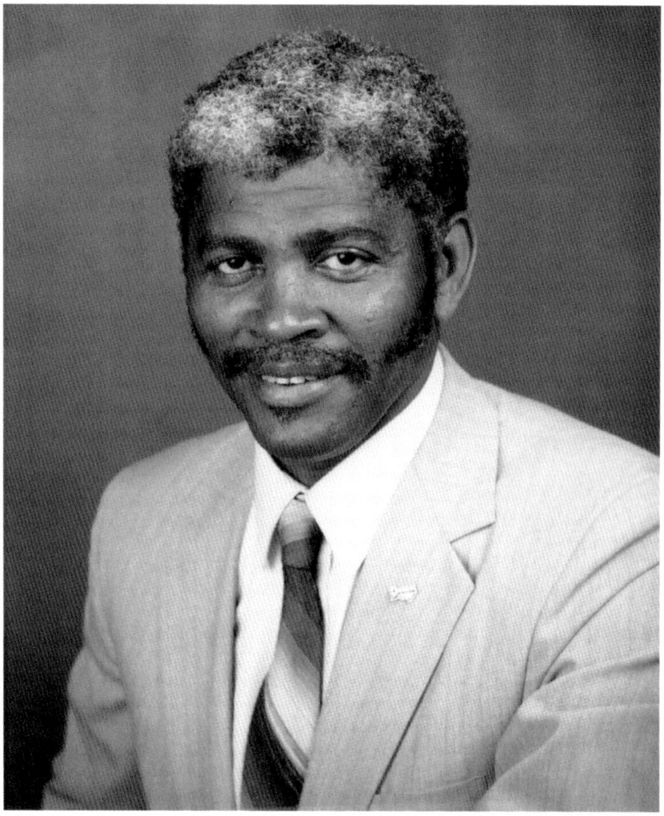

Robert Lee Mathis
Mathis was raised in poverty in the part of town he (and others) called "the black bottom." After joining the Navy in 1951, he turned away from alcoholism and self-pity and learned that "by helping others be their best, doors open for me to be my best." In 1981, Mathis became Concord's first African American public official, serving on the city council for 16 years. (Courtesy of Concord Public Library.)

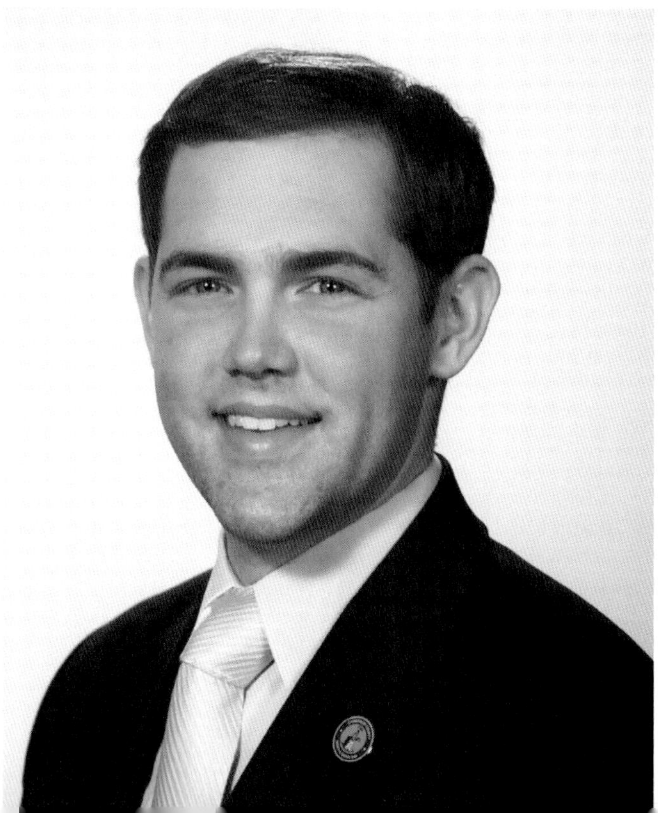

Chris Measmer
By the time this 23-year-old became North Carolina's youngest county commissioner in November 2010, Measmer had already garnered political experience under Congressman Robert Cannon "Robin" Hayes and Sen. Richard Burr. A graduate of Central Cabarrus High School, Measmer is extremely active with several community organizations. Outside of public service, he works alongside his parents at their family business, the regional chain of Wayside Restaurants. (Courtesy of Cabarrus County Governmental Center.)

CHAPTER TWO

Community Builders

For the burgeoning community of Concord, the cotton mills fomented great promise. Yet that promise could not have been realized without the investments and inventiveness of citizens devoted to the common good.

There were no news cameras or Twitter feeds to trumpet the accomplishments of the father-and-son team of Daniel Branson Coltrane and Lester D. Coltrane Sr. when they provided Concord with its financial and telecommunications infrastructures; they grew their businesses and improved their city merely because it was the right thing to do.

Were they not of impeccable character, Charles A. Cannon, J. Roy Davis Jr., and Mariam Cannon Hayes might have rested on their laurels, enjoying the life their families' wealth afforded them. Instead, they sought ways to enhance the lives of their neighbors—those they knew, and those they would never meet.

Believing that the arts and history nourishes the soul, cultural patrons such as Ruth Coltrane Cannon, Janie Patterson Wagoner, the Lore Sisters, and Historic Cabarrus Association, Inc., orchestrated efforts large and small to nurture creativity and preserve the past. Jimmy Murphey fed a different type of hunger, for years opening his door—and his heart—to those without food.

Politicians often avoid risk, opting to appease their constituents by doing only what is expected of them. However, a succession of forward-thinking mayors exercised the courage to help Concord transition into new economic territories and the savvy to convince naysayers that change was in their best interest.

Whether their efforts were publicly lauded through fanfare and commemorative plaques or performed quietly with little or no recognition, these community builders laid the groundwork for the lifestyle we are privileged to enjoy today.

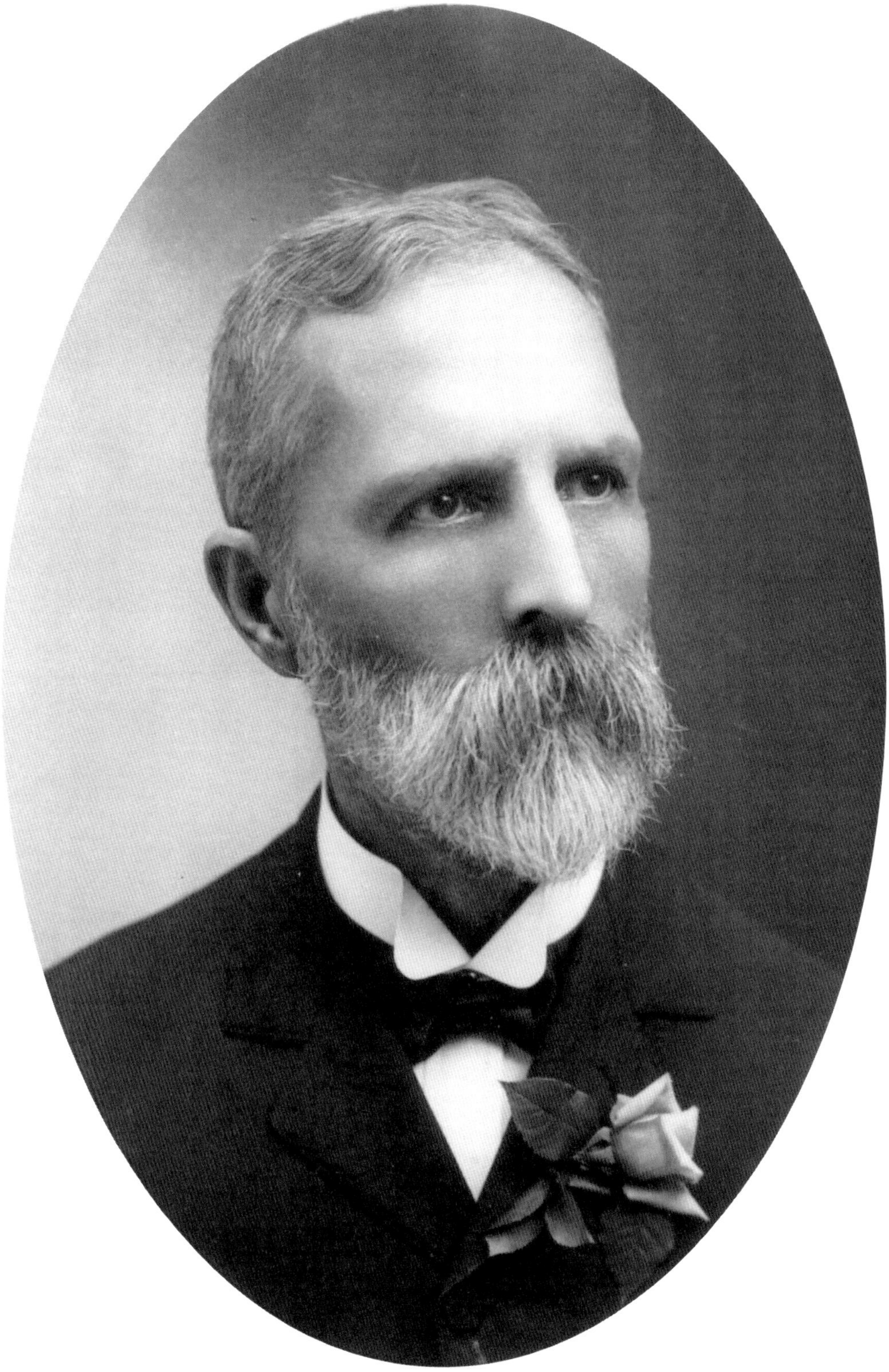

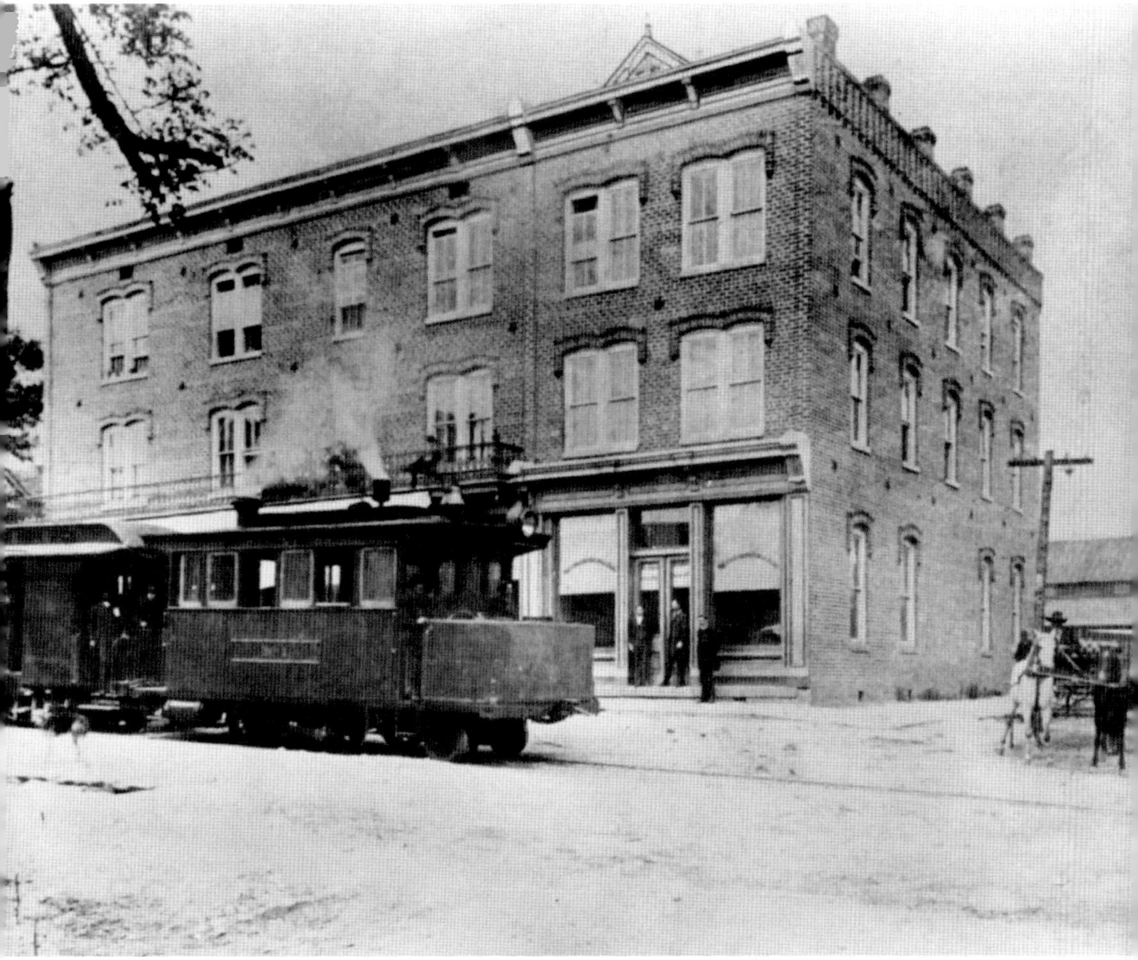

Daniel Branson Coltrane (ABOVE AND OPPOSITE PAGE)
Concord's thriving textile industry precipitated the need for a local financial institution, prompting Coltrane to help found the Concord National Bank in July 1888. The structure, long the cornerstone of the city square, is shown here in its early days; above the bank is the St. Cloud Hotel, which was later augmented into the Hotel Concord.

Coltrane's extraordinary journey spanned nearly a century and began in a log cabin in Randolph County, North Carolina. In his late teens, he joined the Confederate army, fighting alongside "Jeb" Stuart. Postwar, he worked on the family farm in Randolph County and explored new business horizons in Missouri, but after an accidental train encounter with John M. Odell, he chose Concord as his home and settled here in the late 1880s.

Aghast by the illiteracy he witnessed among bank patrons (some of whom were unable to sign their own names), he helped foster the city's public school system and served as a school board member; the Coltrane (now Coltrane-Webb Elementary) School was named in his honor. He also contributed to the development of Stonewall Jackson Training School. In addition to his banking duties, Coltrane served as president of Kerr Bleaching and Finishing Works (Kerr Bleachery) and held other textile interests in the region. He was fervently committed to Central Methodist Church, and his work with the publication the *North Carolina Christian Advocate* earned him statewide acclaim. Coltrane remained the Concord National Bank's president until his death in 1937. (Left, courtesy of Concord Public Library; above, courtesy of Kannapolis History Associates.)

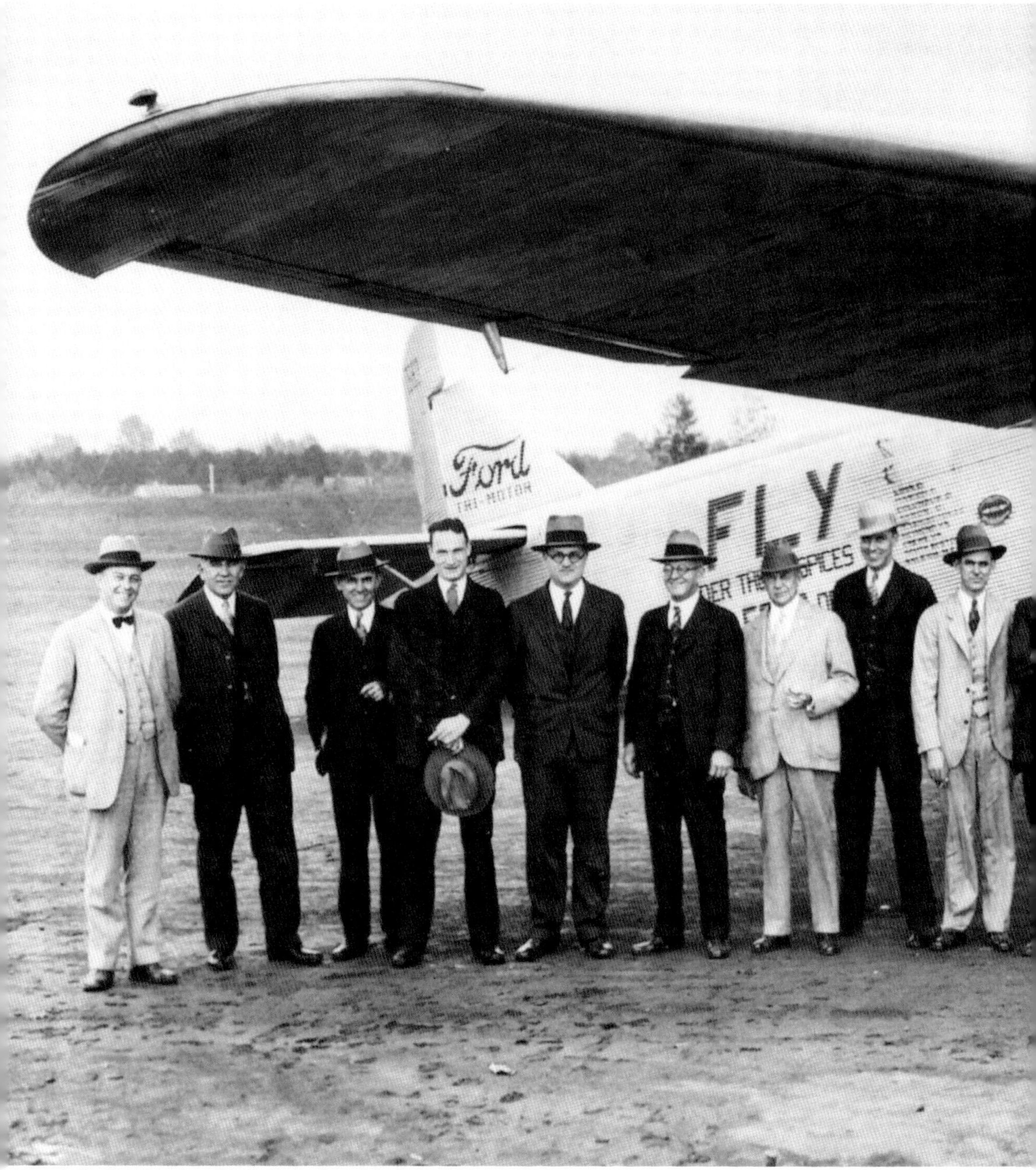

Lester D. Coltrane Sr.

The father of telecommunications in Concord, Lester initially worked for his father, Daniel Branson Coltrane, as a bank teller. When he heard complaints that Charlotte's Bell Telephone was gouging locals with high rates, he created the Concord Telephone Company (CTC) in 1897 as an affordable alternative. CTC's first office was a back room inside the bank building, but later, a two-story office behind the bank was constructed. Coltrane's first residential subscribers paid $10 per year for service, and businesses paid $15 annually. Phone customers originally required assistance from an operator, but in April 1940, CTC introduced its dial system. For more than a century, the Concord Telephone Company, later CTC

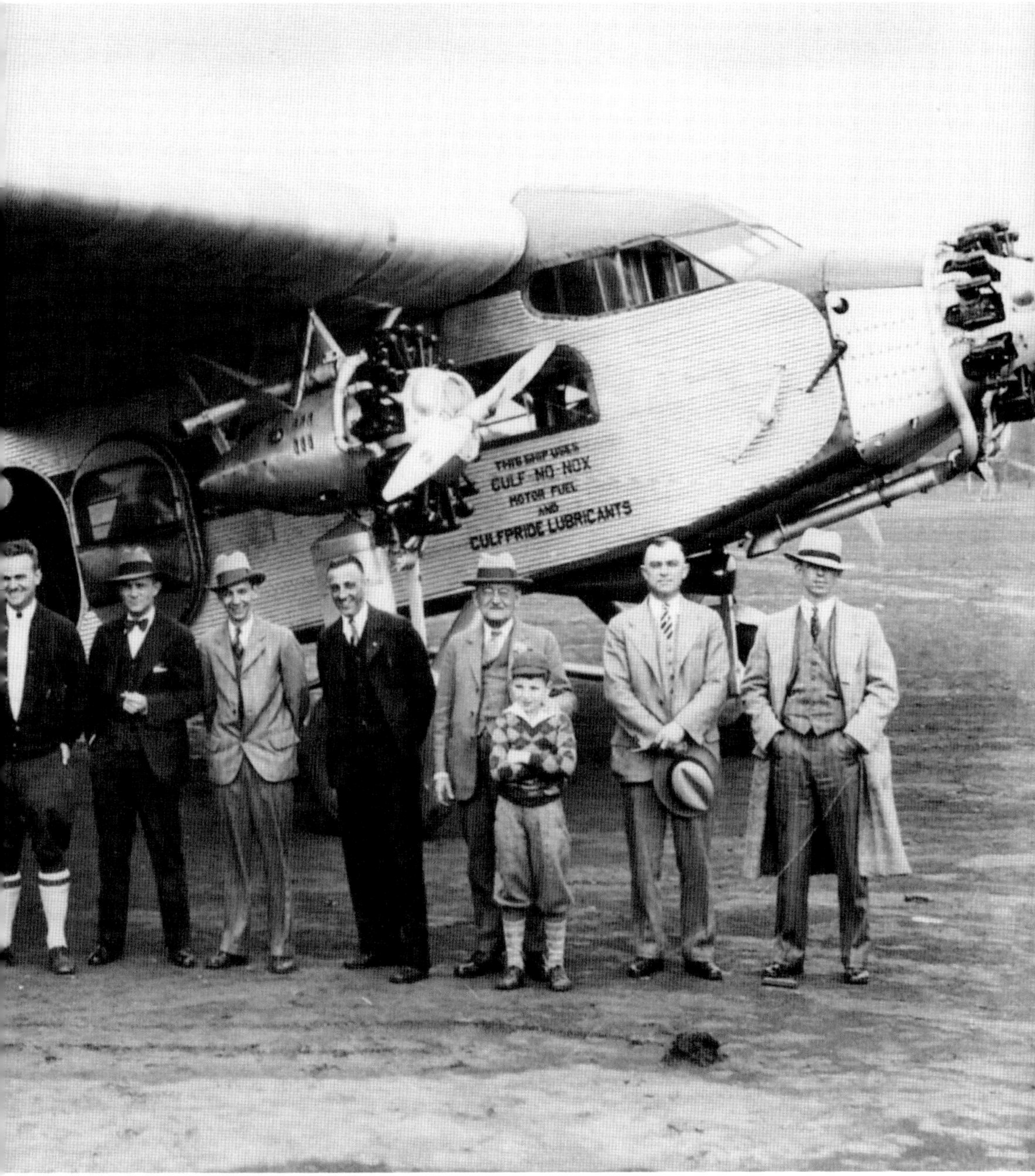

Communications, provided telecommunications services to several counties, with four generations of Coltranes at the helm. It was acquired by Windstream Communications in 2007. In this extraordinary photograph, Coltrane (sixth from left) and a group of Concord's most influential businessmen from the mid-1920s were invited by Noel K. Reid, secretary-treasurer of the Reid Motor Company, on a round-trip flight from Charlotte to Concord in this Ford Tri-Motor plane. From left to right are Reid, A.F. Hartsell, Eugene E. Caldwell, George W. Dowdy, G. Pat Ritchie, Coltrane, Thomas H. Webb Sr., Boyd Biggers, Wyatt H. Moose, Clarence H. Barrier, the pilot (unidentified), Ernest F. Robinson, E. Ray King, James E. Dorton, Eugene C. Barnhardt Sr., Eugene C. Barnhardt III, H. Troy Wallace, and Lone M. Archey.

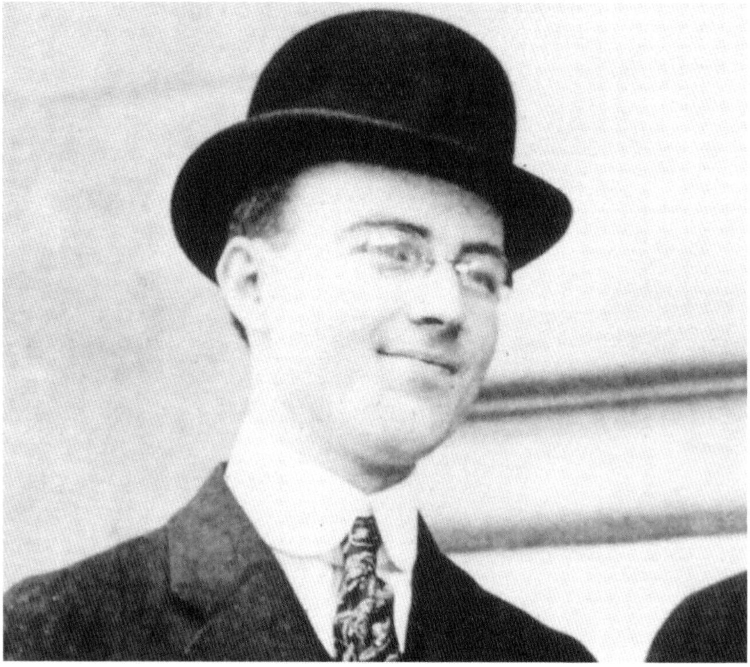

Charles A. Cannon (ABOVE AND OPPOSITE PAGE)

The youngest of the six sons of Cannon Manufacturing Company (Cannon Mills) founder James W. Cannon not only stepped into his father's shoes in 1921 but also into a hornet's nest. A textile workers' strike and unionization attempt paralyzed production and incited riots, prompting Cannon to summon the National Guard to maintain peace. While Cannon resisted the union, over his career, he would implement numerous programs to ensure his employees' well-being and ultimately became one of North Carolina's most successful industrialists of all time.

Born in Concord in 1892, Cannon was shy of his 20th birthday when he was appointed to his first executive position at Barringer Manufacturing Company in Rockwell, North Carolina, rising in the ranks there before becoming vice president of Cannon Manufacturing Company in 1916. Once elected Cannon's president, he amalgamated his father's numerous textile plants and companies into the Cannon Mills Company and continued to run the organization until 1962. As Cannon's chief officer, his product and advertising innovations helped make Cannon Towels a widely recognized brand. At one time, Cannon Mills employed nearly 25,000 workers in the Concord/Kannapolis region, with 300,000 towels produced daily. "His office door was always open for anyone who worked at the mill," William C. Cannon Jr. said of his grandfather in the 2012 textile documentary *Stitched in Time*. Also open was Cannon's heart: he established four charitable organizations, funded community vaccinations, founded Cabarrus Memorial Hospital, and served on a plethora of community and statewide boards. For decades, Cannon was Concord's (and Kannapolis's) unofficial ambassador, entertaining a range of visiting dignitaries. On the opposite page, above, Cannon welcomes Lady Bird Johnson, wife of Pres. Lyndon B. Johnson, as she visited the region during a 1964 campaign for her husband.

Nearly as legendary as Cannon himself is his magnificent Neo-Federal estate at 94 North Union Street, built in 1928 and designed by architect Charles Keen of Philadelphia, shown at the bottom of the opposite page in a 1940s photograph.

Cannon's public and professional presence continued long after his 1962 retirement as Cannon Mills' president. As Cannon Mills' chairman of the board, he very famously returned to his office every day up to the eve of his passing. Cannon's death on April 2, 1971, stunned the community: it had lost its most legendary businessmen, but most importantly, a great friend. (Above and opposite, top, courtesy of Kannapolis History Associates; opposite, bottom, courtesy of Historic Cabarrus Association, Inc.)

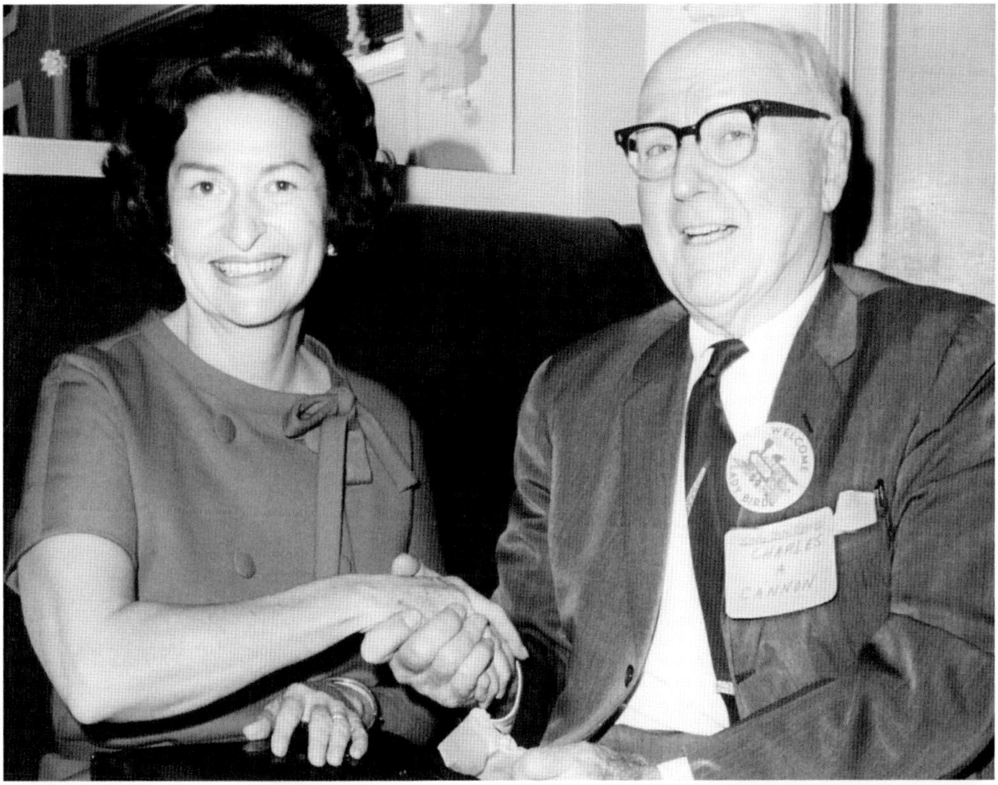
WELCOME
LADY BIRD
CHARLES
A
CANNON

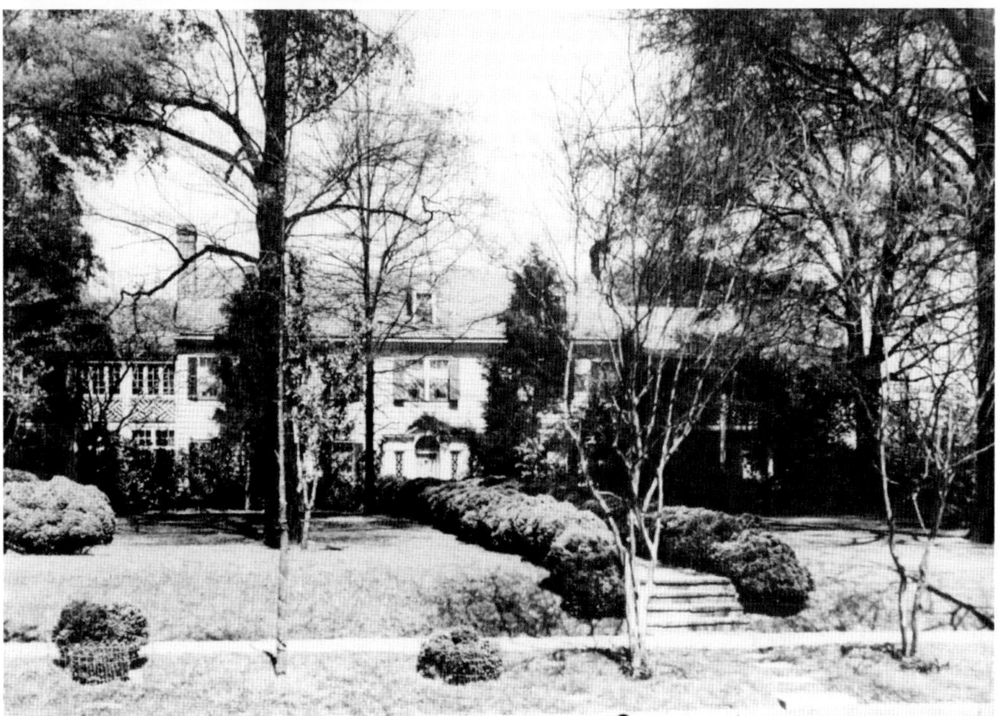

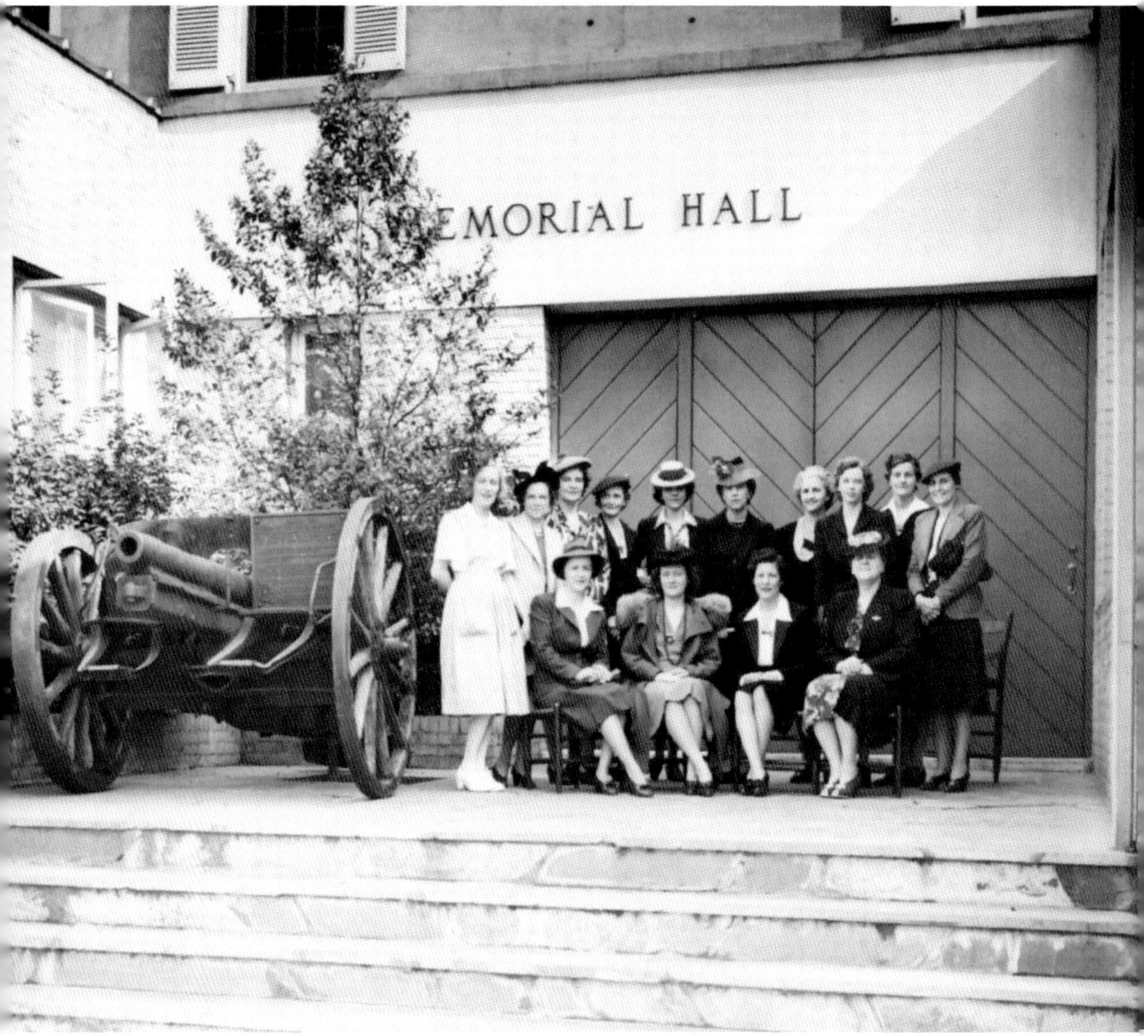

Ruth Coltrane Cannon

Concord's two most prominent families became one when Ruth Louise Coltrane married textile tycoon Charles A. Cannon in 1912. Daughter of Daniel Branson Coltrane, Ruth honored her father's Confederate military heritage through active membership in the United Daughters of the Confederacy (UDC) and by orchestrating Concord's annual commemoration of Confederate Memorial Day. At the request of the city's aldermen, she was fundamental in the 1939 establishment of Memorial Hall, Concord's history museum. Cannon's zeal for cultural conservation extended well beyond the city limits of Concord: she was president of the North Carolina Society for the Preservation of Antiquities from 1945 to 1956 and contributed to the 1959 restoration of North Carolina's first governor's mansion, the Tryon Palace in New Bern. Since 1948, Preservation North Carolina has presented the Ruth Coltrane Cannon Award, which it calls "the most prestigious preservation award presented for outstanding achievement of statewide significance in historic preservation in North Carolina." She is shown here (seated front row, right) in the early 1940s with fellow UDC members at Memorial Hall.

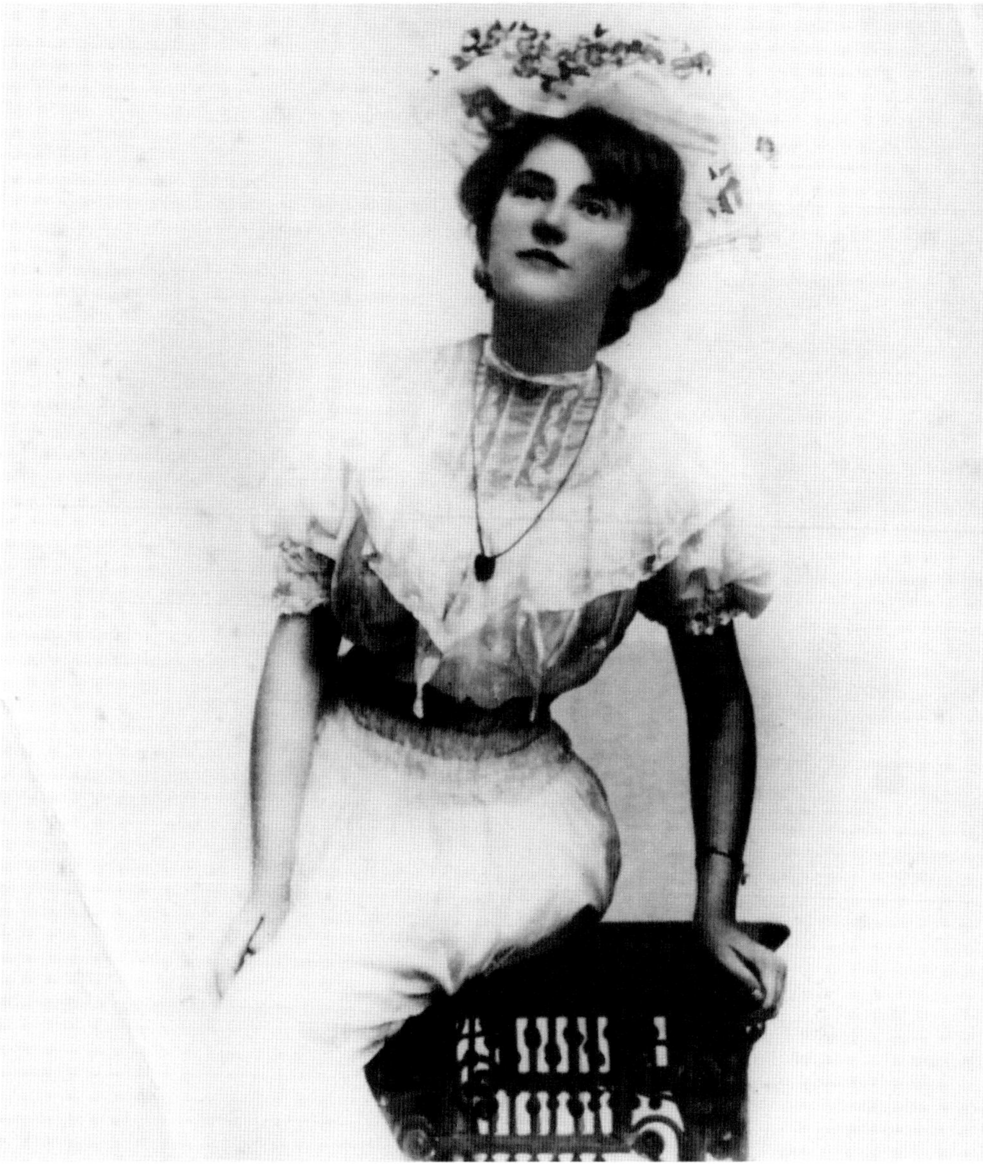

Janie Patterson Wagoner

She was a small-town girl with big-city talent. Born in 1884 to insurance agent John K. Patterson, Wagoner was a New York–trained singer and pianist who counted operatic master Enrique Caruso among her professional acquaintances. The wife of Charles Wagoner, president of the Citizens National Bank, "Miss Janie" enlivened the Concord region's art scene during the first half of the 20th century with her historically based musical compositions and stage productions including "March Mecklenburg," a bouncy wind ensemble arrangement that was performed by John Philip Sousa's band, and the pageant-play *The Beginning of the Art-Song in America*, the story of Betsy Ross's sewing of the US flag. Also noteworthy is her treasure trove of historical clippings, notes, photographs, and postcards, which she archived and catalogued throughout her lifetime. After her death at age 91, her collection was consigned to nephew John K.P. Odell, but upon Odell's passing in the early 1990s, the collection was entrusted to another nephew, Alex Patterson, who contributed this 1905 portrait of his aunt.

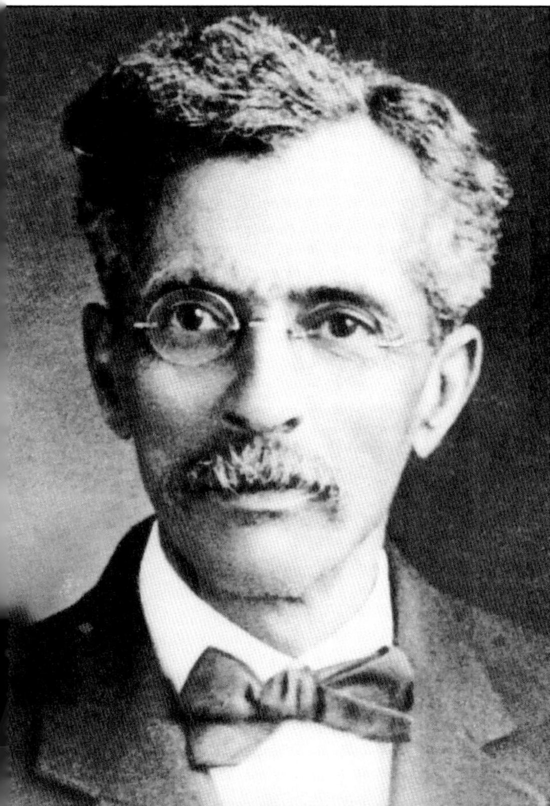

Frank T. Logan

Logan, a former slave and minister from Greensboro, was appointed principal of the Concord Colored School once the city began its public school system in 1891. The facility became Logan School during a 1924 expansion. Logan School closed its doors after desegregation, but today, the entire community surrounding the former school site bears the name of this venerated educator. (Courtesy of Concord Public Library.)

John L. Miller

Concord's first fire chief, when photographed in 1938, had been at his post for nearly four decades. Miller served as chief for a record 52 years. Prior to the establishment of a city fire department in late 1900, firefighting was relegated to bucket brigades of volunteers. Under Miller's watch, the department transitioned from horse-drawn wagons to modern methods, including fire trucks. (Photograph by Zack L. Roberts; courtesy of Concord Public Library.)

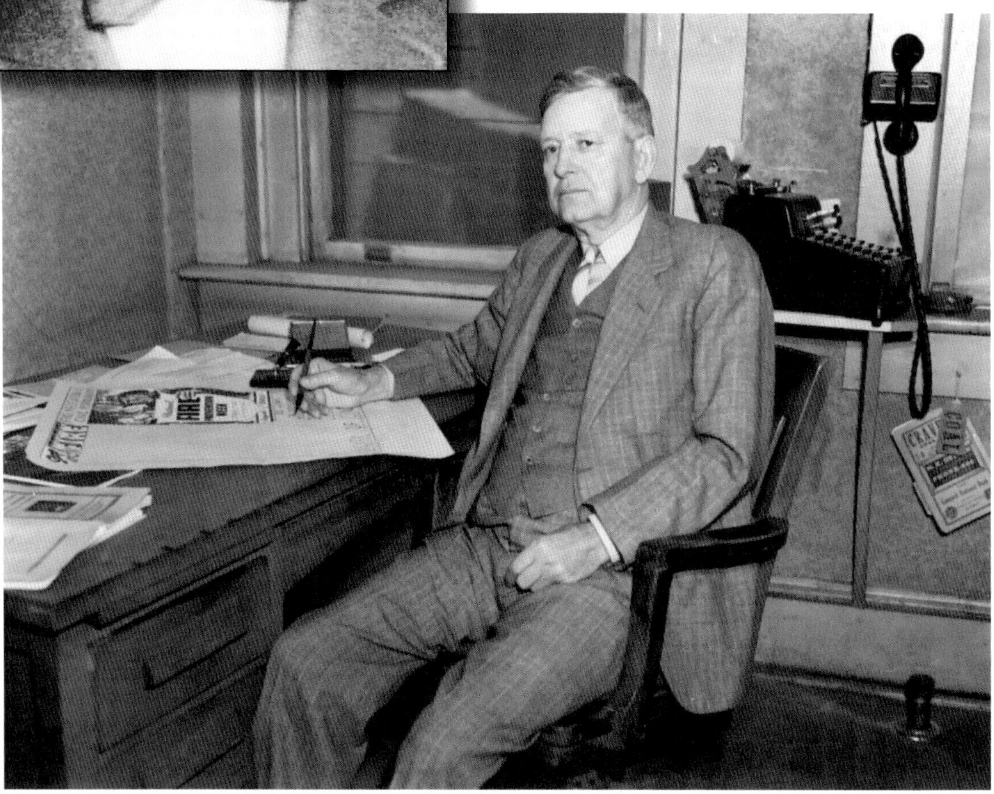

Concord Rotary Club

Like most cities, Concord has boasted a variety of civic organizations dedicated to service projects, but none has experienced the longevity and success of the Concord Rotary Club. Chartered in January 1922, the club's 22 founding members were J. Archie Cannon, W.G. Caswell (treasurer), L.D. Coltrane Sr., Joseph V. Davis, William H. Gibson, Archie E. Harris, Gus Hartsell (vice president), Luther T. Hartsell Sr., Aubrey Hoover, Rev. Thomas Lawrence, Franklin C. Niblock Sr., John M. Oglesby, S. Kay Patterson, Dr. Samuel W. Rankin, L. Maury Richmond, Charles F. Ritchie, William M. Sherrill, Martin Verburg (secretary), Charles B. Wagner, Thomas H. Webb Sr. (president), Albert Shipp Webb, and J.B. Womble. Since 1926, Concord Rotary has met each Wednesday at 12:15 p.m. in the same location, the Hotel Concord ballroom. This photograph, taken from the hotel mezzanine, is of a mid-1930s Rotary dinner that included members' wives. (Rotary membership was limited to males until the 1980s.) The club's roster represents a diverse mix of professions, with members bonded by fellowship and a desire to live up to Rotary's motto, "Service Above Self." Part of a global network of clubs collectively called Rotary International, Concord Rotary has participated in worldwide initiatives, including the eradication of polio and the construction of recreational and medical facilities in South America. Yet, its local projects best resonate throughout the community: Concord Rotary regularly supports Alzheimer's disease research and Meals on Wheels and funded the 2010 construction of the Everybody Plays handicap-accessible playground at J.W. "Mickey" McGee Park. At this writing, the club's new project is Rotary Square, a downtown Concord park that will double as a venue for the Piedmont Farmers Market and local artisans. (Photograph by Zack L. Roberts.)

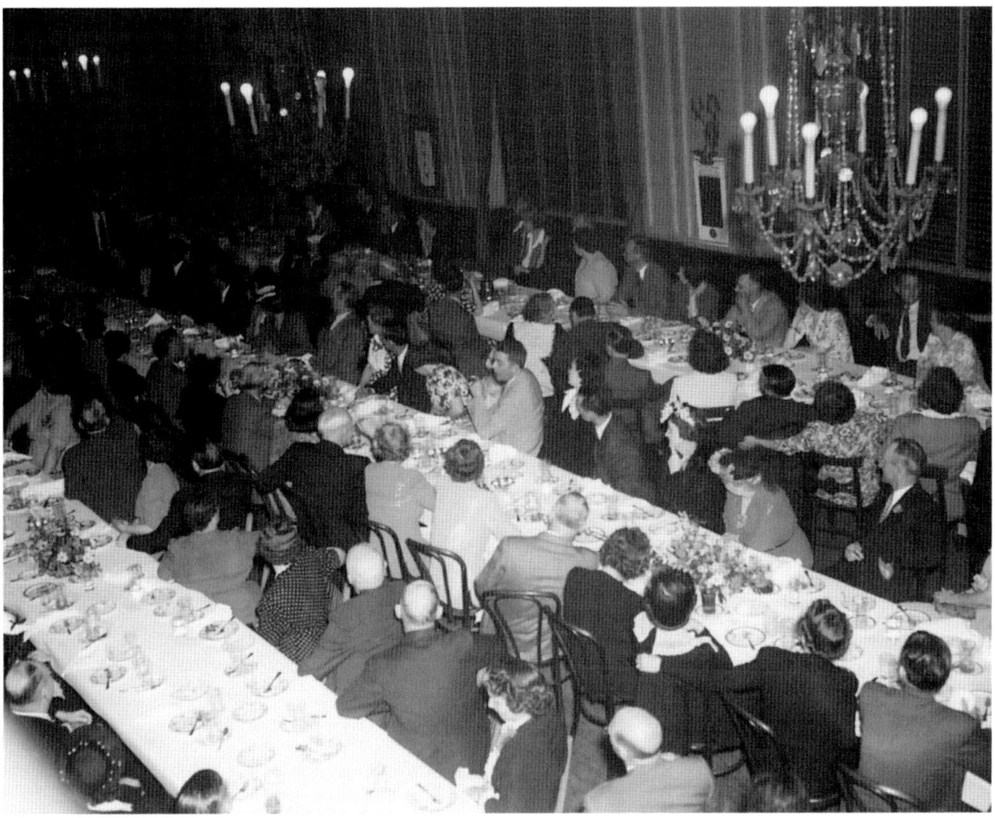

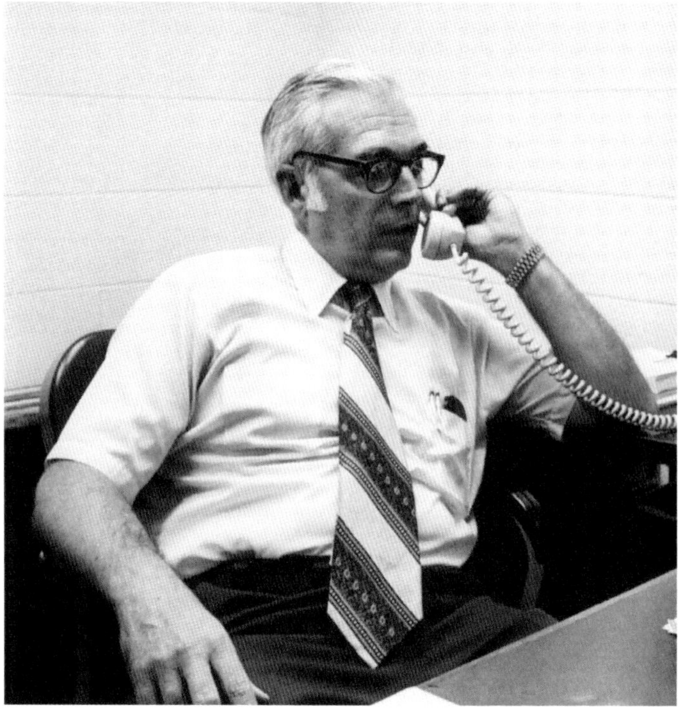

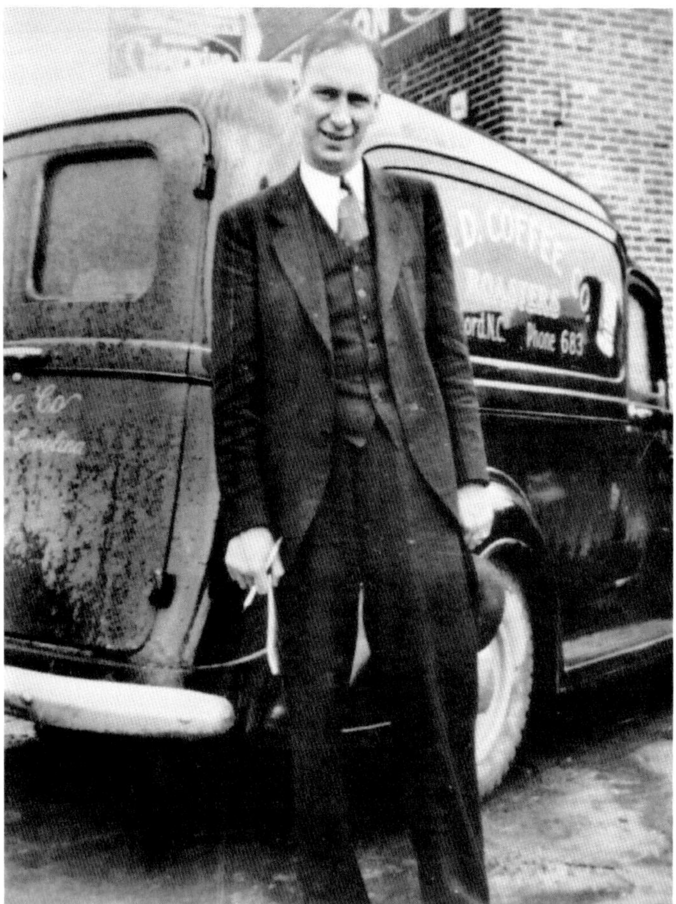

J. Roy Davis Jr.

A Phi Beta Kappa graduate of Davidson College, Davis Jr. (top) joined the family business in 1959. His father, J. Roy "Buck" Davis Sr., and Lawrence Switzer founded S&D Coffee, Inc., in 1927. Once Switzer left the company, William Peden (bottom) became the partner of Davis Sr. Under the leadership of Davis Jr., S&D's territory expanded from regional to national distribution of coffee and tea. Davis Jr. also served on numerous nonprofits' boards, his influence extending beyond the aroma of coffee that engulfs several miles around the Concord plant. Downtown Concord's former county courtroom was refurbished into a 227-seat performing arts facility, the Davis Theatre, largely thanks to the generosity of Davis and his wife, Sue. (Top, courtesy of Concord Public Library; bottom, courtesy of S&D Coffee.)

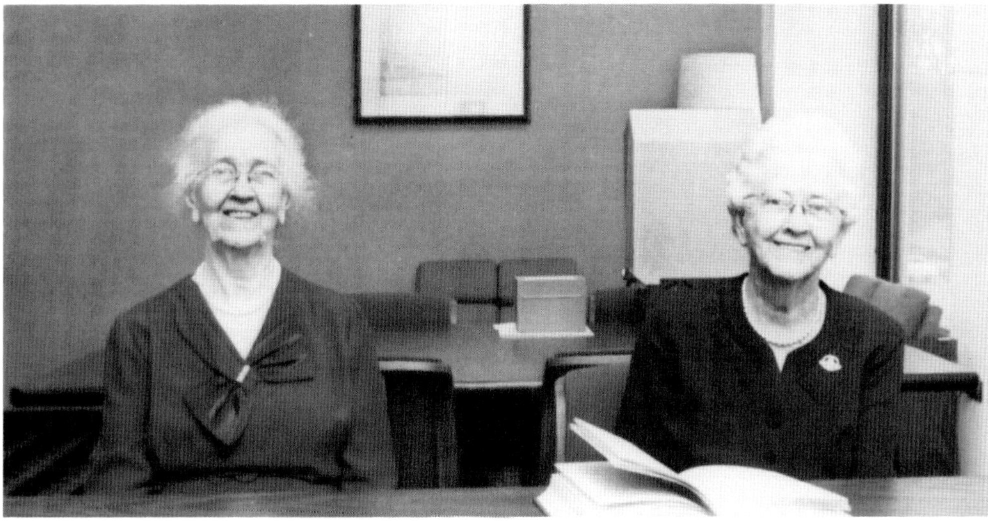

The Lore Sisters

The daughters of a Confederate soldier, siblings Adelaide (left) and Eugenia Lore dedicated their long lives to impeccable research into county history and genealogy. The Lores had three published books to their credit, including *Open the Gates and Roam Cabarrus with Us*. Their preservation coffers provide the backbone of the collection in the Concord library's history room, which today bears their name. (Courtesy of Concord Public Library.)

S. Les Myers

Before serving as mayor from 1965 to 1969, "Concord's most distinguished citizen" was known as an alderman and as president of Union Street Corp., which managed the Hotel Concord. Earlier, Myers was the nation's youngest postmaster at age 21. A 21-acre park on Lawndale Avenue is named after him. This 1968 photograph shows Mayor Myers (left) with aldermen R.R. Cline and Harold B. McEachern. (Courtesy of Concord Public Library.)

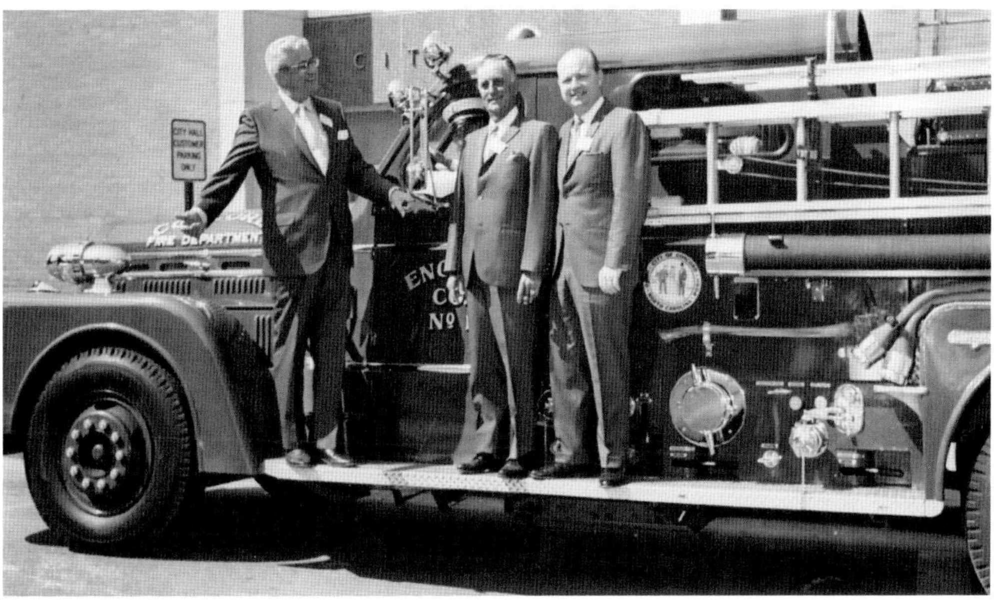

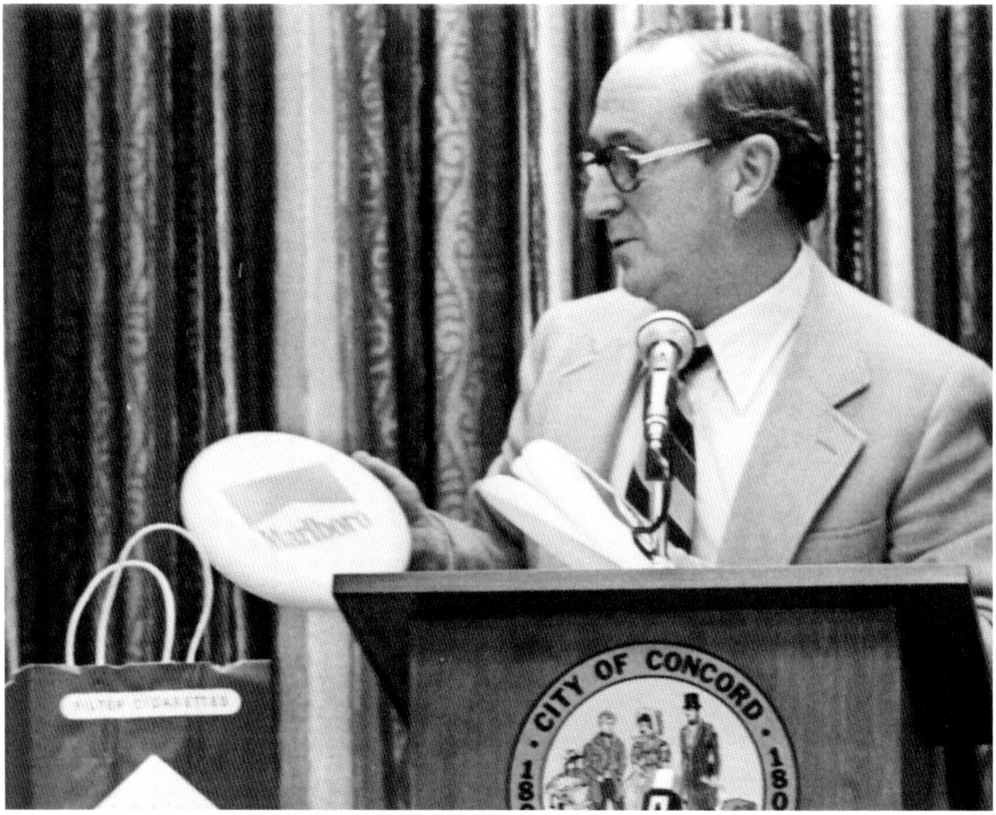

Alfred M. Brown Sr. (ABOVE AND OPPOSITE PAGE)
A lifelong resident, Brown was a Concord High School graduate and maintained a professional profile through several local businesses, including Clear Springs Dairy (founded by his great-uncle A.L. Brown, after whom Kannapolis's high school is named), Brown Mobile Homes, and Brown Realty, the latter of which he operated from the 1970s until his death in 2003. In 1952, he began nearly four decades of community service when he was voted onto the city council, then known as the board of aldermen, for a 25-year stint. Brown was elected mayor in 1969, an office he held until 1977, and returned to the city council in 1989. In 2001, his eldest son, Alfred M. Brown Jr., was elected to succeed him.

A visionary, Brown Sr. supported projects that would bolster the city's economic growth, such as a Philip Morris cigarette-manufacturing plant (announced by the mayor in this 1978 photograph) and the International Business Park on the outskirts of town near Interstate 85. According to his second wife and widow, Frances Bess Brown, "His whole life was a gift back to the city that had nourished him." The city of Concord's operations center bears Brown's name, as does the Brown-Dorton Scholarship (co-named for his colleague James L. Dorton), which is awarded to students at UNC–Charlotte's Master of Public Administration program.

Brown's community service aside, the one-time mayor is affectionately remembered for the red socks he always sported. "The night I was sworn in," Brown Jr. told the *Independent Tribune*, "[the sitting council members] all held their legs up behind the desk so everyone could see their red socks" [they wore in his father's honor].

The 2001 photograph on the opposite page shows Brown's retirement ceremony. In it, Brown is seated with three city councilmen collectively elected in 1995: (from left to right) Jim Ramseur, Scott Padgett, and David Phillips. Brown "took us under his wing," said Ramseur, and the trio has followed their mentor's tradition of public service; each has remained on the council to this day, and Padgett has served as Concord's major since 2001. (Above, photograph by Frankie Furr; opposite, courtesy of Jim Ramseur.)

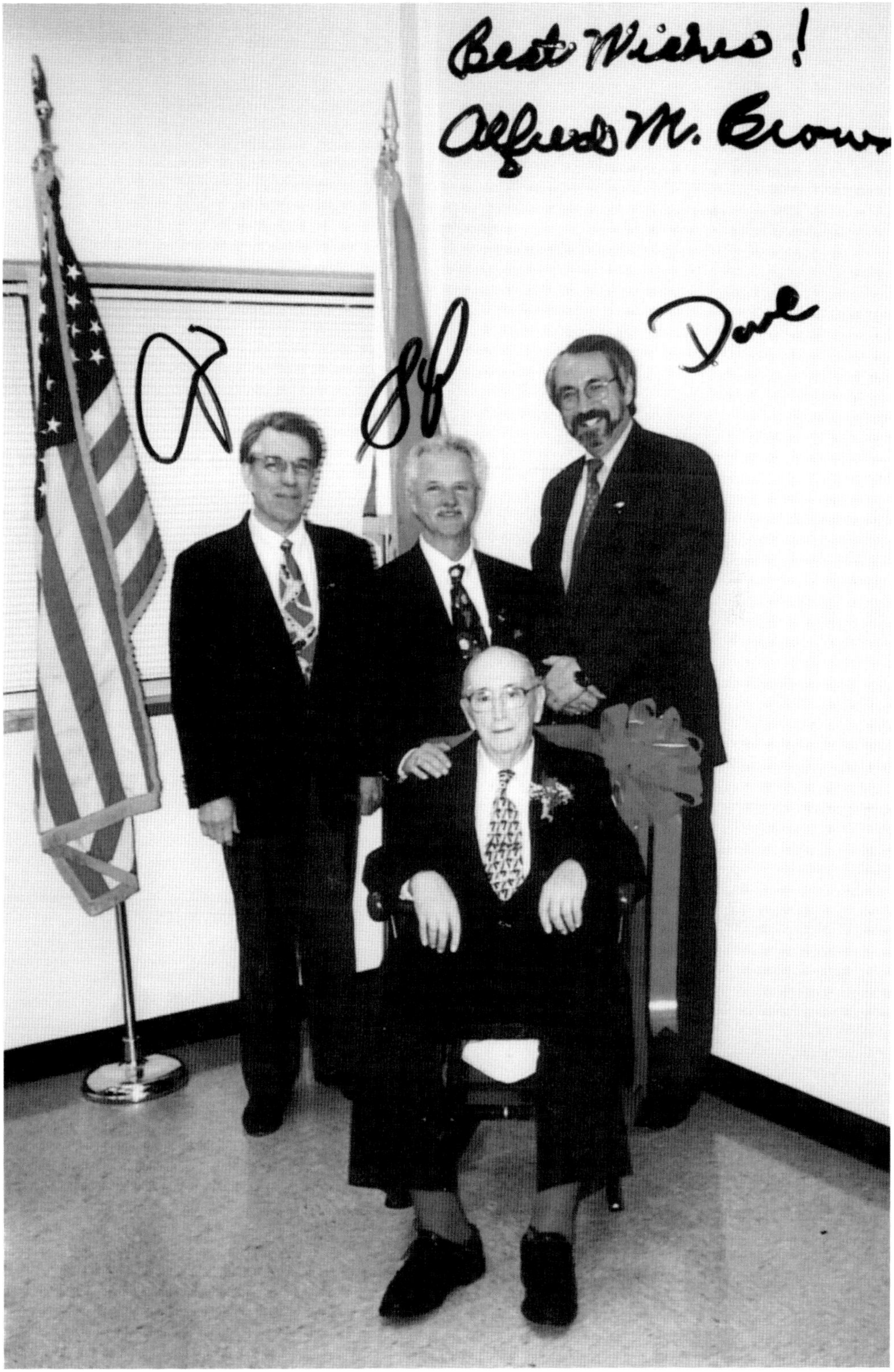
Best Wishes!
Alfred M. Brown
Dave

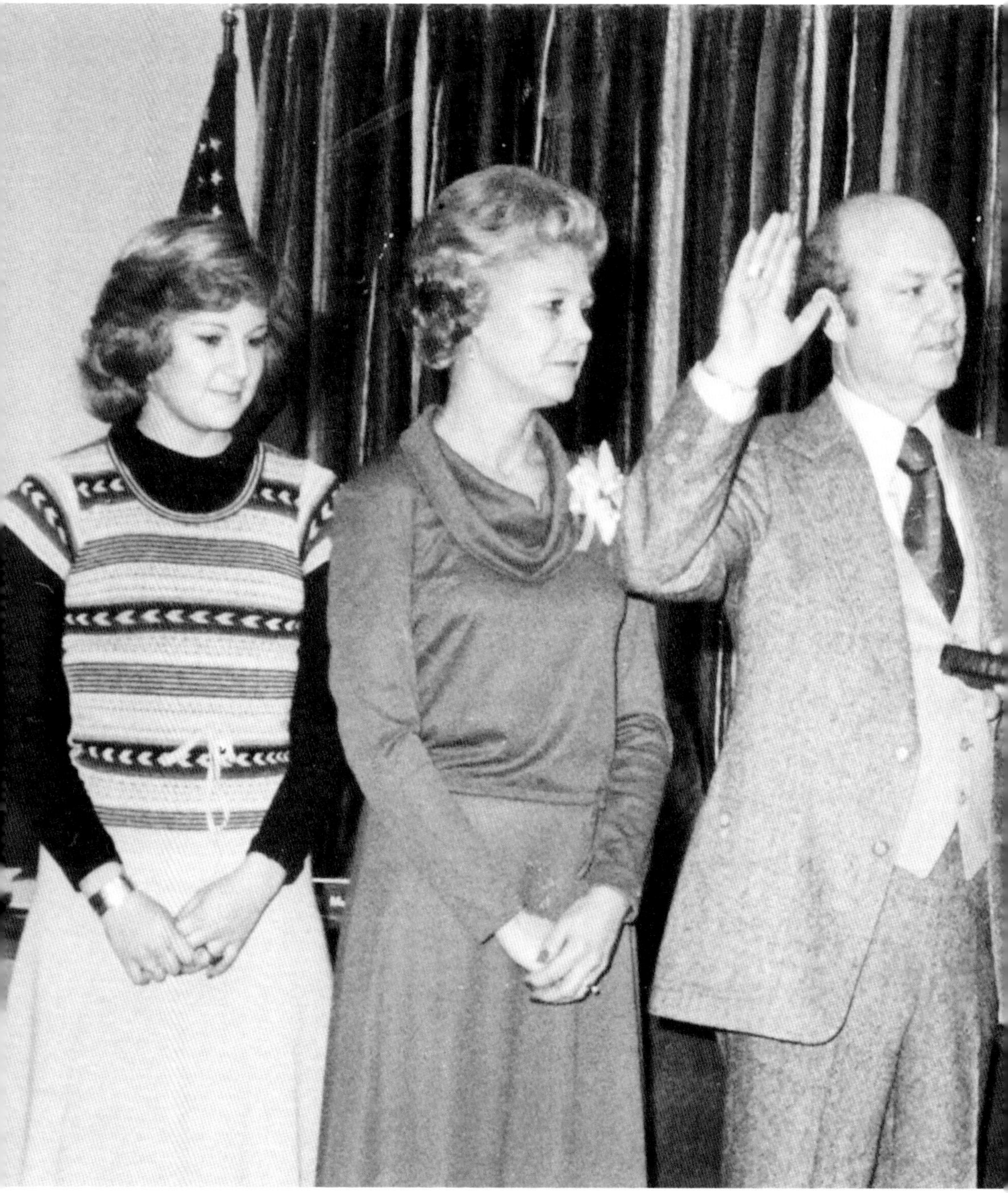

Harold B. McEachern

"The People's Mayor," also known as "Mayor Mac," McEachern held the city's top office from 1977 to 1981, previously serving the community on its board of aldermen from 1965 to 1977. Known as a consensus builder, his calm demeanor often smoothed roiling seas of civic controversy. He was the 2008 recipient of the Order of the Long Leaf Pine, the highest civilian award presented by the state of North Carolina. McEachern's legacy also includes 11 years as the manager of the Cabarrus County Fair,

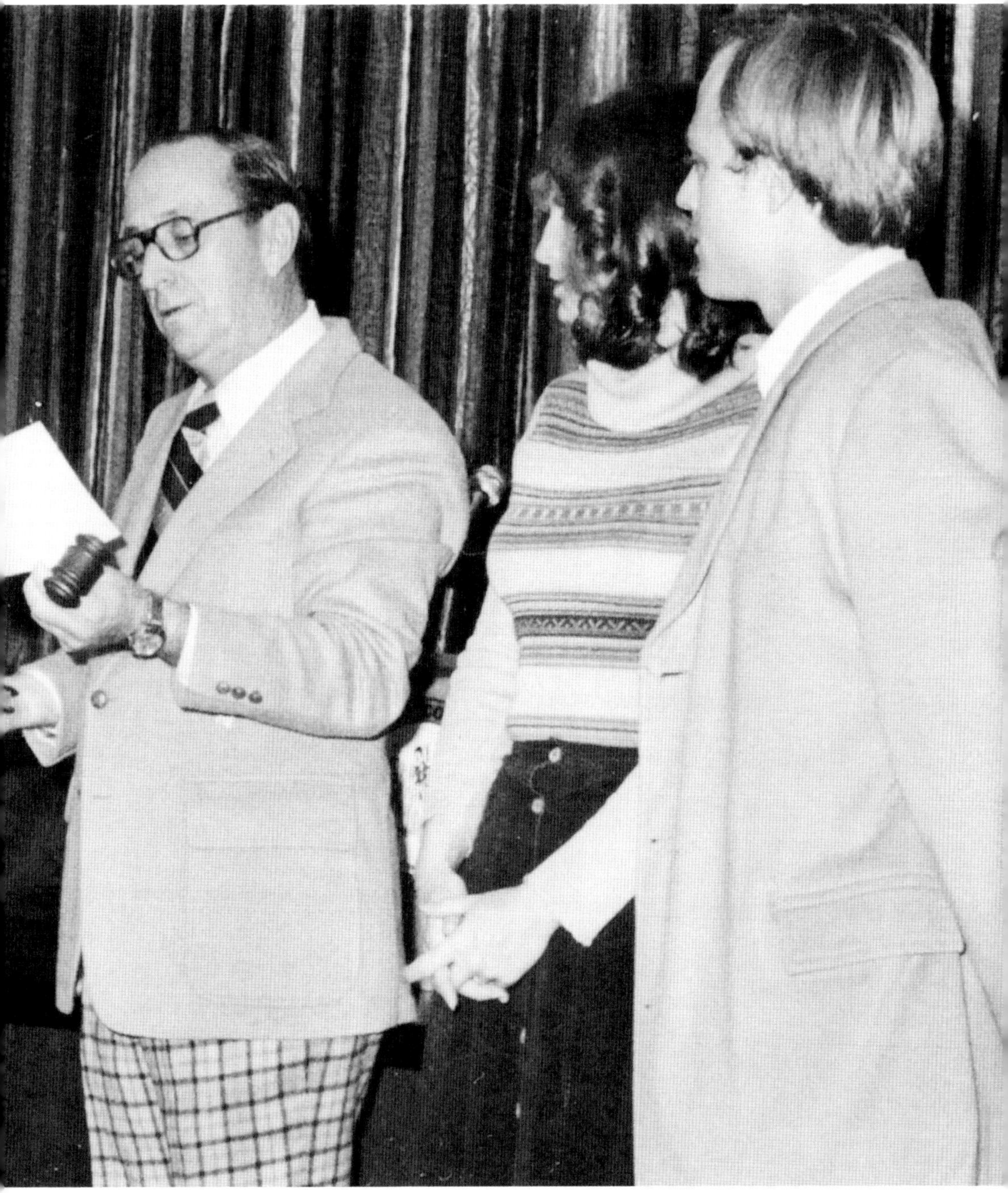

which he ran beginning in 1990. His fascination with this annual attraction began when the fair opened in 1953, when he was in his 20s. A 1.42-mile paved greenway in Concord is named in his honor. He died in 2013 at age 84. This 1977 photograph shows what McEachern's daughter Teena McEachern Boone calls her father's "proudest moment" as he was being sworn in as mayor. From left to right are daughter Teena, wife Reba, McEachern, outgoing mayor Alfred M. Brown Sr., daughter-in-law Martha, and son Dennis McEachern. (Photograph by Frankie Furr.)

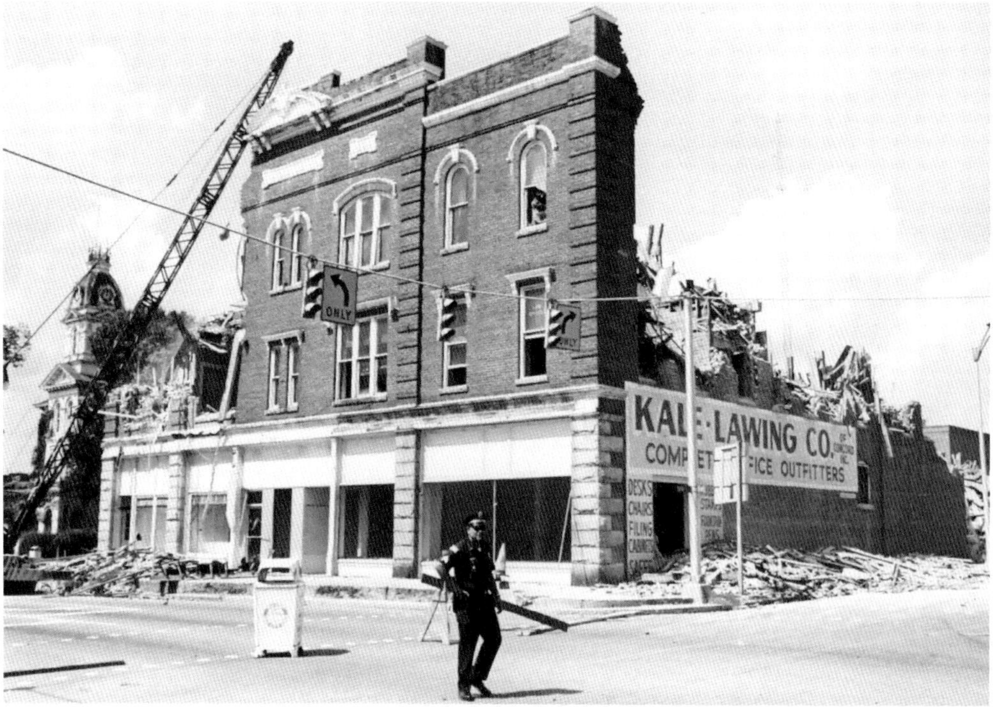
ONLY
LAWING CO.
ICE OUTFITTERS
DESKS
CHAIRS
FILING

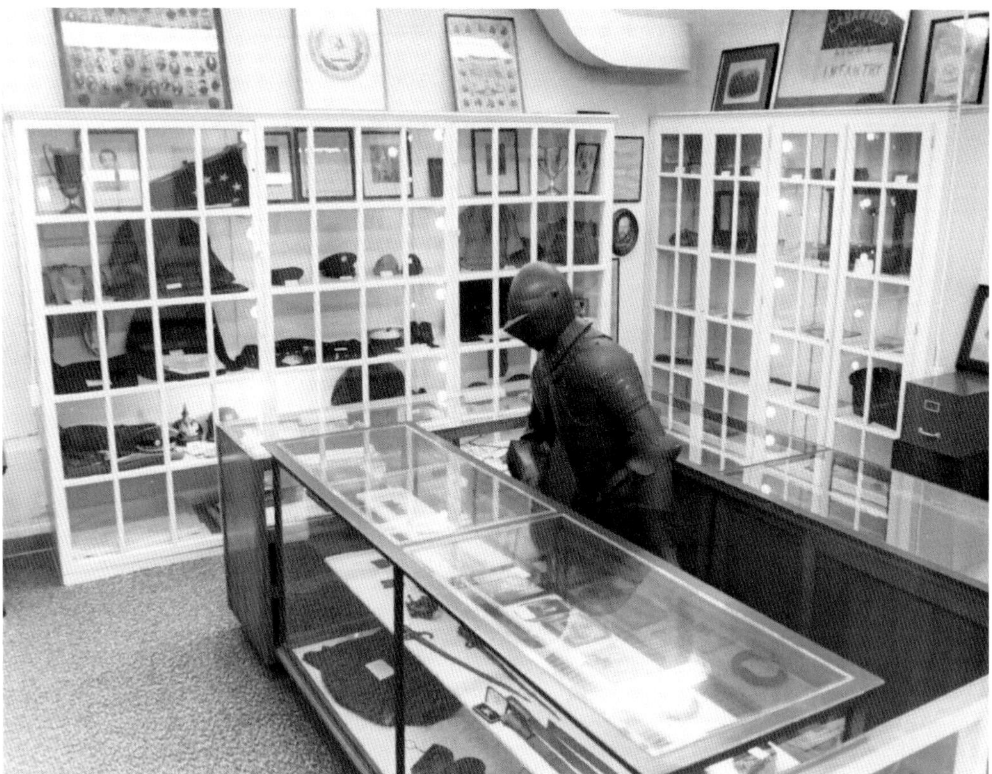
INFANTRY

Historic Cabarrus Association, Inc. (OPPOSITE PAGE)
In early 1967, Cabarrus County officials announced their intention to build a new courthouse in downtown Concord, as the 1876 Historic Courthouse, which stood proudly for nearly a century, had regressed into an overcrowded, ivy-ravaged eyesore with a deteriorating infrastructure. In the early 1970s, businesses occupying the Allison Building at the corner of South Union Street and Corban Avenue vacated. That structure (opposite page, top) was razed to make room for architect George A. Griffin's new courthouse.

Yet, one aspect of the county's plan rubbed many locals the wrong way. As if evoking a lyric from a Joni Mitchell folk song, the once-majestic Historic Courthouse, borne of the drawing board of architect G.S.H. Appleget, would be leveled to "put in a parking lot" for its replacement facility. From across the city, a chorus of voices chimed "No!" to this demolition. Concord's patron saint of historic preservation, Janet Magaldi, galvanized a group of citizens, among them Mrs. C.B. Barber, Mrs. Guy Beaver Sr., Sarah Boer, Mary Snead Boger, Robert L. Burrage Jr., Lester D. Coltrane Jr., J. Roy Davis Jr., George Engstrom, John Foard, John Sharp Hartsell, Mariam Cannon Hayes, Hector H. Henry III, Donald S. and Margaret Holt, Branson Coltrane Jones, Douglas Kelling, Mary Lentz, Eugenia Lore, Alex Patterson, Minnie Walker, and Sylvia Weaver, to take action to preserve this architectural treasure.

The nonprofit organization Historic Cabarrus, Inc., was created to direct this effort. Defying bulldozers and municipal plans, this dedicated group and other concerned citizens raised public awareness and funds to halt the wrecking ball and refurbish the building. The building then became home to a variety of nonprofits, including Memorial Hall (opposite page, bottom; today known as the Concord Museum), and its former courtroom was the location of the newly created Old Courthouse Theatre.

In the wake of this restoration victory, Historic Cabarrus began to produce historical programs and publications. In 2007 the organization merged with the Concord Museum, jointly becoming Historic Cabarrus Association, Inc. Today, it operates two community museums: the Cabarrus County Veterans Museum, located inside the County Governmental Center, and the Concord Museum, appropriately housed inside the Historic Courthouse. Joanne Gonnerman is its current executive director. (Both, courtesy of Kannapolis History Associates.)

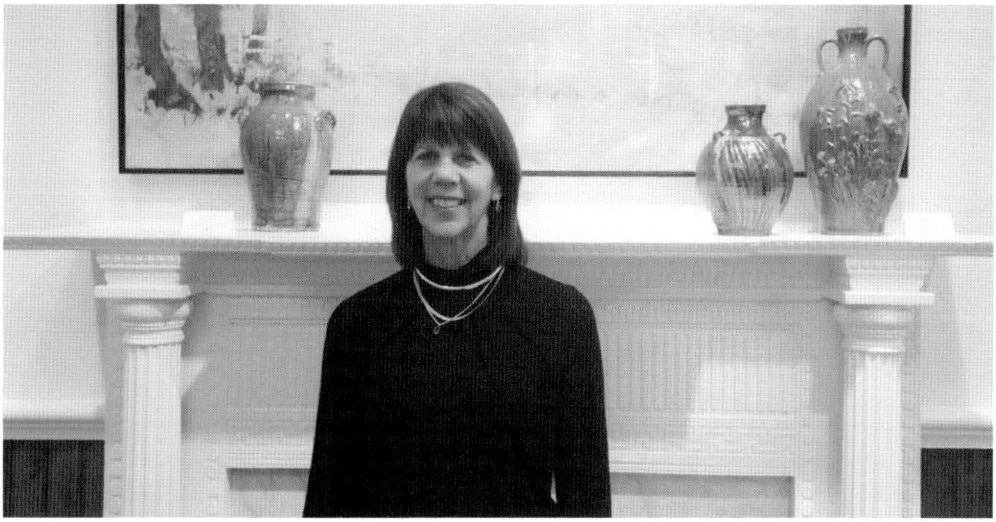

Cabarrus Arts Council
Under the leadership of president and chief executive officer Noelle Rhodes Scott, who joined the organization in 2000, the Cabarrus Arts Council has recreated rustic downtown Concord into a spirited cultural center. Headquartered in the 1876 Historic Courthouse, it operates the Galleries, showcasing rotating art exhibits, and the performance venue, the Davis Theatre. It also sponsors the Downtown Concord Art Walk and arts education programs. (Courtesy of the Cabarrus Arts Council.)

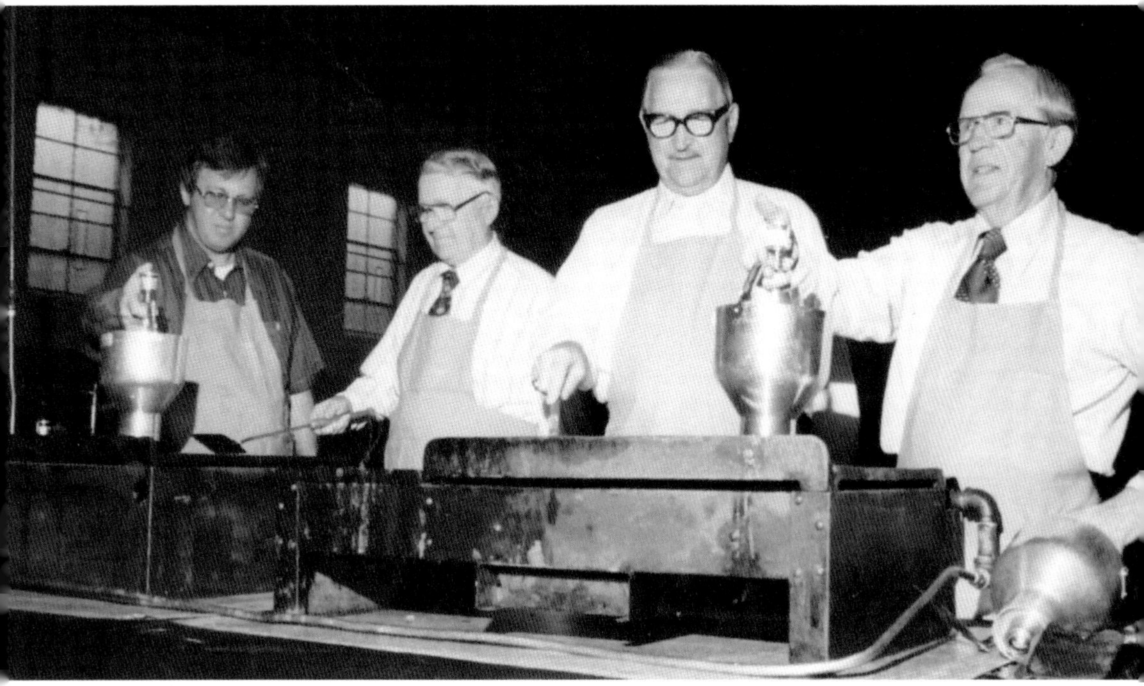

Frank Liske

It is fitting that Concord's 238-acre Frank Liske Park was once part of Stonewall Jackson Training School, since its namesake spent decades working there with troubled youth. Known to many as "Mr. Democrat," this one-time county Democratic Party chairman was also deeply committed to both the Boy Scouts and the Boys Club. Shown above at the Boys Club's 1978 Pancake Day are, from left to right, Phil Tesh, Liske, Harry Martin, and Fred Wilson. Shown below at a Boy Scout event from the late 1970s are, from left to right, Lester D. Coltrane Jr., Liske, and Harold Falls. (Both courtesy of the Boys and Girls Club.)

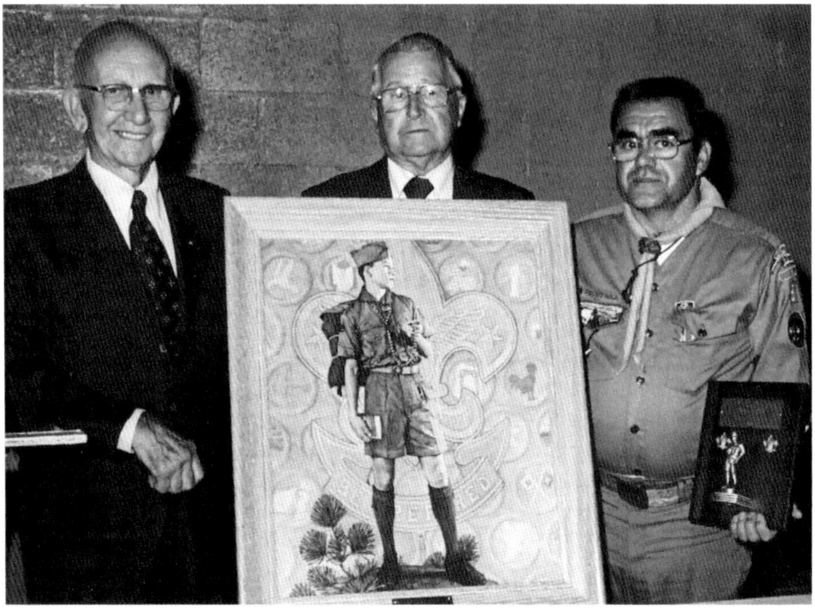

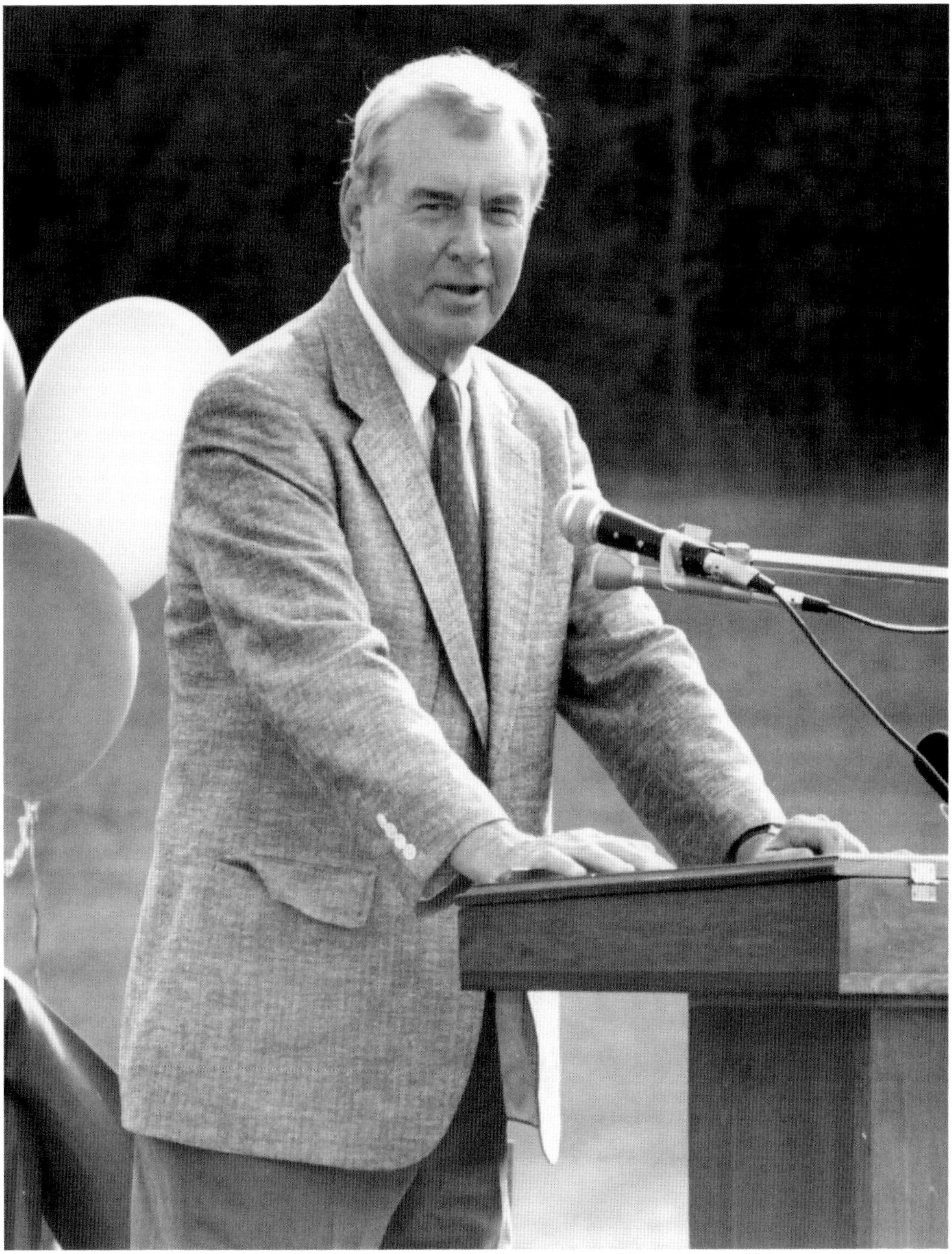

George W. Liles Sr.

This prominent surgeon spent nearly all of his 88 years caring for others, beginning with his service as a World War II medical officer and then continuing through decades of private practice. Upon his 1993 retirement, Liles cofounded the Community Free Clinic with Dr. David Lockhart and was voted into office as Concord's first Republican mayor since Reconstruction. As mayor, Liles laid the groundwork for the development of the Concord Regional Airport and Concord Mills shopping center. A Concord thoroughfare is named in his honor. (Courtesy of Concord Public Library.)

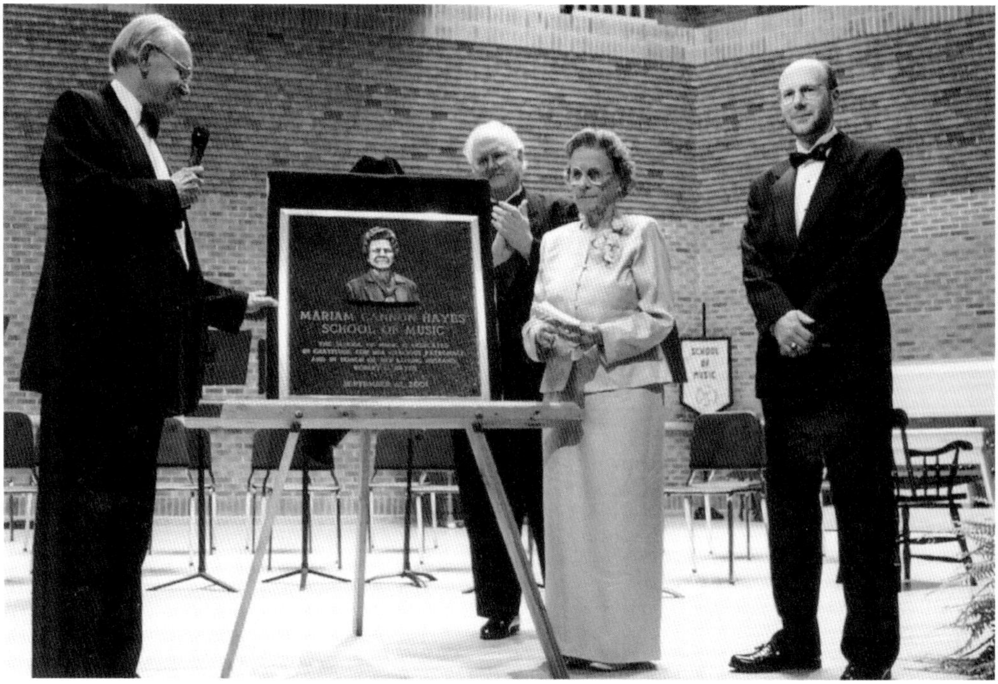

Mariam Cannon Hayes

In 1969, Hayes and her father, Charles A. Cannon, cofounded a summer music camp for high school musicians at Appalachian State University. Her longstanding commitment to the music school culminated with a $10-million endowment in 2001. This photograph shows Dean William Harbinson (left) honoring Hayes at a September 2001 event at which the school was renamed after its Concord-born benefactor. (Photograph by Mike Rominger; courtesy the ASU Communications Department.)

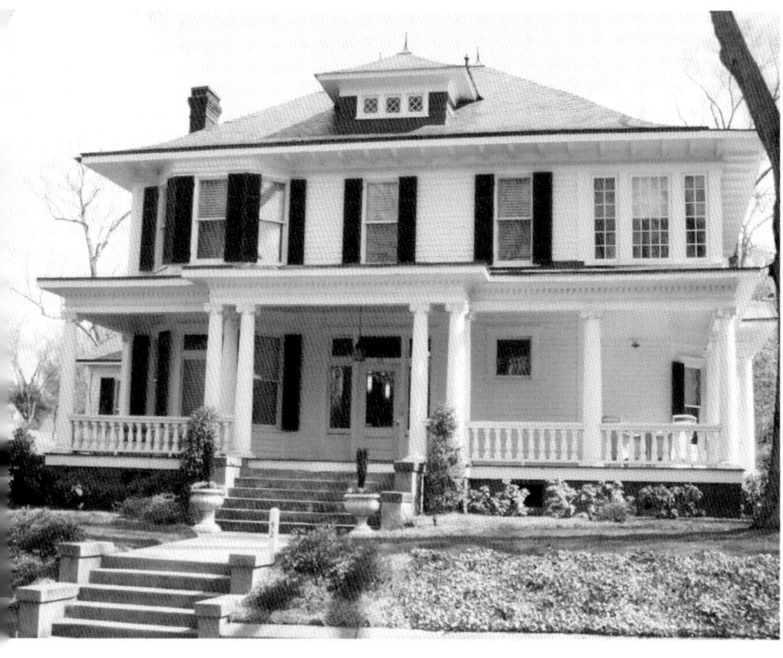

The Cannon Foundation

Once a household name from its mills' towels and sheets, the Cannon legacy today is one of philanthropy. Founded in 1943 by Charles A. Cannon, Cannon Foundation, Inc., annually issues more than $4 million in grants to statewide nonprofit and community organizations. Cannon's grandson William C. Cannon Jr. serves as the foundation's president. The foundation is headquartered in the former home of Mariam Cannon Hayes. (Photograph by author.)

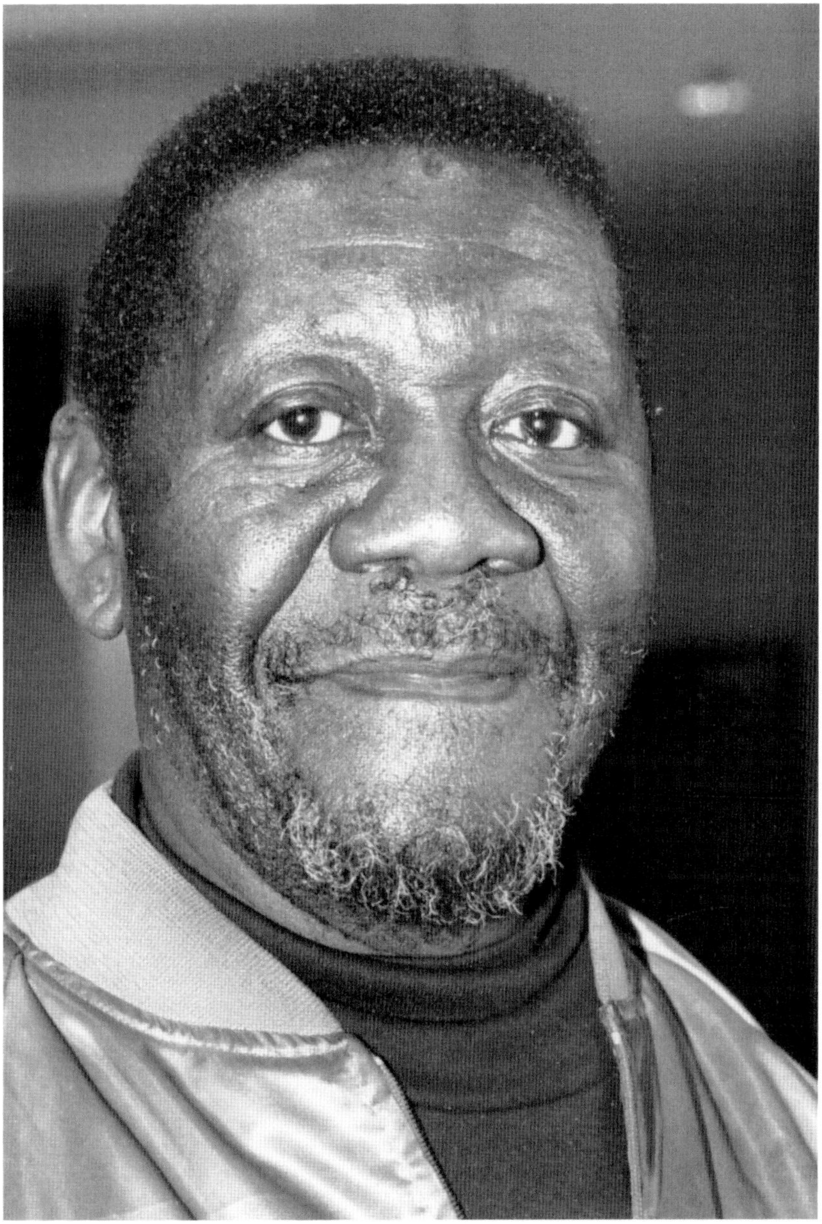

Jimmy Murphey
A hungry stranger knocking at the door might frighten most, but for Murphey, it is a call to action. Raised in poverty by a mother who taught him the importance of sharing, his bottomless heart was a beacon that attracted the needy, sometimes barefoot, to his doorstep each Christmastime. For more than 40 years, Murphey prepared for the holidays by toiling over his stove for days and gathering toys so that no child or parent would endure a joyless Christmas. His personal mission found the support of others in the community, and food and toy donations poured in. While Concord's real-life Santa Claus has since retired from his active kitchen duty, each holiday season, he appeals to locals to help others by donating to the Jimmy Murphey Christmas Fund, which is supported by several Concord organizations. (Courtesy of Concord Public Library.)

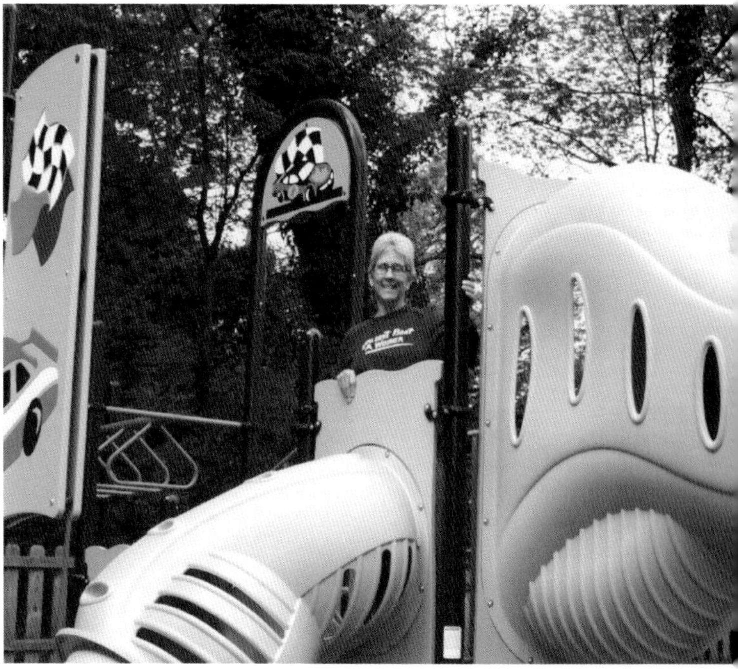

CVAN

Families upended by domestic violence have allies at Cabarrus Victims Assistance Network (CVAN). Founded in 1982, this nonprofit provides support, counseling, and shelter for battered women and children. Thousands of Concord residents have rallied to help CVAN as volunteers and donors through efforts including Men For Change, Women 4 Women, and CVAN's Store. Mary Margaret Flynn, shown here, is its current executive director. (Photograph by Toni Carpenter; courtesy of CVAN.)

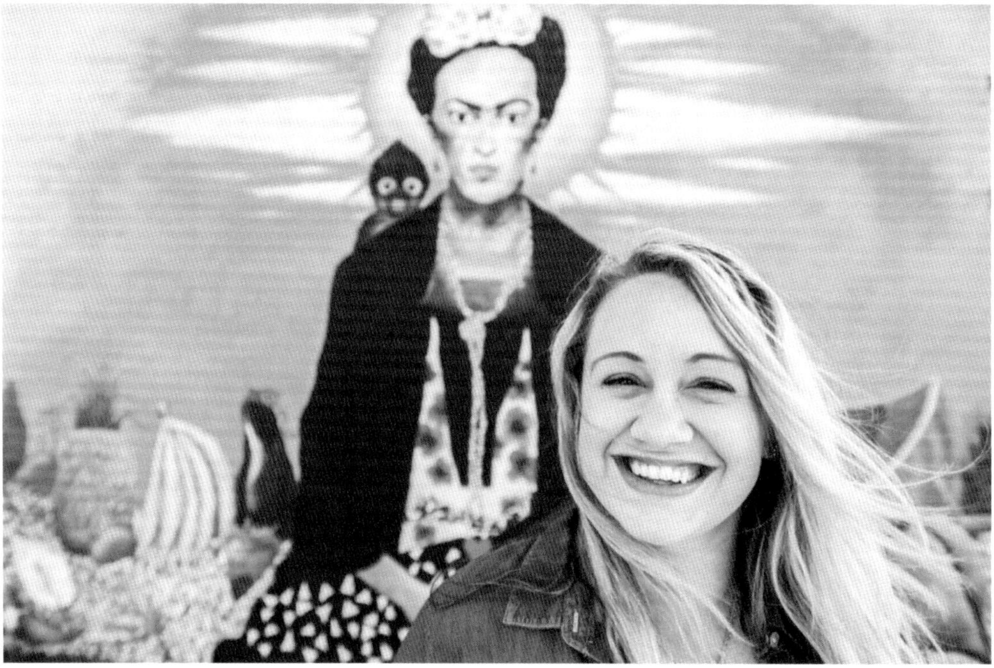

Liz Gray

One person's blight is another's canvas. This effervescent Concord native, who has toiled in Central America and crusaded for social causes, has jump-started a community project to enliven dreary buildings in Gibson Village with splashy street art. Gray's collaborators on the Frida Kahlo mural shown here were Cabarrus County artists Crystal Cronan, Brandi McKenna, Molly Rowland, Lee Sherrill, and Michael Sinclair. (Photograph by James Nix; courtesy of the *Independent Tribune*.)

CHAPTER THREE

Heroes

Each time our nation has taken arms to uphold its values, the men and women of Concord have rallied forth without hesitation. Our plucky patriots now fabled as the Cabarrus Black Boys were among the first American colonists to endanger themselves for freedom; while the passing centuries and political correctness have threatened to diminish public awareness of their fearlessness, their heroism must not be forgotten.

In their tradition have followed thousands from Concord, forsaking the comforts of home and uttering in some cases what would become final farewells as they ventured into the uncertainty of combat. Many were lost to battle, including Charles A. Cannon Jr. Some, like Quincy Collins Jr., were captured and subjected to unfathomable barbarism. Others went missing in action, leaving behind heartbroken families who never knew their loved ones' fates.

On the home front, Concordians have long showered the military with support: wives and mothers sewed battle flags for departing Confederate soldiers, civic organizations and school children collected money for War Bonds, and hundreds have lined the streets for the triumphant homecoming of a wounded warrior or the solemn return of a fallen hero's remains. Chief among them were the men and women behind the Concord Canteen of World War II, who packed downtown's Memorial Hall not only with visiting soldiers but also with profound hospitality.

One must not overlook Concord's valiant law enforcement agents, firefighters, and medical personnel, who have unflinchingly safeguarded their neighbors' lives and property. Many, like longtime sheriff James B. Roberts, served their country in the armed forces and then served their community behind a badge.

The select heroes honored in this chapter represent the thousands of others who have made Concord proud.

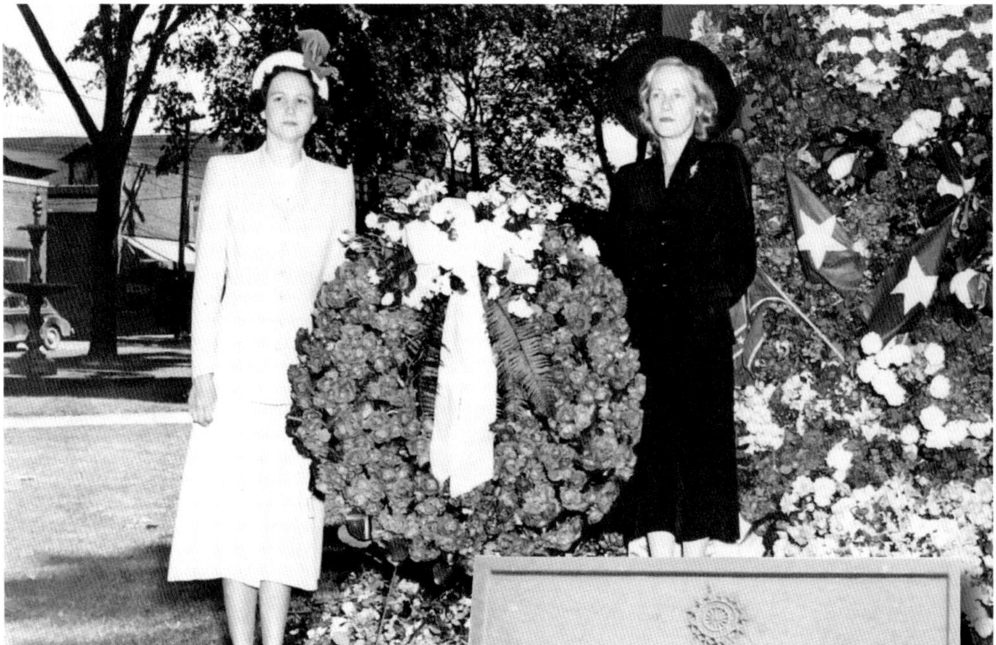

The Cabarrus Black Boys

Were fate not so fickle, the names James Ashmore, Robert Caruthers, Benjamin Cochran, Robert Davis, Joshua Hadley, James White, John White, W.M. White, and William White would be granted an eminence deserving of their feat of radical nationalism. These young colonials from the Rocky River area near what would become Concord (then Mecklenburg County) became pre–Revolutionary War heroes on May 2, 1771, two years before the Boston Tea Party. The fuse of their "gunpowder plot" was purportedly ignited by Presbyterian minister Rev. Alexander Craighead, whose blistering sermons demanded liberty and provoked these youths (in their late teens and early 20s) into covert action. (Many historians contend that their actions were in response to the Regulator movement in Hillsborough, North Carolina.) Blackening their Caucasian faces with soot and disguising themselves as American Indians, these camouflaged patriots bravely destroyed a British munitions shipment en route from Charlotte to Salisbury in one of this nascent nation's first strikes against the Crown. King George deemed them traitors and decreed their executions, forcing the youths into hiding until the Revolutionary War. Yet their heroism became legend, and nearly a century later, these "Cabarrus Black Boys" inspired a Confederate regiment, Company B, 20th North Carolina Troops, to take their name in honor.

In 1914, Concord's Cabarrus Black Boys Chapter of the Daughters of the American Revolution was founded, and two years later, the chapter commemorated the youths' courageous deed by erecting a fountain and historical marker outside of the 1876 Historic Courthouse. The fountain (seen in the left background of the photograph above) is behind Mrs. Joe V. Davis Jr. and Anne Louise Hoover, shown at a commemoration in the late 1930s. Today, the fountain has fallen into disrepair, but the marker, above, still stands. (Note the incorrect date on the plaque's inscription.) In 1926, the DAR also placed a historical marker near the site of the attack in what is known today as the Poplar Tent region of Concord. At the behest of Cabarrus County School Board member and former educator Wayne Williams, Patriots Elementary School, established in 2010, was thusly named as a tribute to the Cabarrus Black Boys. (Top photograph by Zack L. Roberts; plaque photograph by author.)

Nathaniel Alexander

Despite the paucity of medical supplies, Alexander, a surgeon, valiantly saved soldiers' lives during the Revolutionary War. In the late 1700s, he embarked upon a political career that led him to the state's General Assembly, the US House of Representatives, and eventually the governorship of North Carolina. His homestead, on what is now the Charlotte Motor Speedway (in Concord), became the racetrack's souvenir stand in the mid-20th century.

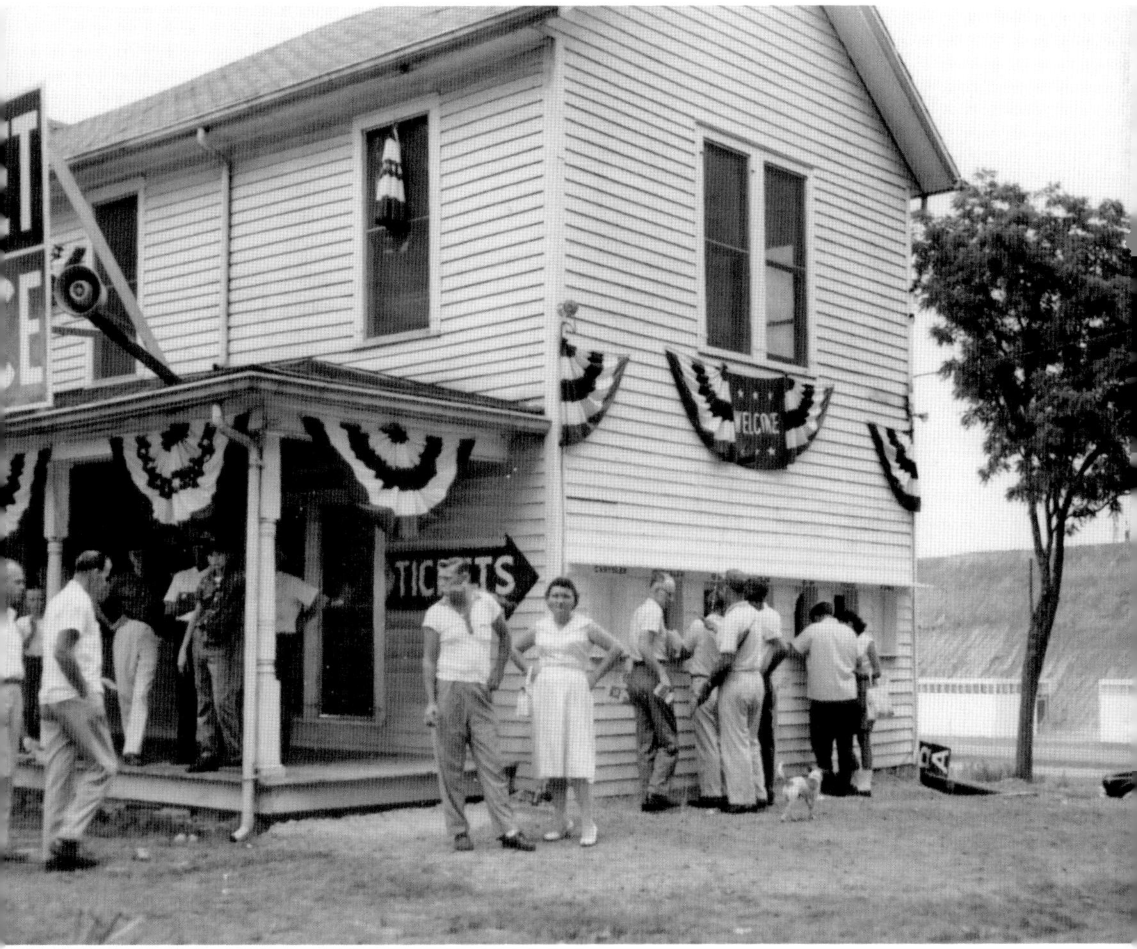

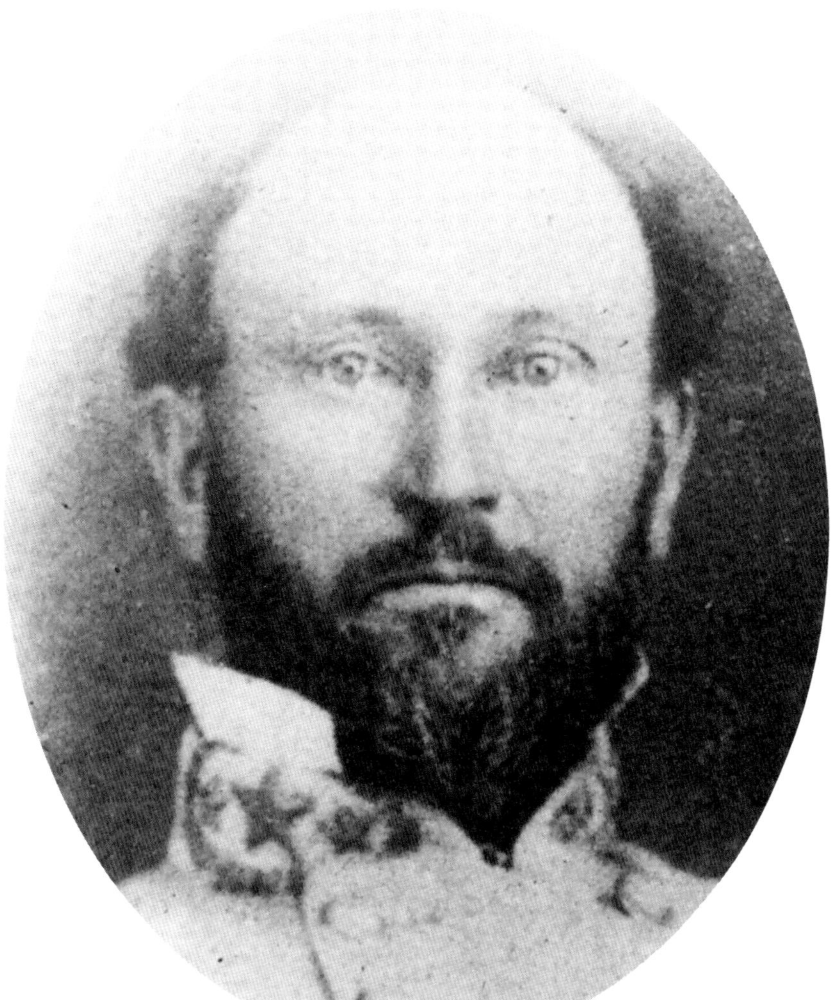

Rufus Barringer

Born in neighboring Mount Pleasant, Barringer established a law practice in Concord in the 1840s and represented Cabarrus County in the state House of Commons from 1848 to 1850. During this period, he fathered two sons born out of wedlock to Roxanna Coleman, a slave; the youngest of those children was black entrepreneur Warren C. Coleman.

As tensions mounted between the northern and southern states, Barringer was vocally supportive of the US Constitution but placed the interests of North Carolina first. Shortly after the state seceded from the Union, he enlisted in the Confederate army and was commissioned as captain of the 100-man Cabarrus Rangers, Company F, 1st North Carolina Cavalry. Barringer galloped into military history by leading his horsemen into combat at the advent of the War between the States. He became brigadier general in 1864, and his battlefield gallantry in 76 battles was so celebrated that upon his capture in April 1865, General Barringer was personally greeted by Pres. Abraham Lincoln himself.

Postwar, Barringer resumed his career as an attorney and in the 1880s, was a proponent of the state's railroad system. His first two wives, Eugenia Morrison and Rosalie Chunn, are buried side by side in Concord's Memorial Garden. Barringer died in Charlotte in 1895 and was survived by his third wife, Margaret Long. (Courtesy of George M. Patterson.)

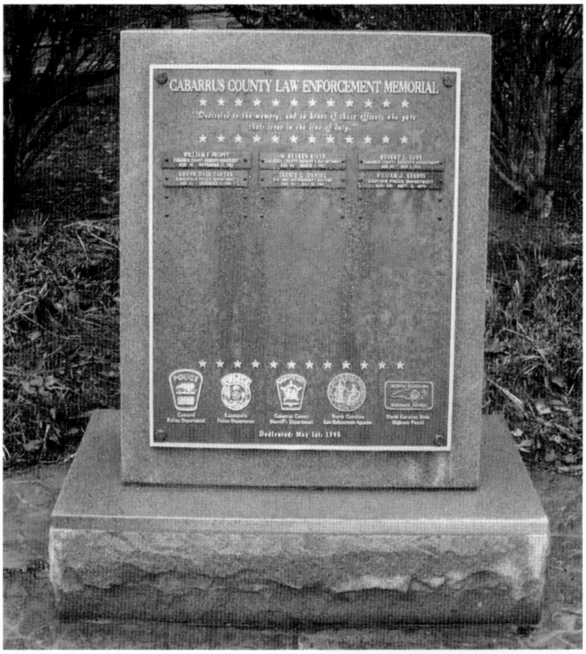

W.J. Kearns
The Concord Police Department's roots began in the 1830s when a constable was appointed. Since then, only one police officer, Kearns, has died in the line of duty; he perished on September 2, 1899, during a skirmish with a group of intoxicated men. The Cabarrus County Law Enforcement Memorial, located beside the County Governmental Center, acknowledges the sacrifices of Kearns and several county peacekeepers. (Photograph by author.)

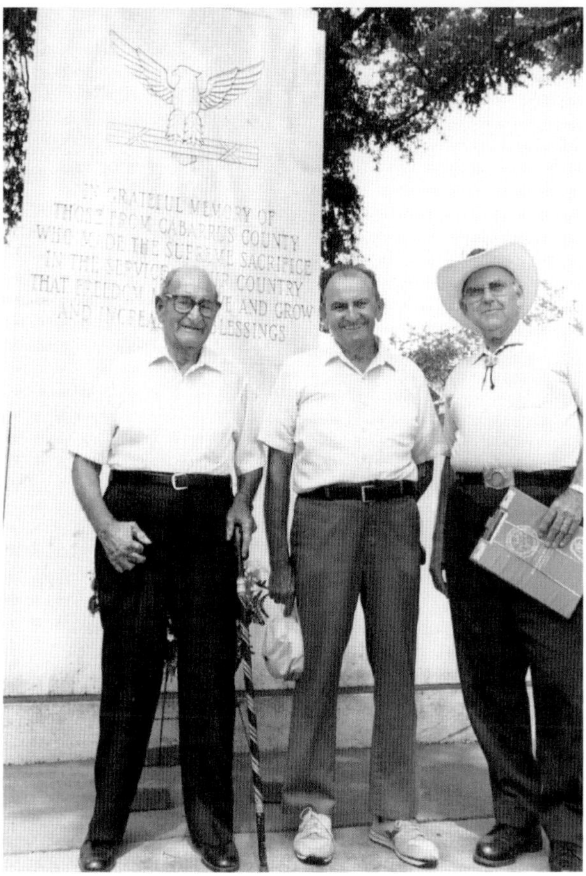

Cabarrus County Veterans Monument
The Cabarrus County Veterans Monument honors locals from all branches of the US military "who made the supreme sacrifice in the service of our country." It is located in downtown Concord at the corner of North Union and Killarney. Shown paying their respects in this undated photograph are veterans, from left to right, Leon Martin, Eddie Stelmack, and Norman Galloway. (Courtesy of Concord Public Library.)

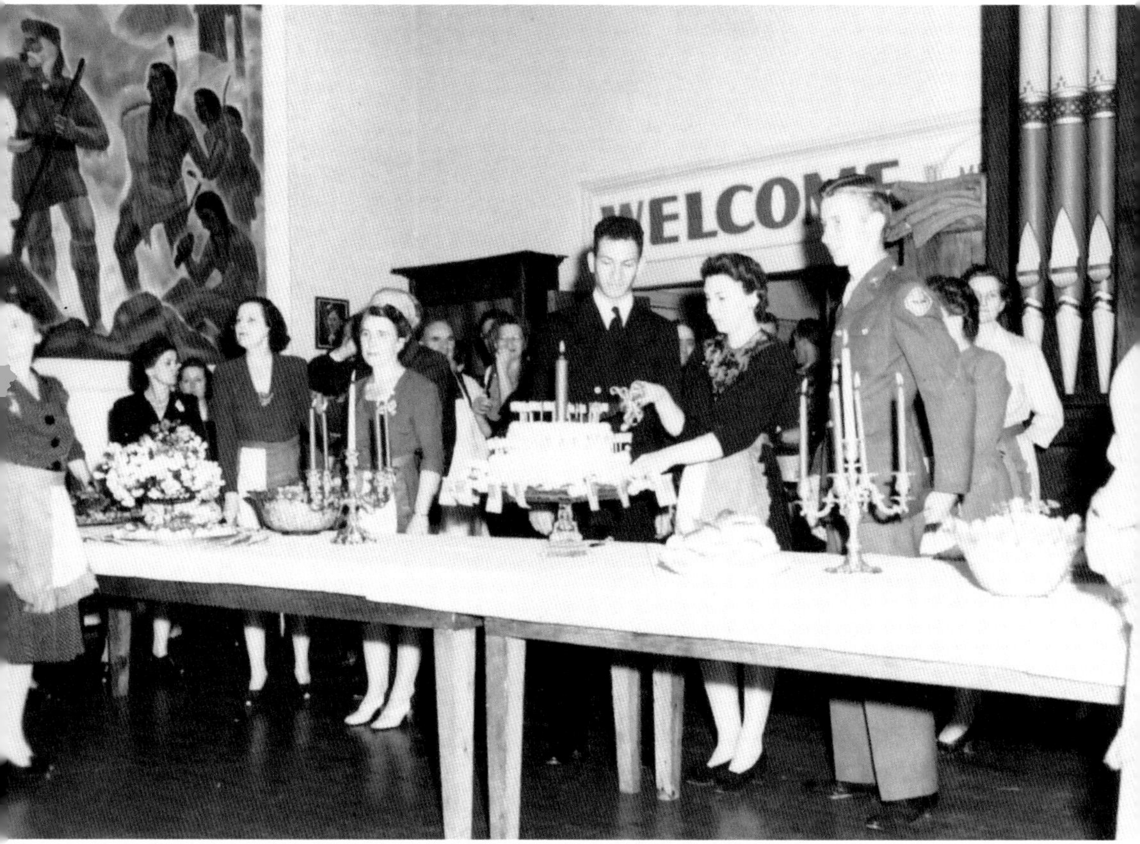

Concord Canteen

Wartime heroes do not always wear uniforms. Downtown Concord's imperial Memorial Hall, which showcased a collection of regional historical treasures gathered and managed by the Coltrane-Harris Chapter of the United Daughters of the Confederacy, took on a new life as the Concord Canteen during World War II. Opening its doors to USO-sanctioned dances for "our boys" on leave from various ports of call, this once-austere site of lectures and research was electrified by live big band music, with visiting soldiers and Concord bachelorettes jitterbugging before the unlikely backdrop of artist James McLean's Cabarrus County history mural. Once the soldiers departed town, the ladies continued their support by becoming pen pals. The Concord Canteen's mailbox was routinely stuffed with heartfelt thank-you letters from military bases across the globe, including this cartoon sent by an unidentified soldier. (Photograph by Zack L. Roberts.)

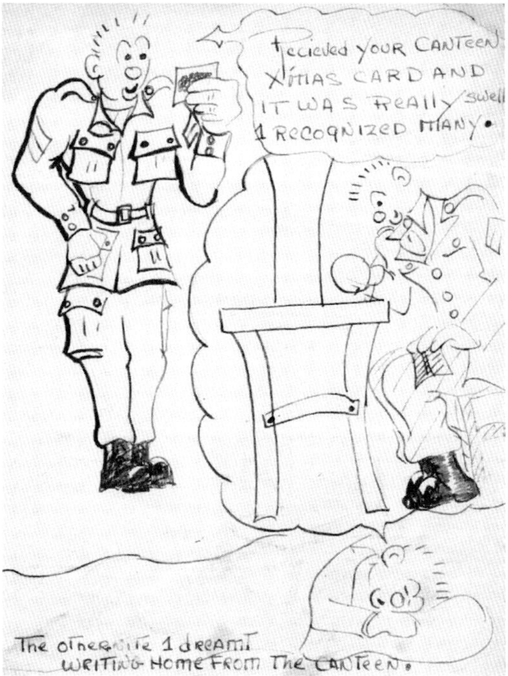

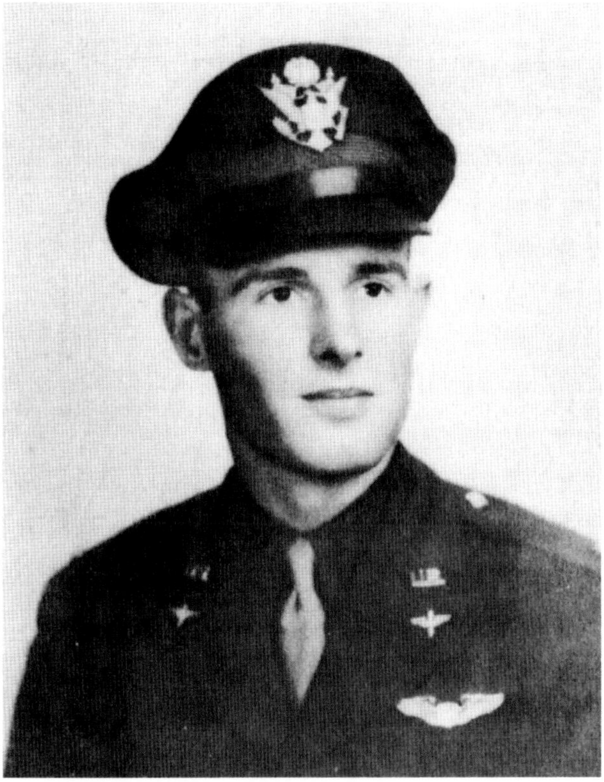

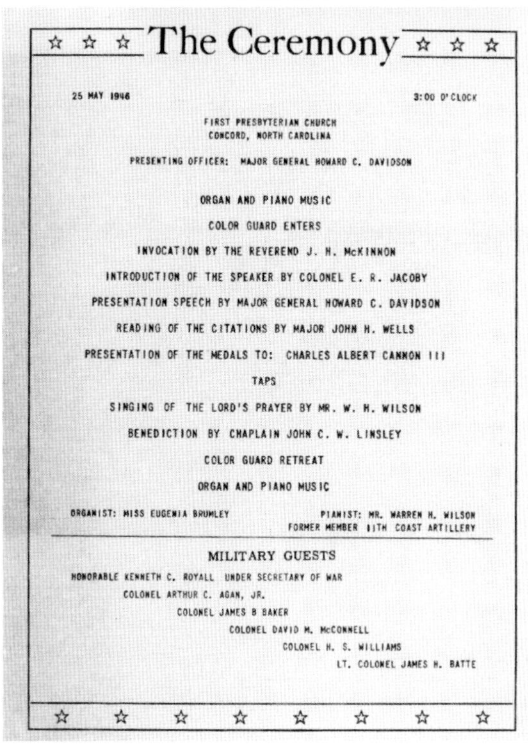

☆ ☆ ☆ The Ceremony ☆ ☆ ☆

25 MAY 1946 3:00 O'CLOCK

FIRST PRESBYTERIAN CHURCH
CONCORD, NORTH CAROLINA

PRESENTING OFFICER: MAJOR GENERAL HOWARD C. DAVIDSON

ORGAN AND PIANO MUSIC

COLOR GUARD ENTERS

INVOCATION BY THE REVEREND J. H. McKINNON

INTRODUCTION OF THE SPEAKER BY COLONEL E. R. JACOBY

PRESENTATION SPEECH BY MAJOR GENERAL HOWARD C. DAVIDSON

READING OF THE CITATIONS BY MAJOR JOHN H. WELLS

PRESENTATION OF THE MEDALS TO: CHARLES ALBERT CANNON III

TAPS

SINGING OF THE LORD'S PRAYER BY MR. W. H. WILSON

BENEDICTION BY CHAPLAIN JOHN C. W. LINSLEY

COLOR GUARD RETREAT

ORGAN AND PIANO MUSIC

ORGANIST: MISS EUGENIA BRUMLEY

PIANIST: MR. WARREN H. WILSON
FORMER MEMBER 11TH COAST ARTILLERY

MILITARY GUESTS

HONORABLE KENNETH C. ROYALL UNDER SECRETARY OF WAR
COLONEL ARTHUR C. AGAN, JR.
COLONEL JAMES B BAKER
COLONEL DAVID M. McCONNELL
COLONEL H. S. WILLIAMS
LT. COLONEL JAMES H. BATTE

☆ ☆ ☆ ☆ ☆ ☆ ☆ ☆

Charles A. Cannon Jr. Cannon, the son of Charles A. and Ruth Coltrane Cannon, successfully completed 29 combat missions as a World War II pilot. While on a March 1945 assignment in the China-India-Burma theater, his B-25 aircraft failed to reach its destination and was presumably shot down. The US Army Air Force officially declared Lieutenant Cannon dead more than one year later. On May 25, 1946, the Air Medal with Oak Leaf Cluster and the Purple Heart were posthumously awarded to him and presented to his young son Charles A. Cannon III. Shown here is a page from the ceremony's program.

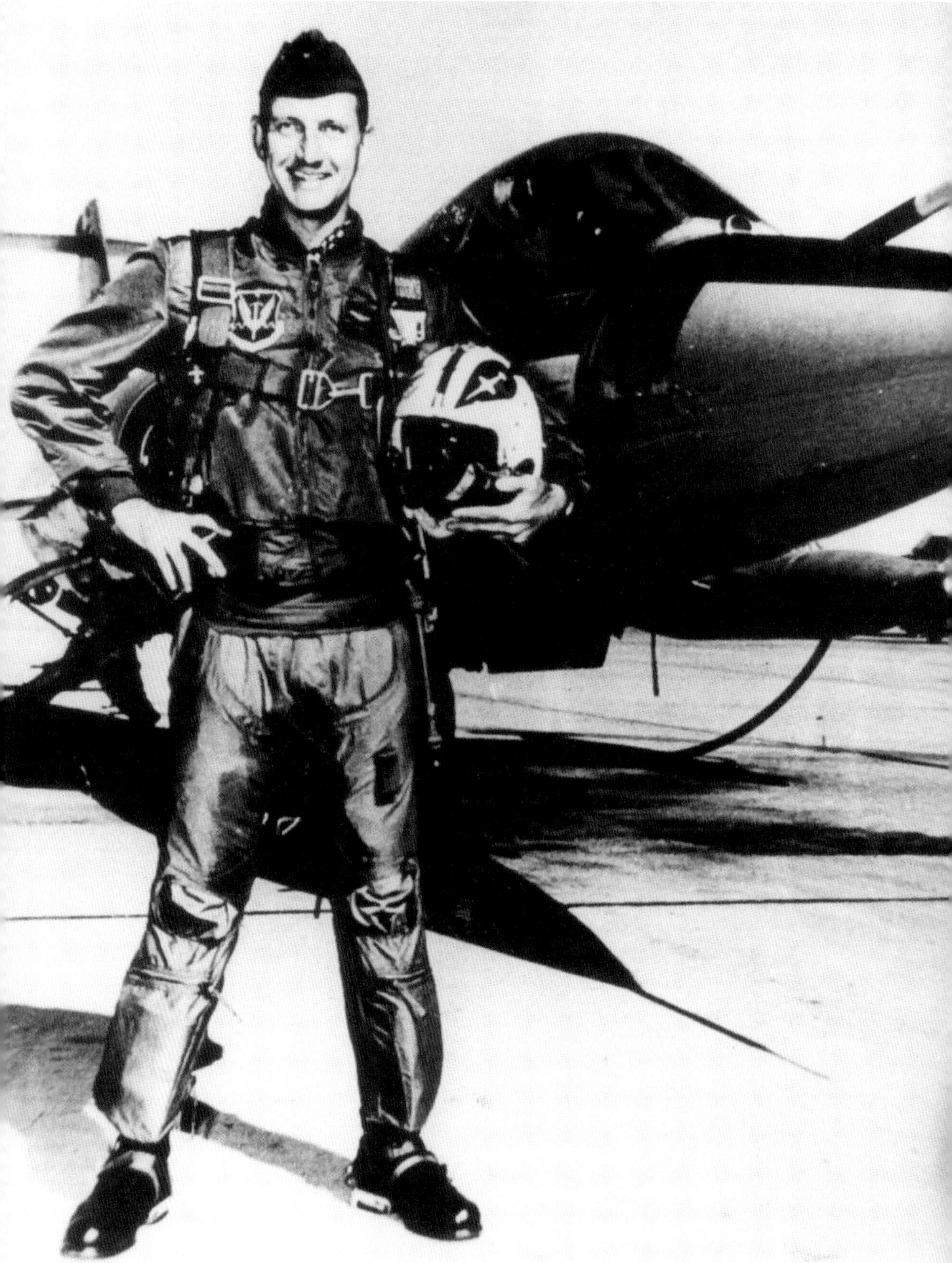

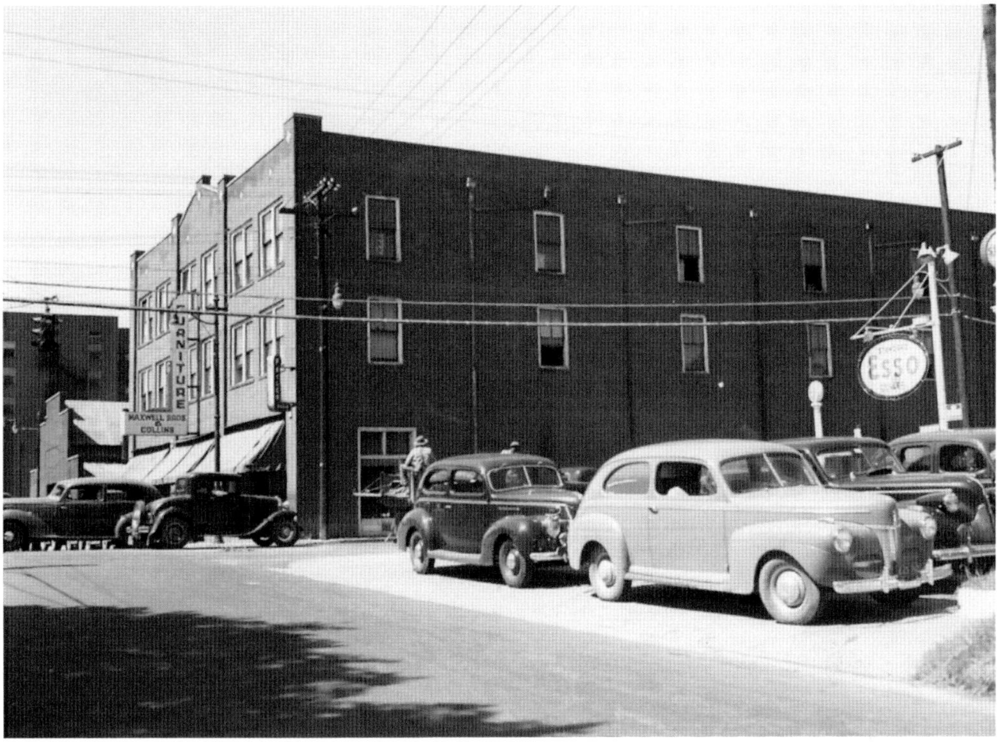

Quincy Collins Jr. (ABOVE AND OPPOSITE PAGE)
Described by a classmate as Concord High School's "best-looking, highest-stepping drum major," the sky seemed to be the limit for this son of prominent local businessman Quincy Collins Sr. of the Maxwell Brothers and Collins furniture store (which is shown here in the late 1930s). The junior Collins graduated from the Citadel in 1953 and fast-tracked into the Air Force, logging over 3,000 hours of jet time during his extraordinary 21-year career as a pilot and flight commander. His classmates from Clara Harris School and CHS expected no less from their exceptional friend.

No one in Concord, however, could have anticipated the depth of their friend's resolve. On September 2, 1965, while piloting an F-105 fighter-bomber, Colonel Collins was shot down by the North Vietnamese and spent more than seven years as a prisoner of war in and around Hanoi, along with fellow captive John McCain, who would later become famous as a US senator and 2008 presidential candidate. Collins's cell was small and windowless, with a bucket as a toilet. He was fed a paltry diet of rice and soup "seasoned" with random animal parts. Collins was, at one time, bound naked in a dark cell for days, mosquitoes feasting upon his tortured flesh. He attributes his faith in God for helping him through this ordeal and often bolstered his fellow prisoners' spirits with uplifting messages. To maintain his sanity, Collins would also remember the names and faces of those back home who loved him and even recite the names of his Clara Harris classmates, saying in 2013, "Growing up in Concord gave me a very balanced outlook, and showed me the importance of caring and love."

For nearly three years, Collins was considered Missing In Action, until his mother spotted a picture of him taken by a Cuban photographer that circulated through the news media. Upon his release on February 12, 1973, he returned to a world he no longer recognized: his wife had moved on and his three sons regarded him a stranger. Once again drawing on his faith for support, Collins started over. He married Catherine, the love of his life, becoming a father anew to her three daughters; he repaired his relationship with his estranged children from his first marriage, and he has enjoyed success in the private sector and through civic and political activism in Charlotte. Today, he is an in-demand inspirational speaker. (Opposite courtesy of Quincy Collins Jr.)

MIA\ ONLY HANOI KNOWS

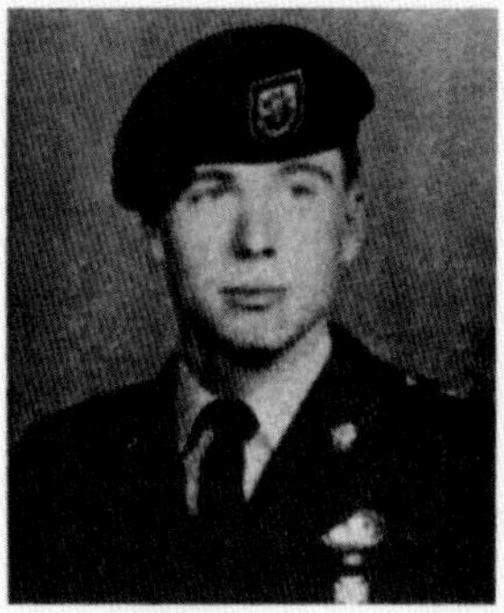

Where Is Donald Shue?

SSGT. DONALD M. SHUE
U. S. Army - Special Forces
Age: 24
Hometown: Concord, N. C.

Sergeant Shue has been missing in action in Laos since November 3, 1969. His mother and sisters are left in limbo.

IS HE ALIVE OR DEAD??

In signing The Paris Agreement, North Vietnam promised a "complete" accounting of all American POWs/MIAs in Southeast Asia.

Out of 1,925 men held prisoner or missing, there are still over 1200 unaccounted for.

Fifty-three (53) known POWs were not listed. We cannot repeat the tragedy of the Korean Conflict, when 389 known POWs were left behind.

THEY NEED YOUR HELP!

– CONTACT –

AMERICANS WHO CARE

Post Office Box 100,000 • Fayetteville, N. C. 28303

Worth Printing Company
Professional Printers of Fayetteville, Inc

Donald M. Shue (BELOW AND OPPOSITE PAGE)
"Donnie" Shue came home on Saturday, April 30, 2011. But it took him over four decades to do so. Born in Concord in 1949, Shue's affability and infectious smile helped him persuade his obstinate father, Wesley Shue, to allow him to drop out of A.L. Brown High School in 1967 to join the US Army during the Vietnam War. "He was on his knees, begging my daddy to let him go," Shue's sister, Peggy Shue Hinson, told the *Independent Tribune* of her brother's devotion to serving his country. In November 1969, Sgt. First Class Shue, assigned to the 5th Special Forces Group, was one of three men who went missing during a reconnaissance mission in Laos. His devastated family nonetheless held out hope that Shue was still alive. The military's designation of "Killed In Action/Body Not Recovered" for Shue seemed to dash that hope in 1979, casting a pall over a commemorative plaque that was erected in the missing soldier's honor a few years earlier at Concord's downtown post office. Yet members of the Joint POW/MIA Accounting Command, like those who grew up with Shue, never forgot him. Through an investigation that included an interview with a witness to the attack that took Shue's life, the remains of all three missing soldiers were discovered in 2010, affording their bereaved families some measure of closure. With thousands lining the streets to pay their respects, the fallen hero was brought home for burial in Concord in a procession led by the Rolling Thunder veterans motorcycle group, a fitting return since teenage Shue enjoyed wheeling around town on his bike. Buried alongside his parents, who died before their son's fate was known, Donnie Shue was finally reunited with his family. (Photograph by James Nix; courtesy of the *Independent Tribune*.)

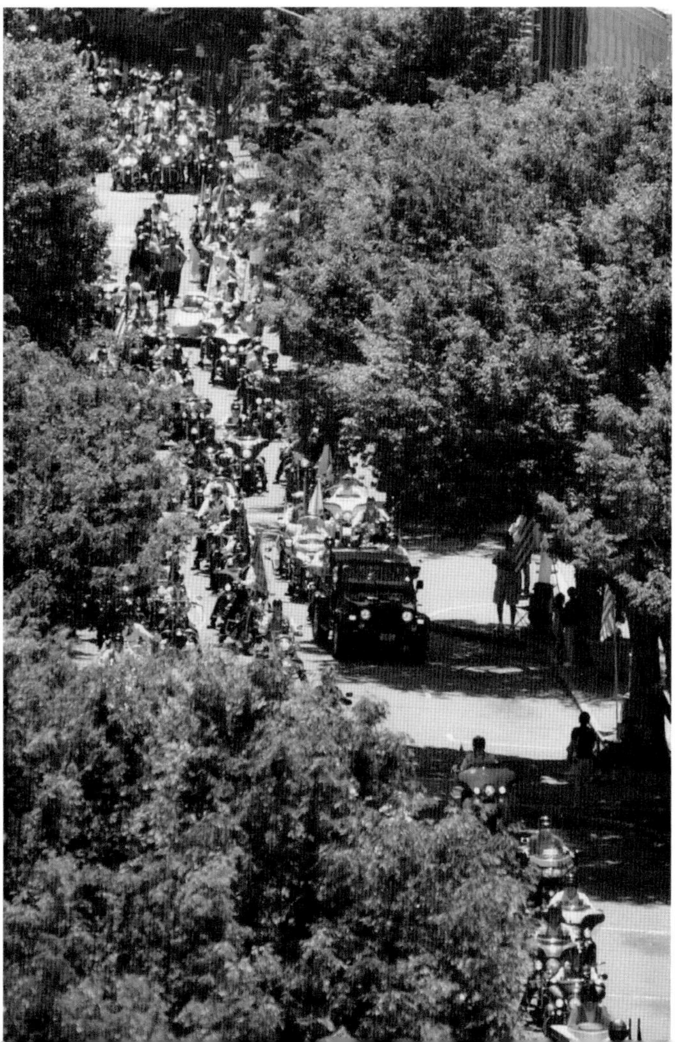

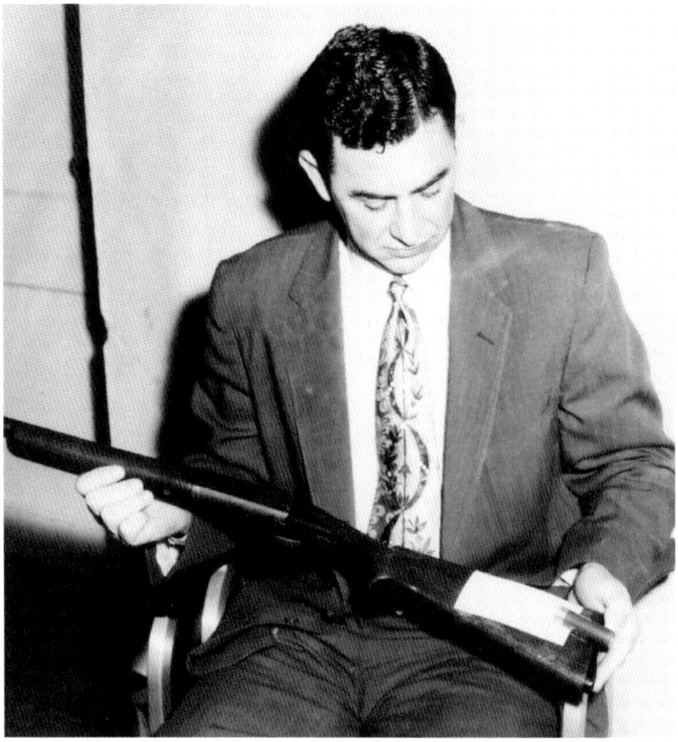

James B. Roberts
Cabarrus County's most durable sheriff cheated death during World War II, surviving for hours in the Pacific Ocean after the Japanese sank the Navy ship on which he served, the USS *Yorktown*. He joined the sheriff's department as a deputy in 1951 and was tapped to replace Sheriff E.M. "Tubby" Logan in 1956. Roberts was sheriff for nearly three decades, until 1984. (Courtesy of Concord Public Library.)

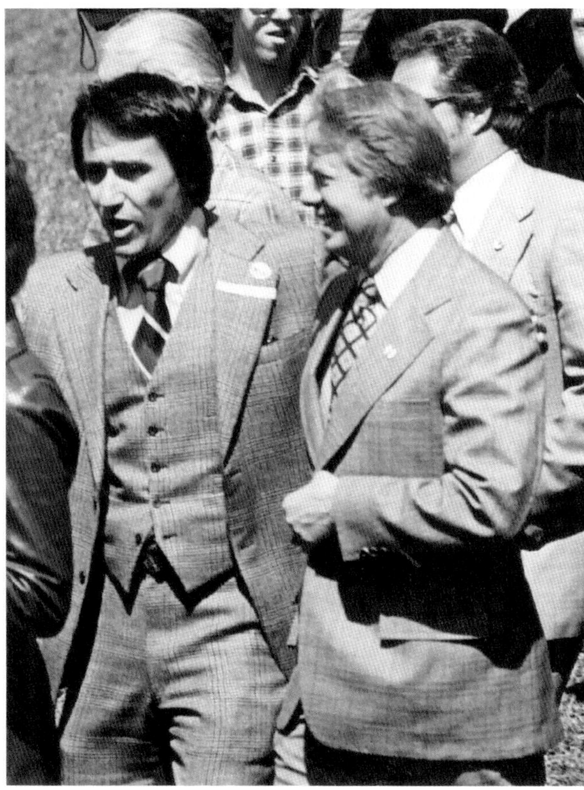

Hector H. Henry II
During his 1976 presidential campaign visit to Concord, Jimmy Carter quickly discovered that it is tough to keep pace with this human dynamo. A pediatric and adult urologist and a colonel in the US Army Reserves Medical Corps, Dr. Henry has held a seat on the city council since 1973, with only a four-year break. Even during medical deployments to Afghanistan and Iraq, Henry managed to attend council meetings via Skype.

CHAPTER FOUR

Business Leaders and Professionals

For most of the 20th century, Concord was economically buttressed by the powerhouse Cannon Mills and by numerous smaller but profitable plants, including Kerr Bleachery and Willis Hosiery. While textiles provided jobs and spending power, entrepreneurial locals saw great promise for new ventures, and businessmen from other communities rushed to Concord to ply their trades.

It did not take long for these startups to discover that in this intimate community, their name recognition was tantamount to their product. Oliver A. Swaringen and James F. Jackson Sr. guided multiple boards of directors, yet in the minds of Concordians, they would forever be remembered as grocers. Drop the family names Burrage, Morrison, Propst, Troutman, and Young, and identifiable businesses spring instantly to mind. One local stalwart needs no surname to evoke her brand—a simple "Neta's" will do.

Concord's citizens have been well insulated by highly competent municipal governors, medical practitioners, law enforcers, and legal representatives. Some of them have enjoyed multifaceted careers, including Manly Llewellyn, the crusading lawyer who was once a teammate of New York Yankee Babe Ruth.

As the city's saga unfolded, homegrown reporters and photographers captured each day's events for an inquisitive public. Zack L. Roberts and Lawson Bonds are among a long line of locals committed to telling it like it is (or *was*, in the case of "A Look Back" columnist Helen Arthur-Cornett).

A yen for public service directed many of Concord's captains of industry beyond their private practices and car dealerships to loftier positions in local, county, and state government.

From the perennial merchant to the convivial go-getter, these business leaders and professionals netted premiums that raised the bar for those who have followed.

Manly Llewellyn

Known in town as "Lawyer Llewellyn" and "Judge Lew," this lanky Oak Ridge Military Institute graduate received his law degree from UNC-Chapel Hill in the early 1920s and went straight to the major leagues, becoming New York Yankees teammate Babe Ruth's favorite batting practice pitcher. As his pitching arm weakened, Llewellyn dropped down to the minors and eventually the semipros. He was the manager of the Concord Weavers during the legendary "shirt-tail shower" of 1927, an unexpected (and according to some, divine-inspired) downpour that doused a near-riot between heated Concord and Kannapolis fans and players during their championship game. In the late 1920s, he opened a law practice in Concord and in subsequent years earned respect throughout Cabarrus County's African American community by defending falsely accused blacks. Llewellyn later became a Concord judge while maintaining an involvement with baseball, mentoring young players as commissioner of the Junior World Series. Llewellyn died in 1969 and is buried at Oakwood Cemetery. He had recently opened his law practice in downtown Concord at the time of this 1928 photograph. (Courtesy of Concord Public Library.)

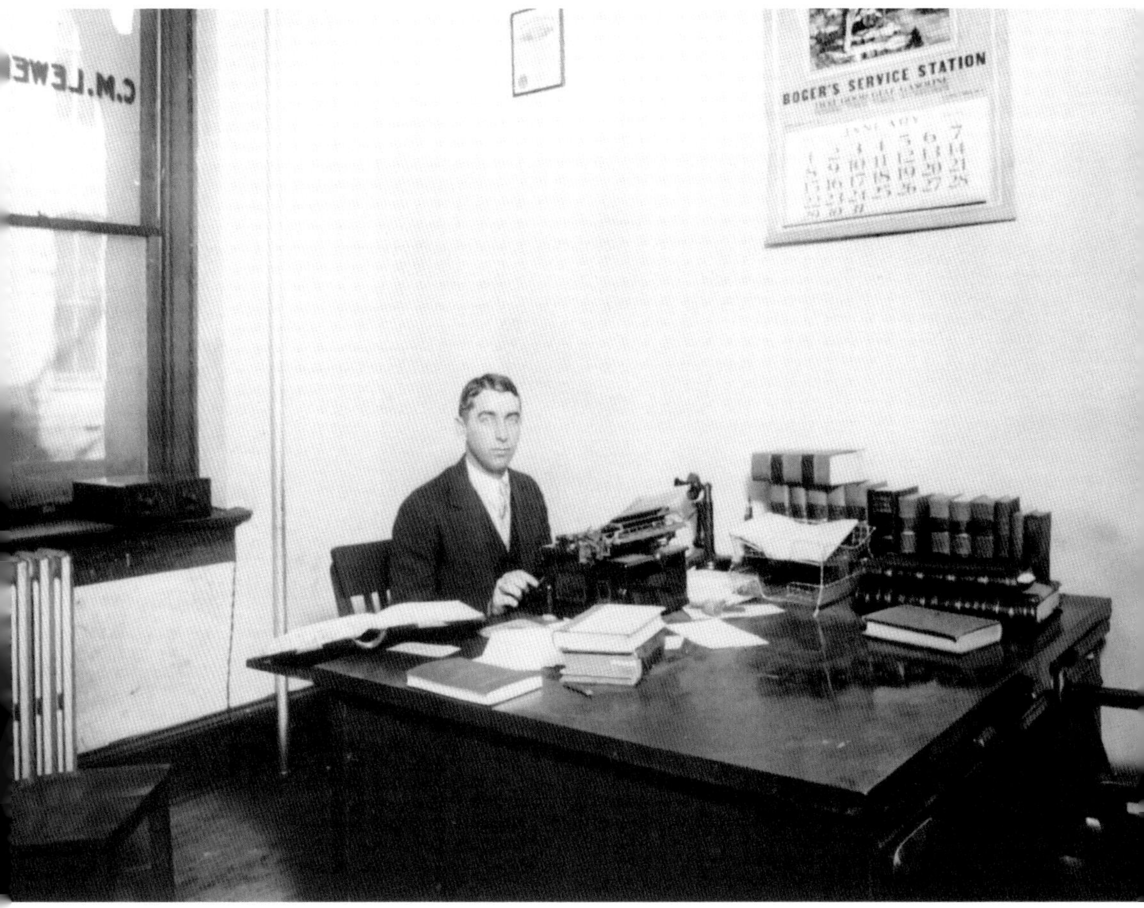

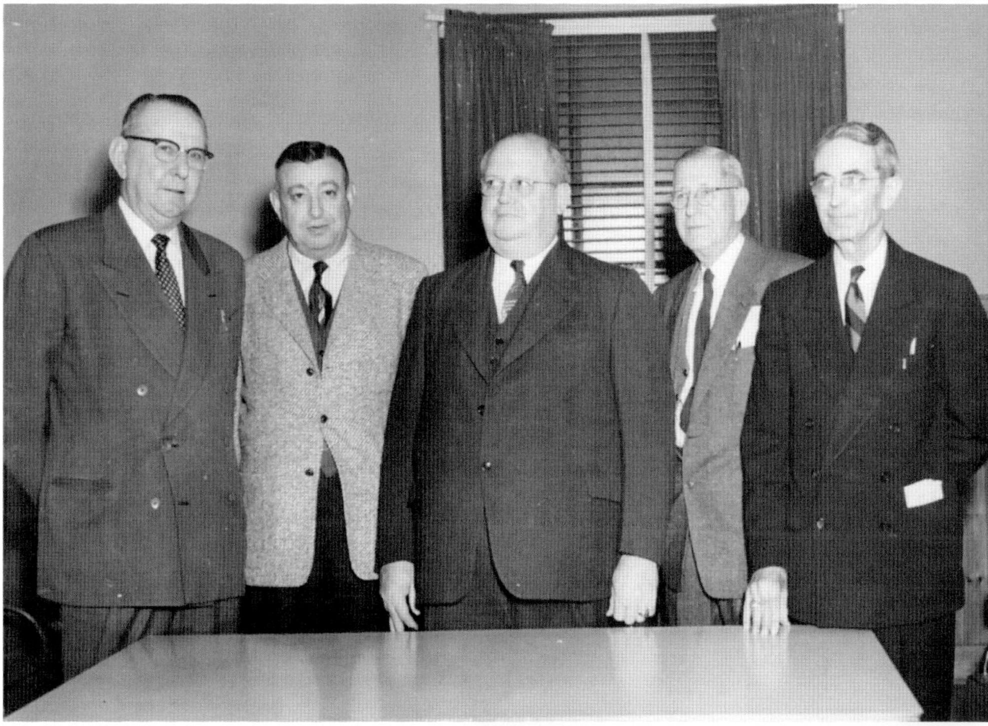

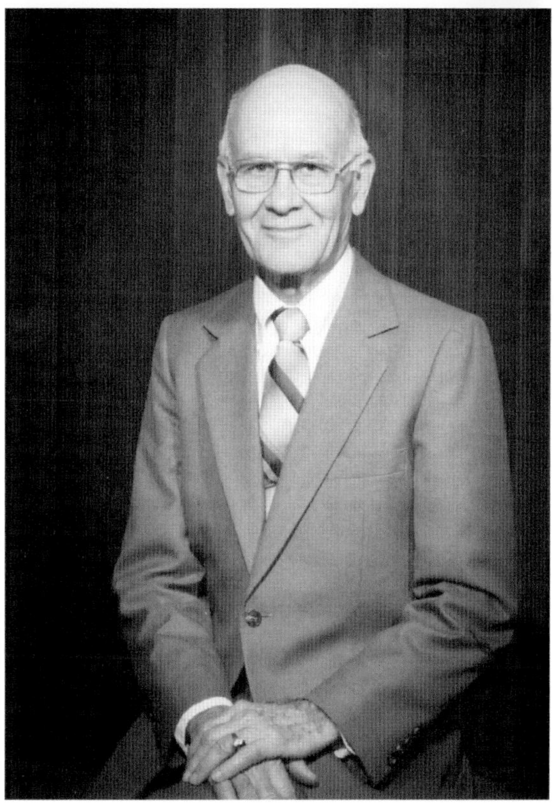

Oliver A. Swaringen
Swaringen became a grocer in 1918 with the Cabarrus Cash Grocery, and in 1939, he and partner James F. Jackson Sr. opened Concord's first supermarket, the Food Centre. A five-term president of the Concord Merchants Association, Swaringen, acutely active in many civic groups, was the father of longtime Concord High School teacher Evelyn Campbell. From left to right are Robert Sasser, "Mac" McEachern, Swaringen, unidentified, and Ray McEachern.

James F. Jackson Sr.
In 1935, Jackson partnered with veteran grocer Oliver A. Swaringen, and four years later, they introduced Concord's first supermarket, the Food Centre. His generosity to pastors of his church inspired Central United Methodist to name its Methodist Men group in his honor. Jackson served on many local and state boards and was a former director of the North Carolina Food Dealers Association. (Courtesy of Pat and William Jackson.)

Robert Burrage Family

Beginning in the early 1900s, dairy farmer Robert L. Burrage Sr. bottled milk under the names Burrage Dairy and the Co-Operative Dairy before a 1924 merger formed a company that would survive for decades, Cabarrus Creamery Company, Inc. In 1931, the Cabarrus Creamery opened a storefront location on South Union Street, and in 1940, an expanded facility on North Church Street was unveiled, which included an expansive onsite production and distribution facility (opposite, bottom). Burrage's failing health led him to recruit his son, Robert L. Burrage Jr., to take over the family business. (Burrage Jr. is shown here in a 1940s photograph with his daughter Jackie in the bicycle basket. This customized motorbike was powered with a lawn mower engine and used for business travel during World War II–era gasoline rationing.)

In 1954, the Cabarrus Creamery joined the All Star Dairy Association, entitling it to All Star's packaging and promotional materials. The creamery's interior ice cream parlor and scrumptious, freshly

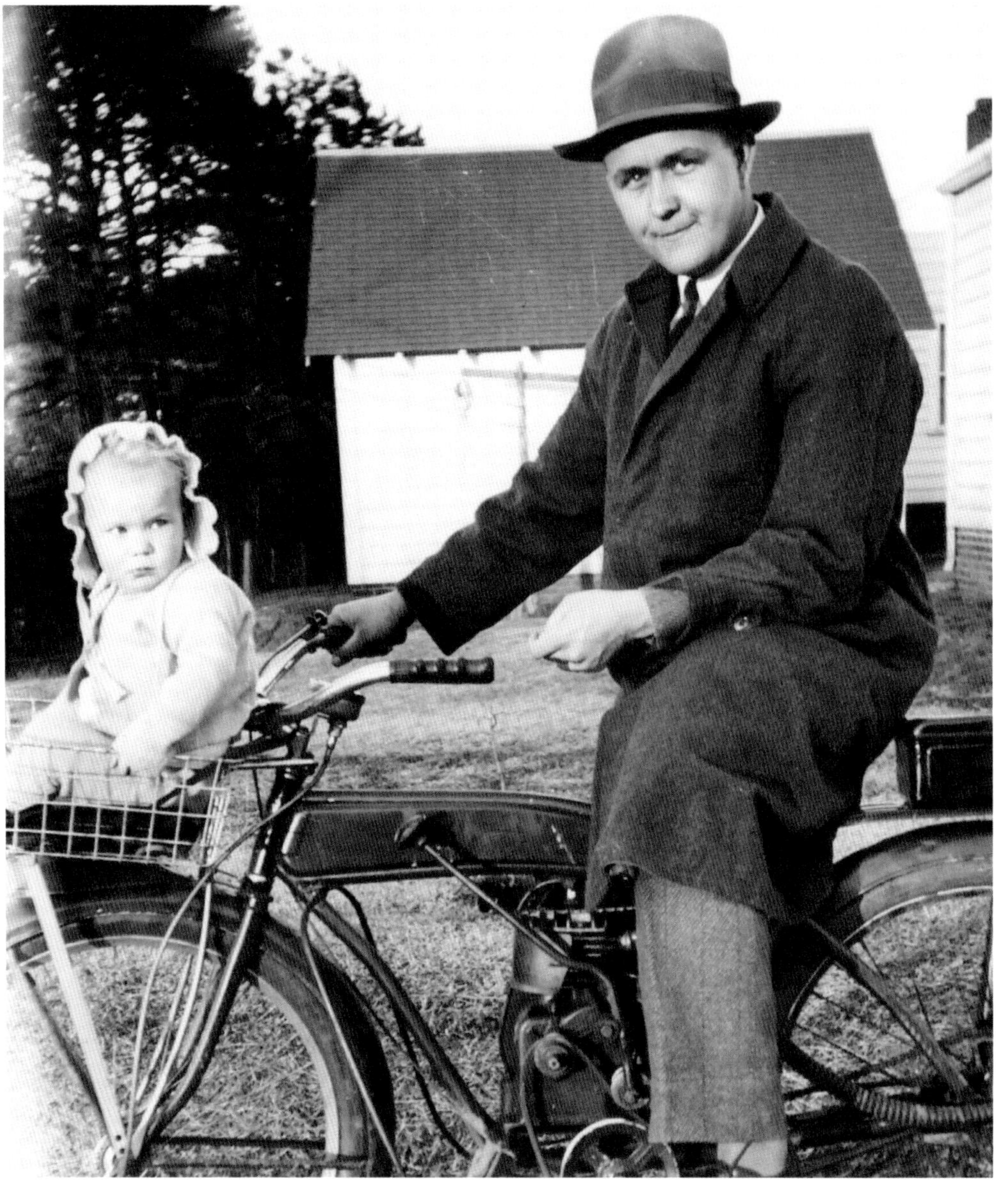

manufactured products made it one of the county's most popular eateries; on hot summer days, it was not uncommon for a line to form around the building. The Cabarrus Creamery exemplified the family business, with numerous Burrages working there in some capacity and with family members appearing in local newspaper advertisements. An extended family of longtime workers made careers there, and for many teens in Concord, scooping ice cream at the Cabarrus Creamery was their first job.

Robert L. Burrage Jr.'s son Robert E. Burrage Sr. eventually took over the family business. His son Robert E. "Little Robert" Burrage Jr., shown as a toddler in the 1975 advertisement below, was the heir apparent to the business, but in 1999, shifts in the marketplace forced upon the family the difficult decision to close the creamery. Today, Little Robert owns Lil' Robert's, a popular downtown Concord hangout that sells craft beers, which coincidentally is located next door to the new Cabarrus Creamery, now an ice cream parlor operated by a different owner. (All courtesy of Robert E. Burrage Sr.)

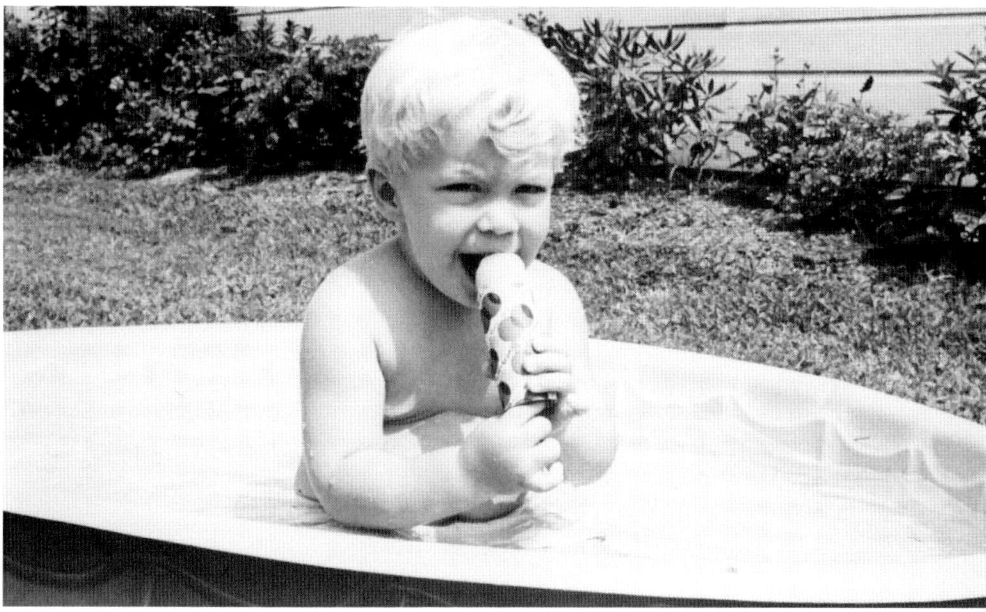

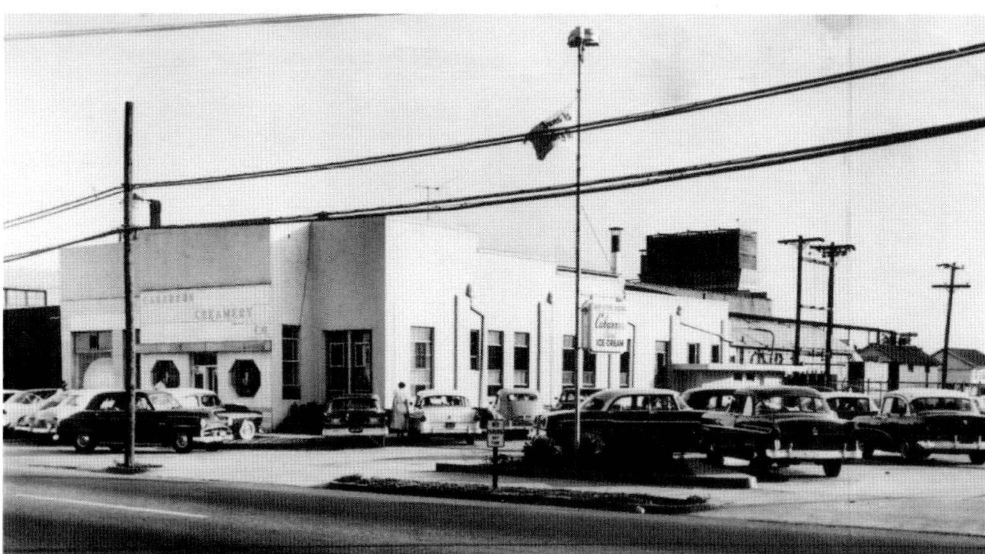

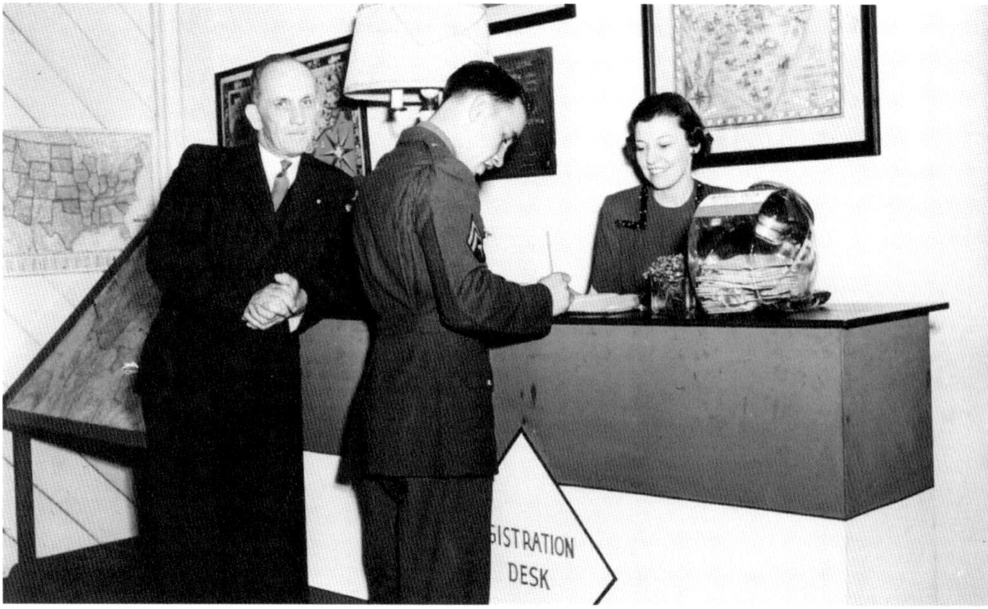

Lester D. Coltrane Jr.

Following his father's footsteps in 1948 at the helm of the Concord Telephone Company (CTC), Coltrane methodically learned the ropes of the business. Graduating from North Carolina State University in 1914 with an electrical engineering degree, he toiled as a "troubleman" (darting around town on a motorcycle) and other positions before rising to assistant manager in 1931. In 1955, Coltrane led the company's expansion into a larger facility on Cabarrus Avenue. Many remember him for starting *Progress* magazine, a periodical that merged historical articles with the company newsletter. *Progress* began in 1967 and ceased publication in 1986, the year after Coltrane's death. Shown above at the Concord Canteen registration desk in 1943 are, from left to right, Coltrane, an unidentified soldier, and hostess Jennie Brown. The photograph below shows CTC operators in the early 1940s. (Both by Zack L. Roberts.)

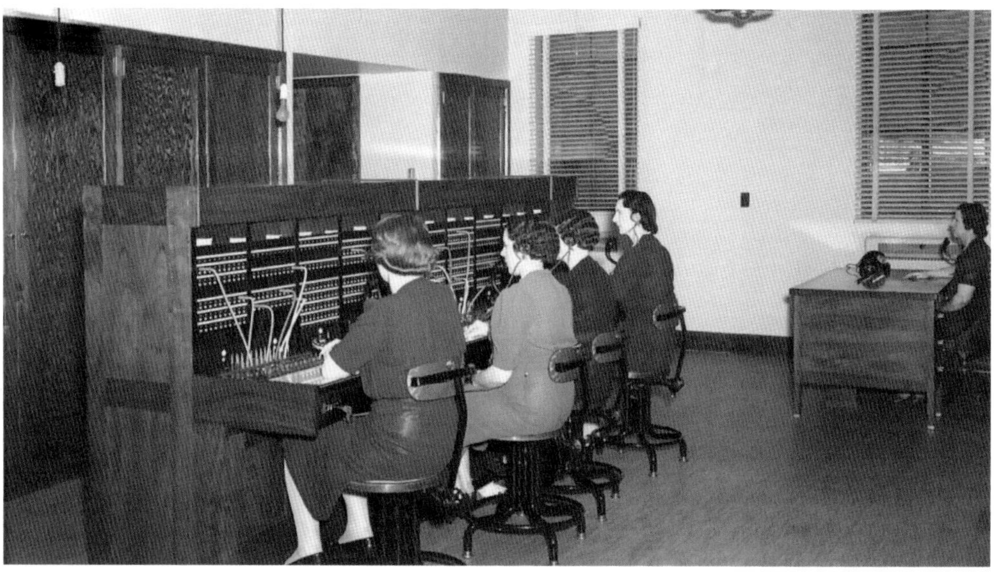

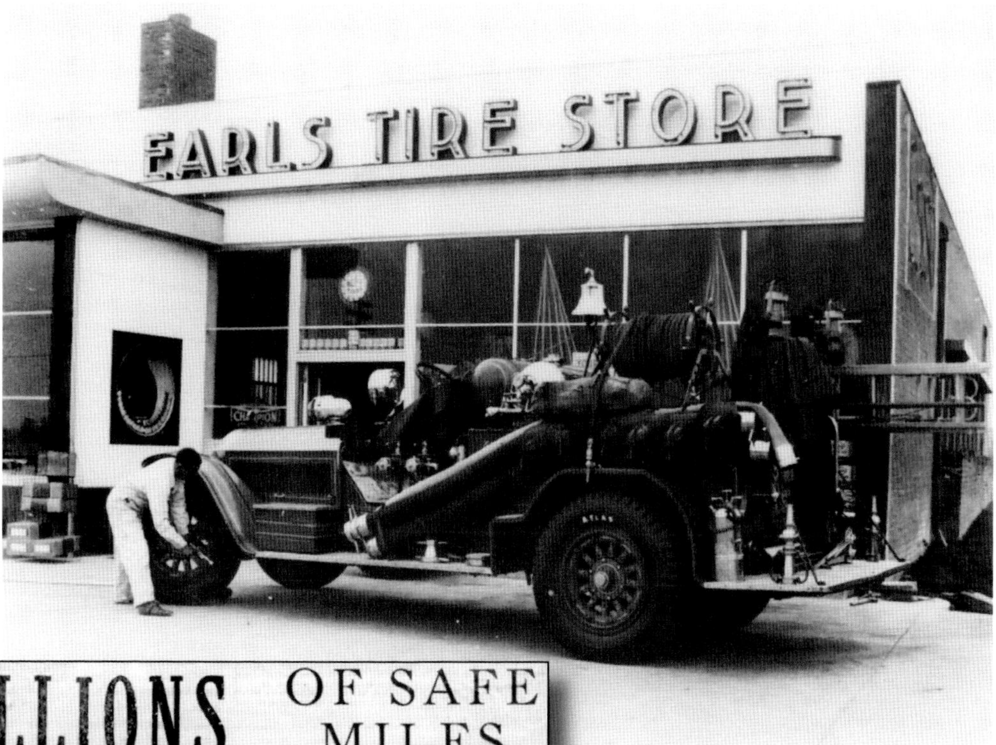

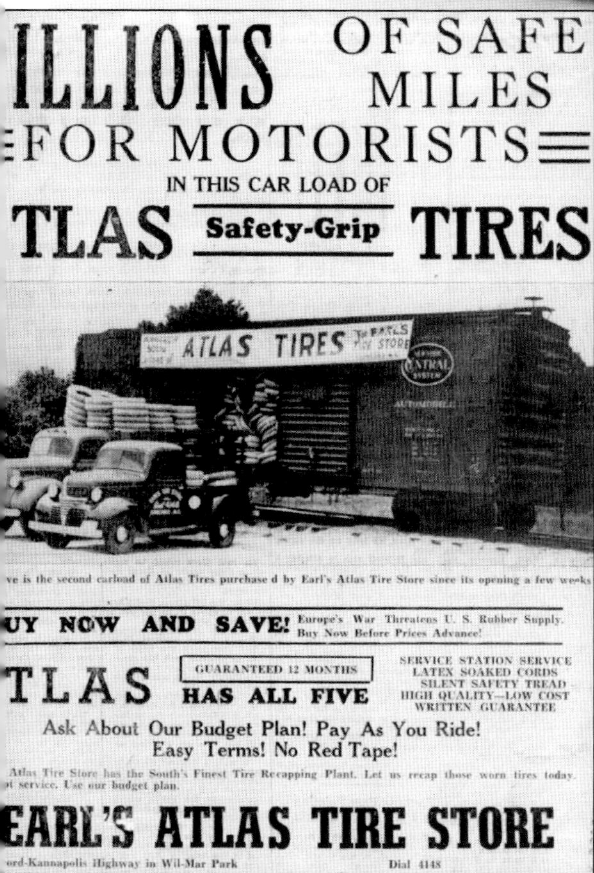

Propst Brothers

William Propst Jr.'s 1937 purchase of 140 acres on North Church Street became Wil-Mar Park, its name chosen in a contest from an entry that combined his name, William, and his wife's name, Margaret. Propst and siblings Clyde, Earl, Carl, Ben, and Phil foresaw the emerging car culture and developed appropriate businesses, including the hauling company Propst Transport, fuel distributor Propst Brothers, the Pine Tavern roadside lodge, and Colonial Motor Court, which operated in north Concord across from what today is Carolinas Medical Center NorthEast. Earl's Tire Store opened on North Church Street in March 1940 and was a longtime Concord fixture. As this newspaper advertisement shows, the business was originally Earl's Atlas Tire Store; it responded to World War II tire rationing by adding recapping services. (Courtesy of Kenny Propst.)

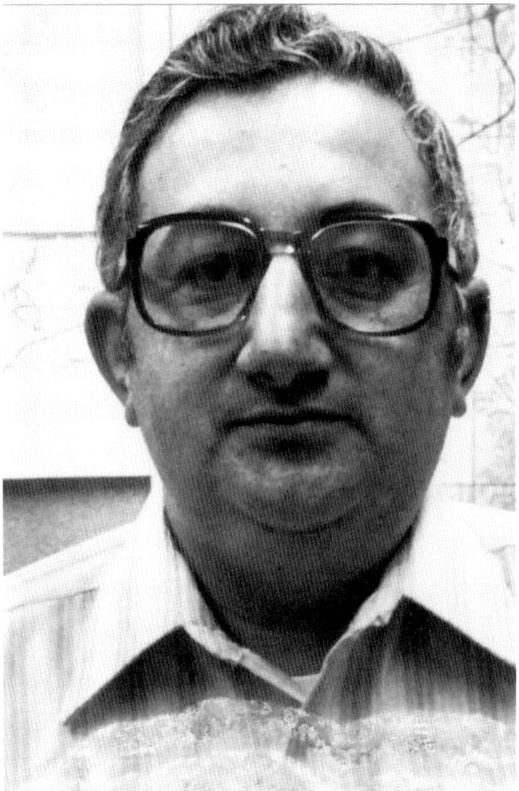

Tommy J. Williams

Williams was only seven when he joined his older siblings to work at Williams Candy Kitchen, a newsstand/lunch counter and popular downtown Concord hangout for nearly 60 years. His parents, Lebanese immigrants J.B. and Rosa Williams, started the business in 1929 beside North Union Street's Pastime Theatre, shown in this 1942 photograph; in 1945, it relocated to Barbrick Avenue. Williams and his wife, Lorraine, took over the Candy Kitchen after his father's passing. His mother, known as "Mom" Williams, was a petite firecracker who often warned everyone from businessmen browsing the sports page to kids flipping through comic books that "This ain't no liberry!" Williams closed the Candy Kitchen in 1988 when the building's block was razed to build a parking lot. He ran a real estate business until his death in 2013.

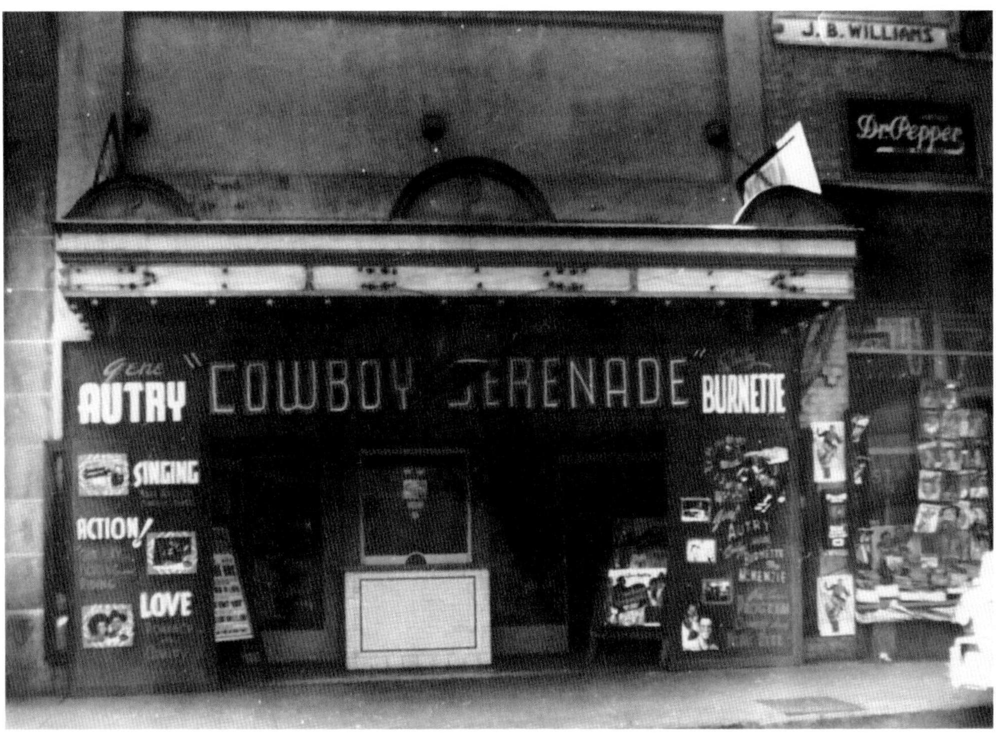

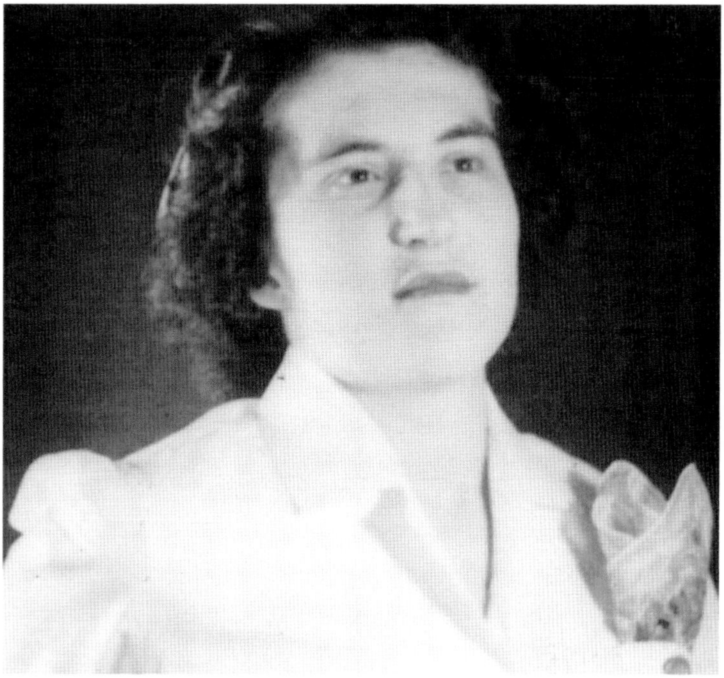

Bea Goodnight
This native of Rowan County served her country during World War II as a member of the US Army Nurse Corps. Her uniform is part of the permanent collection of the Cabarrus County Veterans Museum and can occasionally be seen on display there. Postwar, Goodnight was well known as a nurse anesthetist at Concord's Cabarrus Memorial Hospital for 40 years.

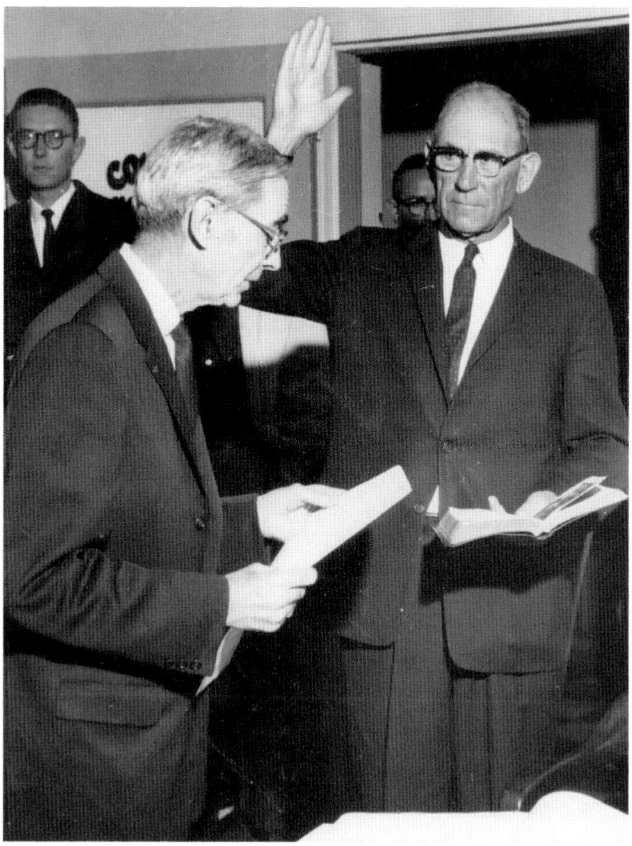

John Boger Sr.
Boger (right) served a long, midcentury stint as the city's register of deeds. In this early 1960s photograph, he is being sworn in to the position by Ray McEachern while his son, attorney John Boger Jr. (background, left), observes. Boger was also seen around town in a baseball uniform as the coach of Concord's Babe Ruth All-Stars and continued his youth advocacy as Boys Club president.

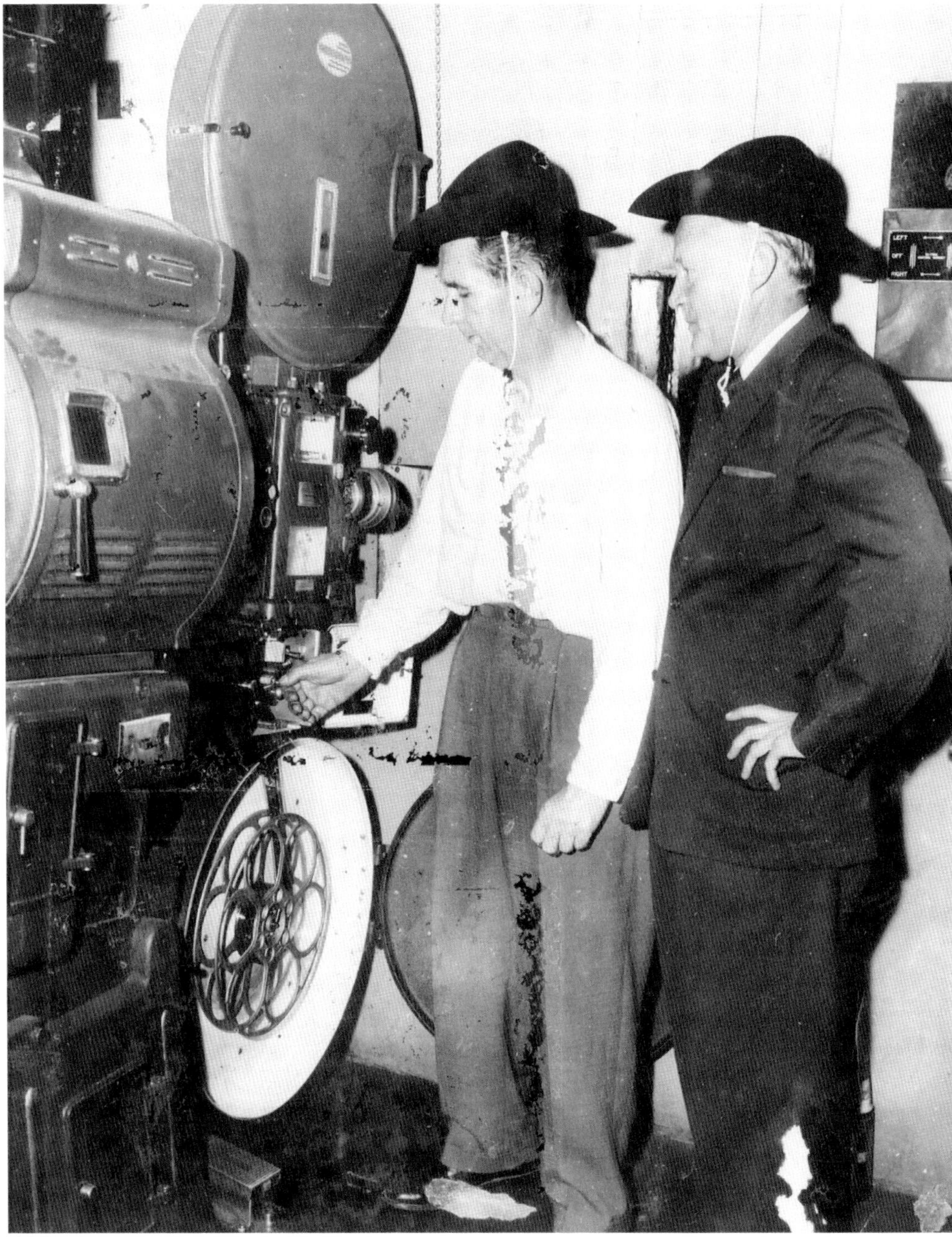

Malcolm Purnell

"Purnie" moved to Concord in 1950 to take over downtown's Cabarrus Theatre from previous manager D.B. Austell and managed the movie house until it closed in the early 1980s. Purnell used his Rotary Club connections to invite a pre-Mayberry Andy Griffith to town in 1957 to promote his film *A Face in the Crowd.* Purnell is shown here at right, with projectionist Bud Morgan. (Courtesy of Sally Purnell Howard.)

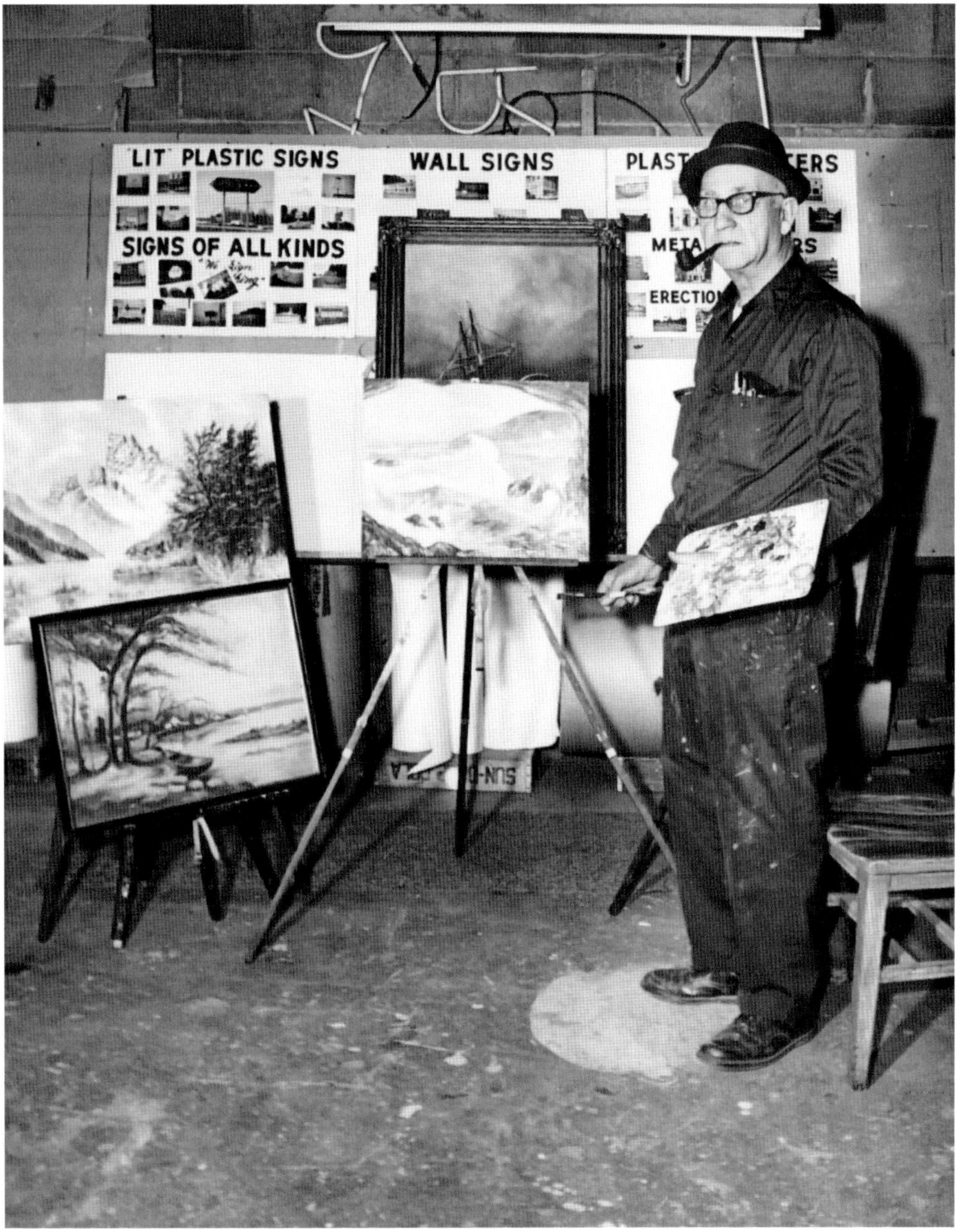

Badger Franklin Broome

This mid-1960s photograph shows that "Badge" Broome's artistic talents extended beyond his sign-making business; in addition to landscape painting he was constantly sketching, on napkins, church bulletins, whatever he could find. Broome Sign Company has been in the same Spring Street location since 1964 and in that neighborhood since its 1927 opening. Its founder died in 1973, but two subsequent generations have kept the business vibrant. (Courtesy of Lennie Turner.)

Zack L. Roberts

It was through Roberts's eyes that Concord's most significant events of the 1930s through the 1940s were seen. As the chief photographer of the *Concord Tribune*, he took thousands of photographs, many of which have been immortalized in the archives of the Concord Museum. The city's mayor from 1953 through 1957, Roberts was also well known for the camera shop he operated at the town square. (Courtesy of Concord Public Library.)

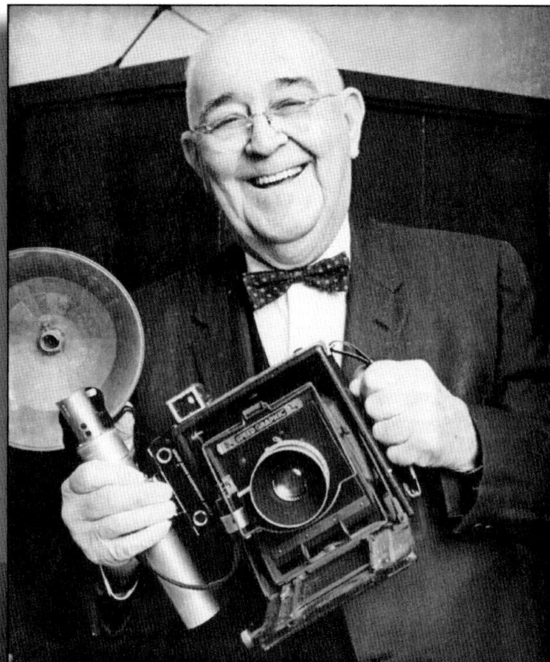

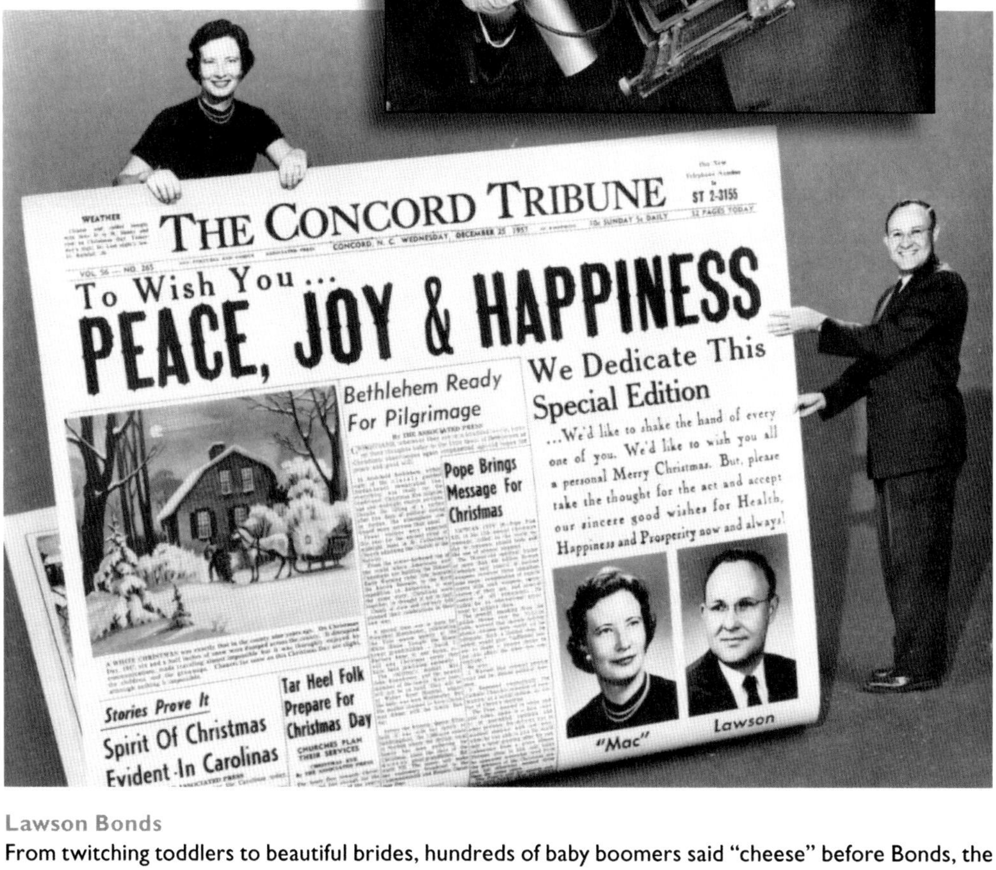

Lawson Bonds

From twitching toddlers to beautiful brides, hundreds of baby boomers said "cheese" before Bonds, the "Olan Mills" of Concord, and his wife Maxine "Mac." When he wasn't snapping smiles in his downtown portrait studio, located upstairs at 38 Union Street South, Bonds was a photographer for the *Concord Tribune*. His studio was in operation from the mid-1950s until 1988. Bonds died in 2010. (Courtesy of Concord Public Library.)

 70

Call

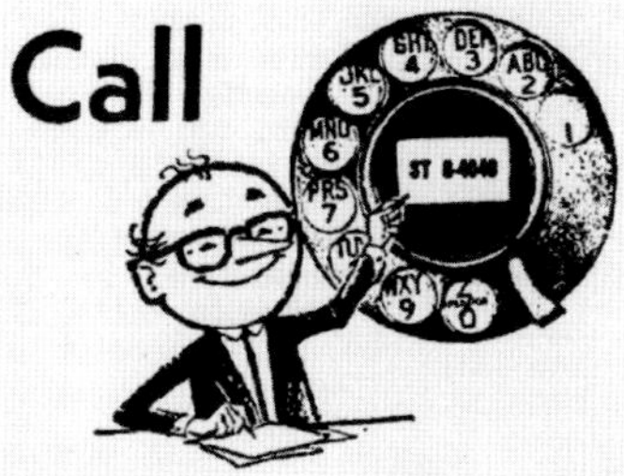

Mr. Trib

Mr. Trib is happy to answer questions telephoned in by readers of The Tribune. Persons who have questions should call Mr. Trib at ST 6-4040 between the hours of noon and 8 p.m. As many questions as possible of general interest will be answered each day in The Tribune.

Q. Mr. Trib, we'd like to know more about this liquor still that is now on display on Highway 29. Can you tell us how much the present owners paid for the still, how they came about acquiring it, anl if they can legally display this still and charge admission? Also, why didn't Cabarrus County keep the still and put it on display if this is legal? H. E. C. T., B. H., and others.

A. The moonshine liquor still, which is now on display on Highway 29, at Kiser's Auto Parts, was traded to the present owners for their assistance in helping destroy the operational still in southern Cabarrus County. When the still was discovered, Alcohol and Tobacco Tax Unit Agents first planned to destroy the still with high explosives, but later decided against this. Manuel and Rufus Kiser offered their services in removing the equipment from the site in exchange for the remains of the still. ATTU agents agreed to this and the Kisers uncovered the underground still and removed it from the site. A hole was cut in each vat to insure that it could not be used as a liquor still. The display is perfectly legal and Cabarrus County cannot operate a private business for the purpose of making money.

Mr. Trib
In the 1960s and 1970s, before Google made information instantly accessible, curious Concordians' queries about myriad subjects—from the "World's Largest Moonshine Still" on Highway 29 to Hollywood trivia—were answered in a daily feature, "Mr. Trib," in the *Concord Tribune*. Despite a rumor to the contrary, there was no singular "Mr. Trib"; the column was produced by rotating staffers.

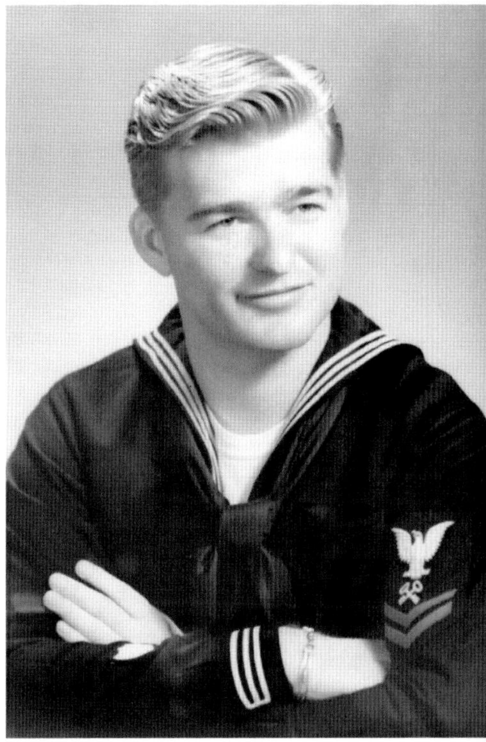

Marvin L. Eury
"Will I be able to play the piano?" this veteran newsman asked his doctor after losing a fingertip in a mid-1970s accident. After being told yes, Eury quipped, "Good. I never was able to before." This quick-witted reporter covered many of the region's most significant stories, and his personality profiles made even the most ordinary Concordian shine. An active youth leader, Eury died in 1983. (Courtesy of Aggie Eury.)

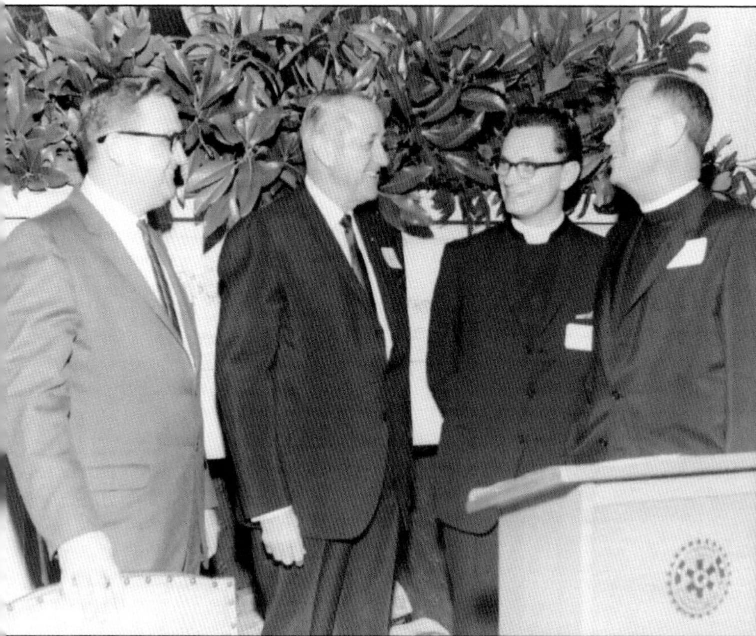

Ray Cline
The gregarious spokesman for Concord's business district, Cline was manager of Belk department store for decades and employed numerous Concordians. One would be hard-pressed to find a civic organization that did not include him on its roster, including the Concord Rotary Club. From left to right are Brown Holbrooks, Cline, Rev. T.C. Plexico, and unidentified. (Courtesy of St. James Lutheran Church.)

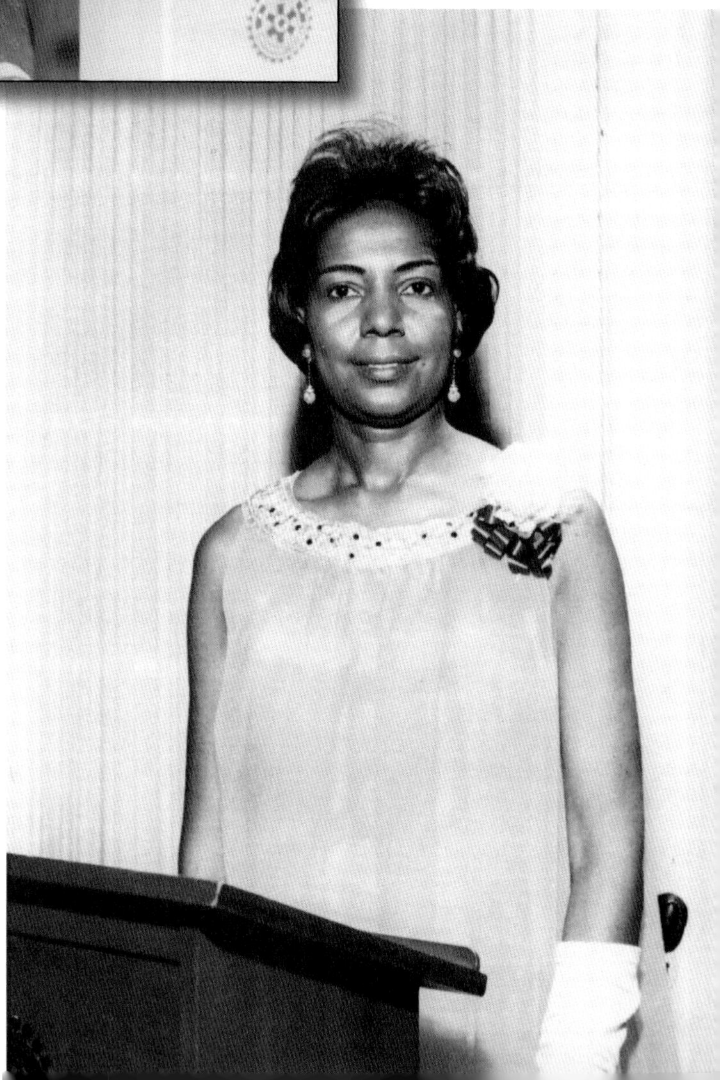

Mildred Florence Stevenson Harvey
At a time when professional opportunities for African Americans were limited to the classroom or the clergy, Harvey became Concord's first black banker in 1962. This Logan High School and Barber-Scotia College graduate commuted to Charlotte as head teller and trainer and, later, branch manager for Mechanics and Farmers Bank for nearly three decades. Harvey was a lifelong member of Price Memorial A.M.E. Zion Church. (Courtesy of Concord Public Library.)

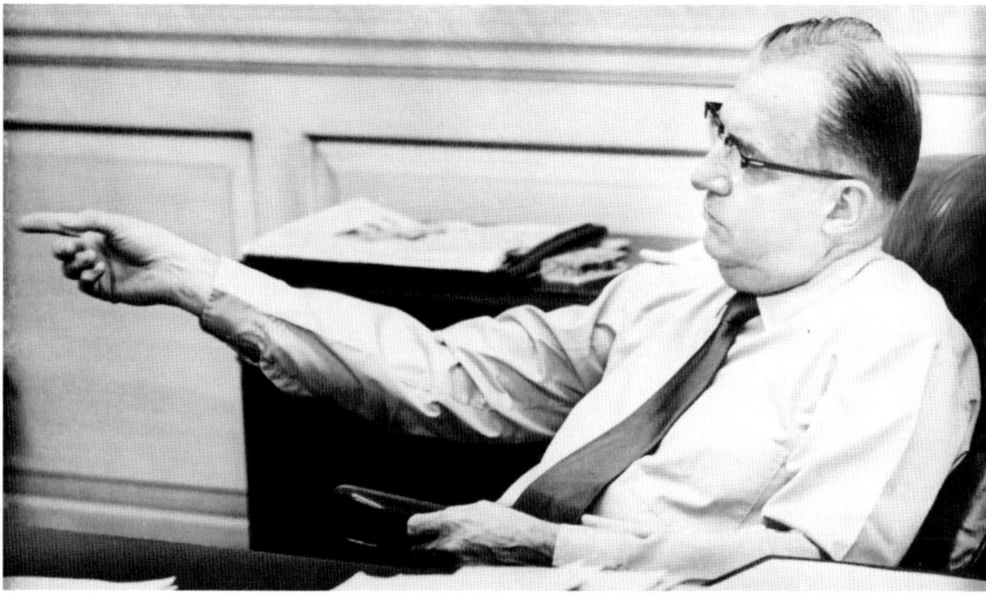

Donald S. Holt

Locals could barely imagine anyone other than Charles A. Cannon at the helm of Cannon Mills, but Holt ably succeeded the textile tycoon upon "Mr. Charlie's" 1962 retirement. As president, Holt continued the company's prosperity, adding an 840,000-foot sheet distribution factory in the early 1970s. He and his wife, Margaret, were highly respected philanthropists, with Concord's public library among their favorite charities. (Courtesy of Concord Public Library.)

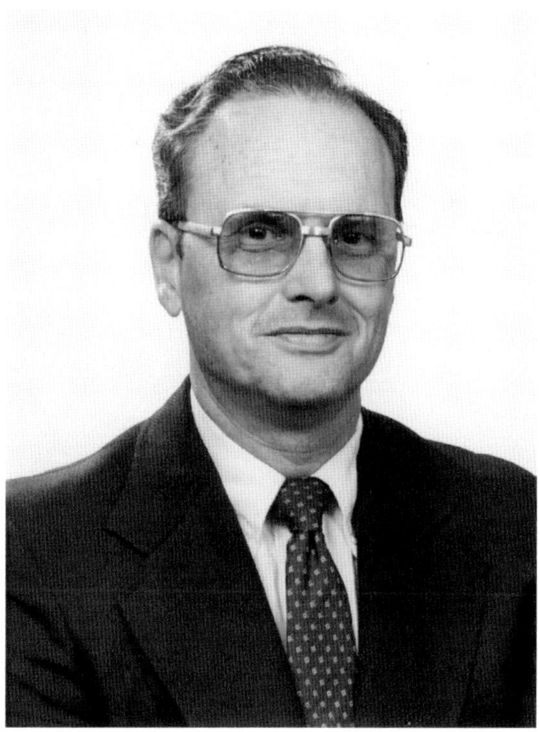

Branson Coltrane Jones

Jones, a World War II veteran and Concord native, personified community service. The grandson of Daniel Branson Coltrane, he was employed in management at Cannon Mills for nearly 40 years and sat on a litany of regional boards and councils for municipal and collegiate organizations. In 2000, Jones was selected as one of Cabarrus County's Most Influential people from the last 100 years. (Courtesy of Concord Public Library.)

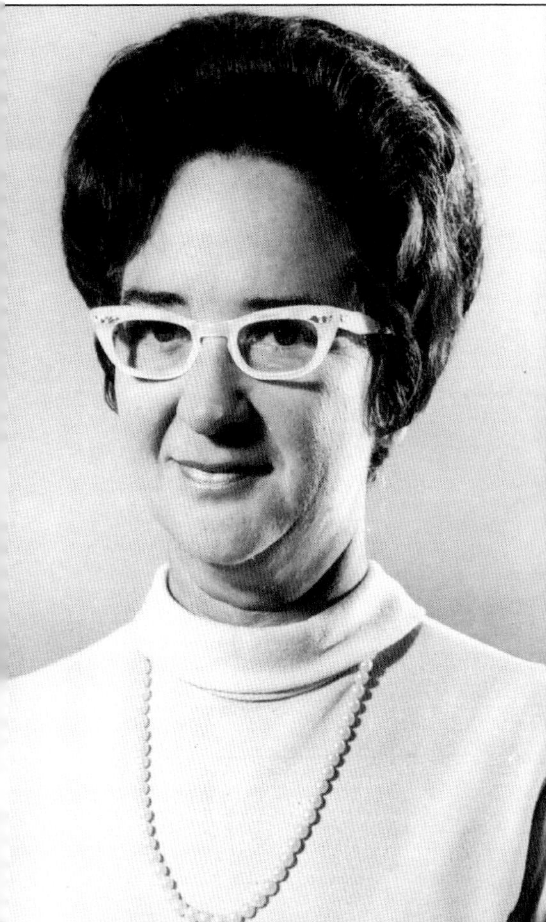

Helen C. Arthur-Cornett

The grande dame of Cabarrus County history took to the subject "like a duck to water" thanks to the inspiration of Concord High School educator Blanche Stewart. Yet the esteemed journalist did not begin "looking back" in print until later in her career, instead reporting on current events, starting at the University of Georgia's campus newspaper. Many old-timers remember her as depicted here in 1971, when she covered the city beat for the *Concord Tribune* (she eventually became city editor). The granddaughter of former Concord mayor J.B. Caldwell, Arthur-Cornett later penned memorable personality profiles for the *Charlotte Observer's Cabarrus Neighbors* section. Her signature feature, "A Look Back," dusted off news items from the region's past and made them sparkle for a new generation of readers. It enjoyed a run of 21 years. The author of several local history books, including collections of her "A Look Back" columns, Arthur-Cornett is shown below with Sissy Howard Mendenhall at a 2009 book signing at the former location of the Concord Museum. (Left, photograph by Frankie Furr, courtesy of Concord Public Library; below, photograph by author.)

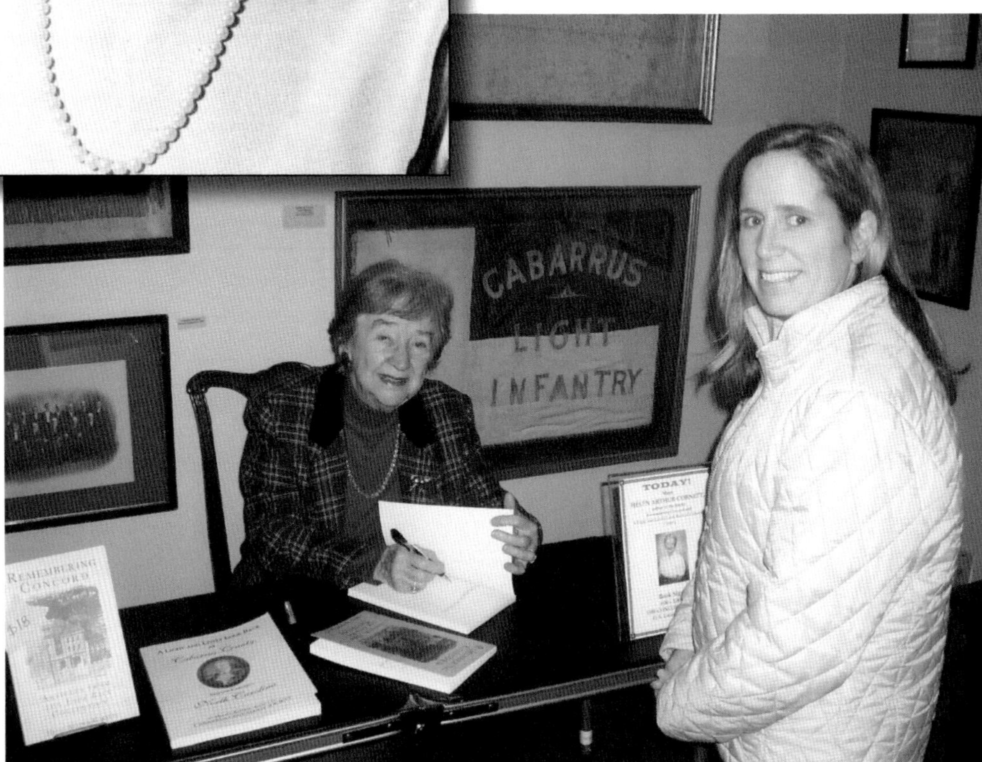

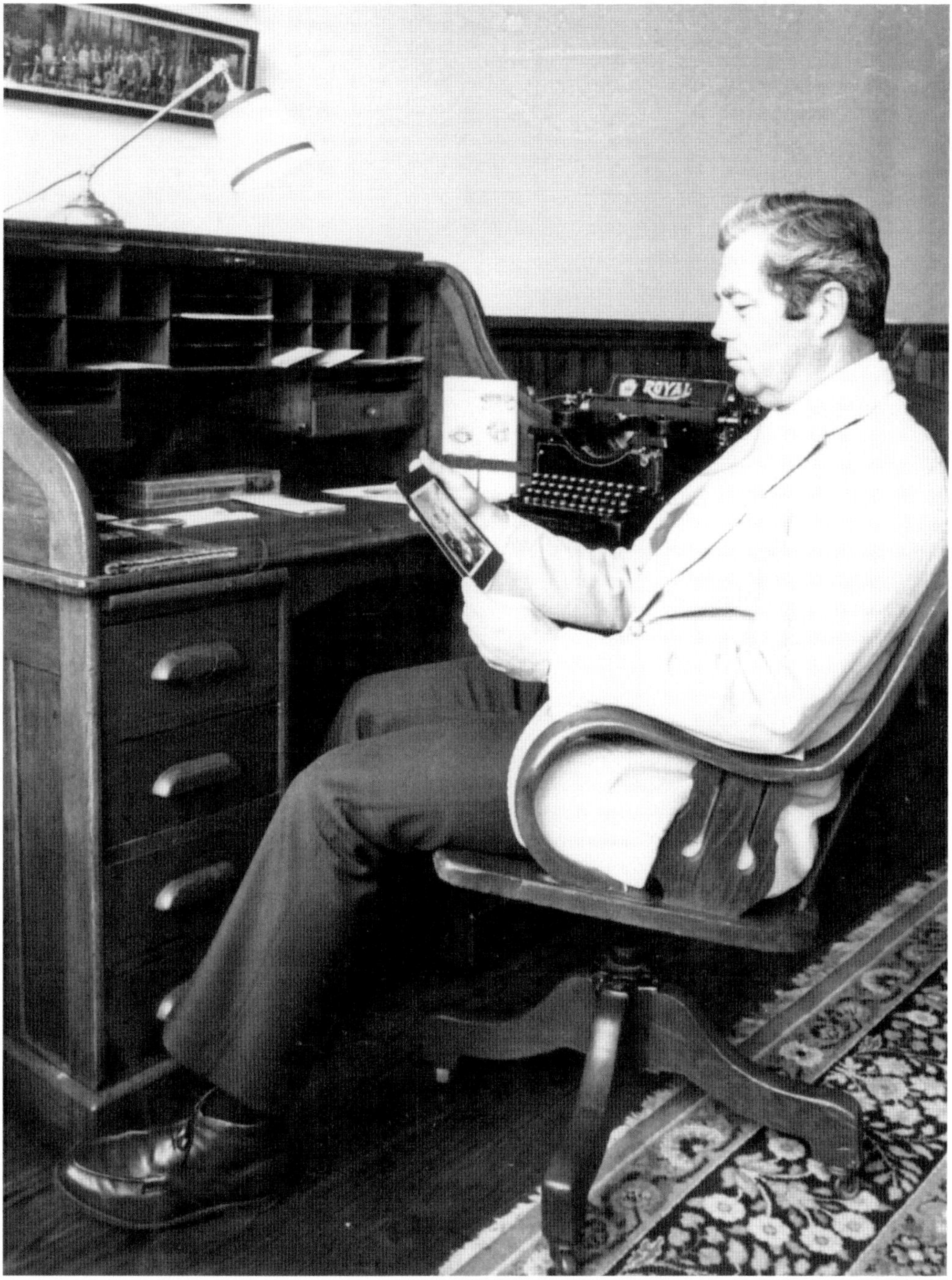

Alex Patterson
This third-generation insurance man might tell you about when his father made a kite sturdy enough to hoist a man off the ground, or when tipsy socialites took a downtown stroll in their underwear, or how Arnold Hatley of the Red Pig was terrified of snakes. Patterson has compiled hundreds of hand-printed, slice-of-life stories about Concord personalities, recalled in remarkable detail with affection and humor. (Photograph by Frankie Furr.)

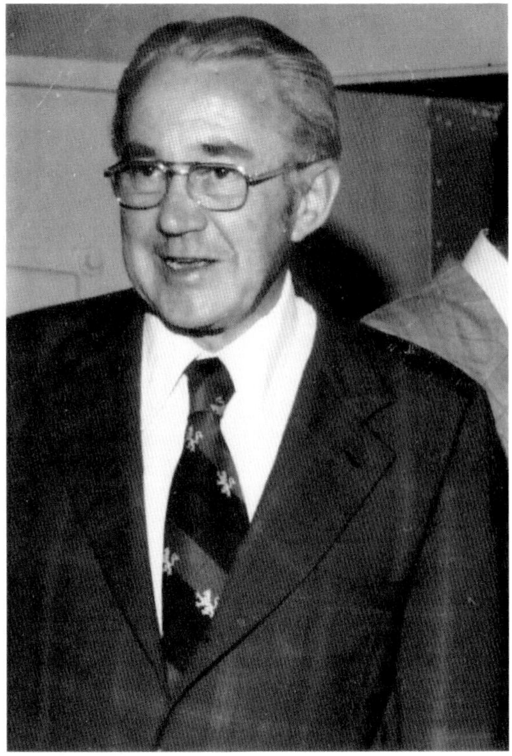

John Sharp Hartsell

If you made a blip on the community radar during the second half of the 20th century, chances are Hartsell kept a file on you, chock full of newspaper clippings. This prominent Concord attorney was once called by the *Concord Tribune* "the person most knowledgeable of the history and families of Cabarrus County." A veteran of World War II, Hartsell died in 2004. (Courtesy of Concord Public Library.).

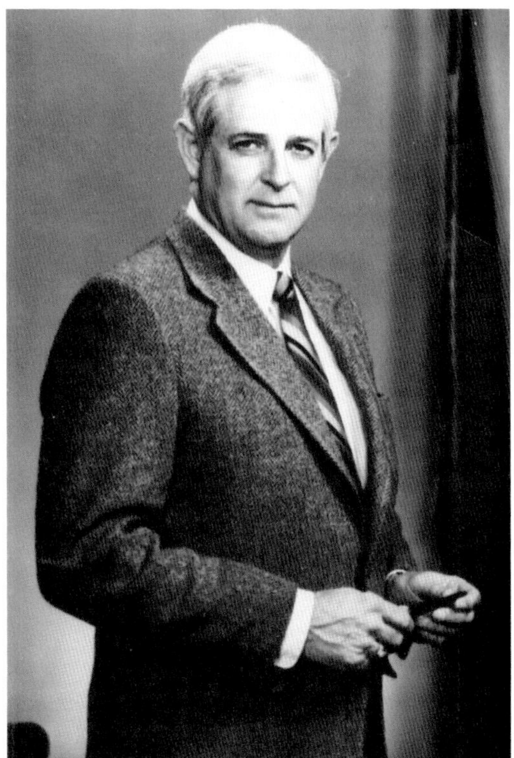

James C. Johnson Jr.

Whether they sat on a jury or in his Sunday School class, Concordians were enthralled by this accomplished orator. A criminal defense attorney, Johnson doubled in Raleigh for multiple terms in both the State House and Senate. He amassed a collection of combat memorabilia that he proudly displayed on his property. Johnson was on the ballot for State Senate when he died unexpectedly in 2008. (Courtesy of Concord Public Library.)

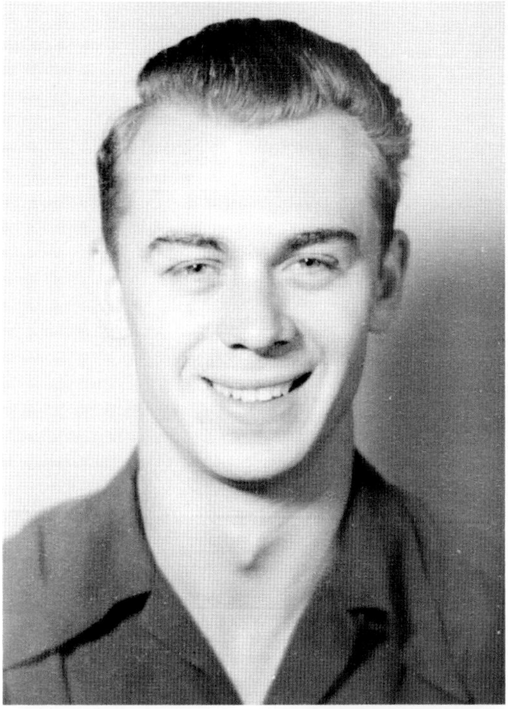

Raiford Troutman
A young businessman in 1944, Troutman eventually became Concord's most versatile entrepreneur. He counts among his ventures a pre-owned car dealership, a real estate business, and popular barbecue restaurants. Today, his three adult children work alongside their father from their automobile lot/office on Highway 29, but as the 1990 aerial photograph below shows, Troutman Motors was previously located in downtown Concord on Church Street, where Wells Fargo is located today. Many locals fondly remember Troutman's putt-putt golf course, which operated in a wooded area of Highway 29 during the 1970s. (Both, courtesy of Keith Troutman.)

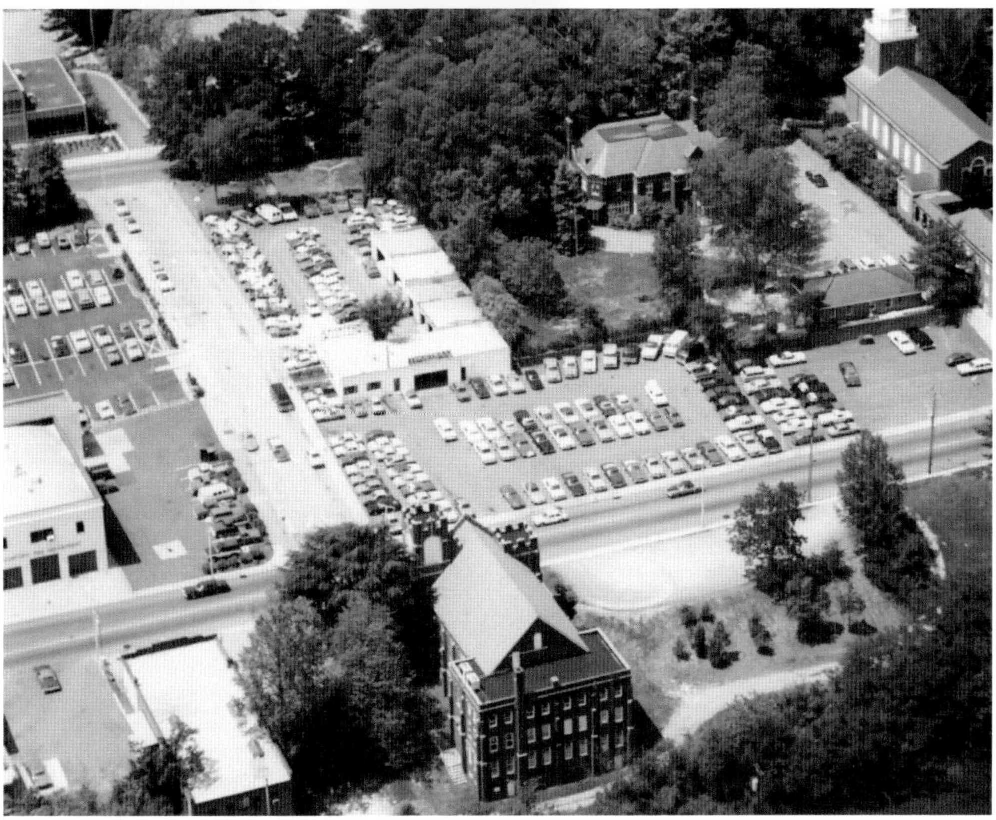

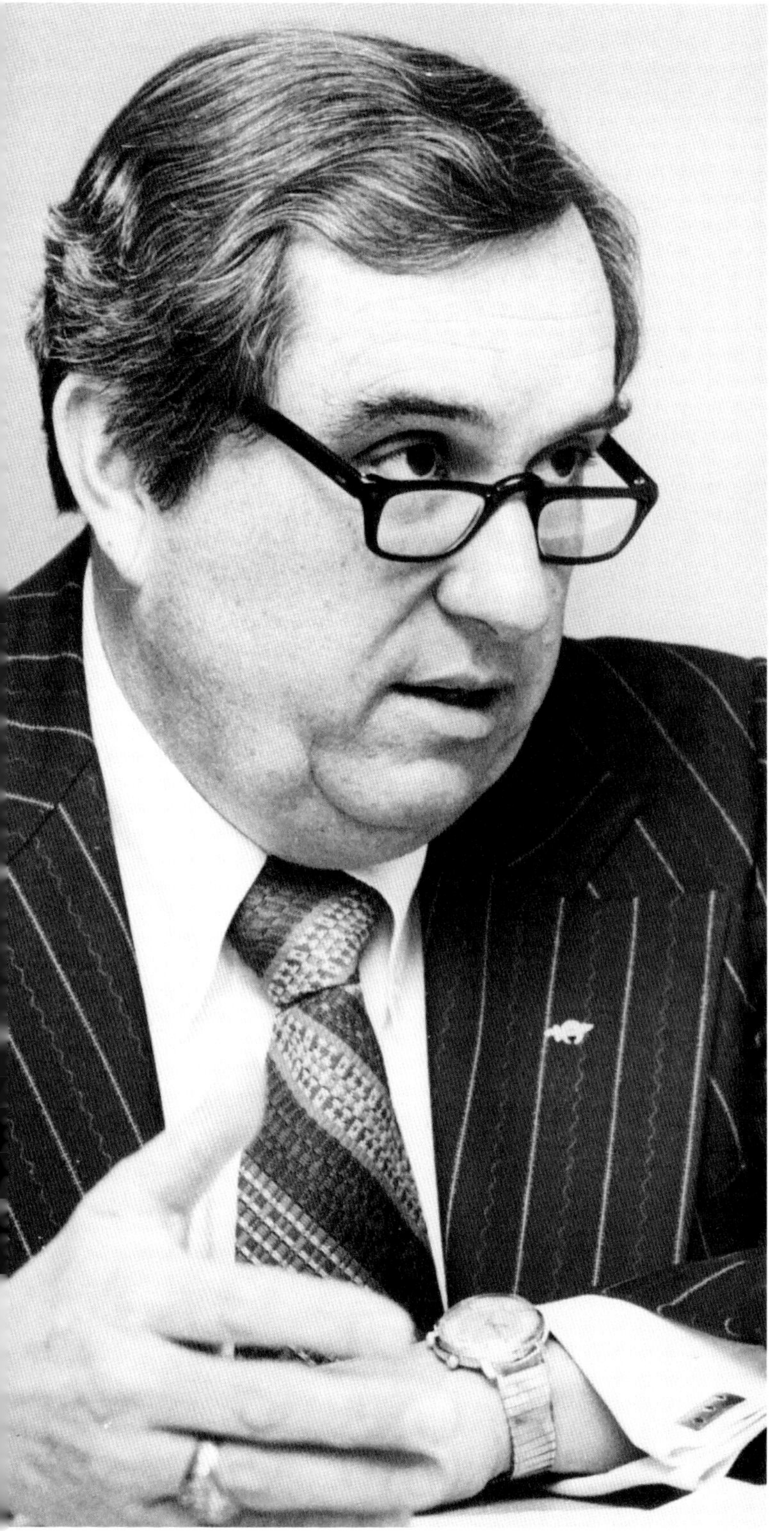

Art and Betty Dorton Thomas

(LEFT AND OPPOSITE PAGE) His death in a 1975 car accident numbed not only Concord but also the entire state: Thomas ran a thriving Chevrolet dealership, was active in numerous civic organizations, and was in his second term as a state representative at the time of his passing. Eighty-five bills comprised his astounding record as a legislator, including the creation of a Youth Service bill. General Motors denied Thomas's wife, a boisterous Democratic Party activist, the opportunity to assume management of her late husband's Chevrolet franchise because of her gender. The North Carolina House of Representatives offered no such barriers, however, and Betty was appointed to fill his seat. She was reelected to the legislature for the nine years following. Issues garnering her support included equal rights for women, education improvements, and "liquor by the drink," resisted by many conservatives but perceived by Thomas as beneficial to local economies. Like her husband, Betty was active with a variety of community groups and boards and received numerous service awards. She died in 2009. The photograph on the opposite page depicts the Thomases at Carowinds amusement park in the mid-1970s. (Left, courtesy of Concord Public Library; opposite, courtesy of Terre Thomas Bullock.)

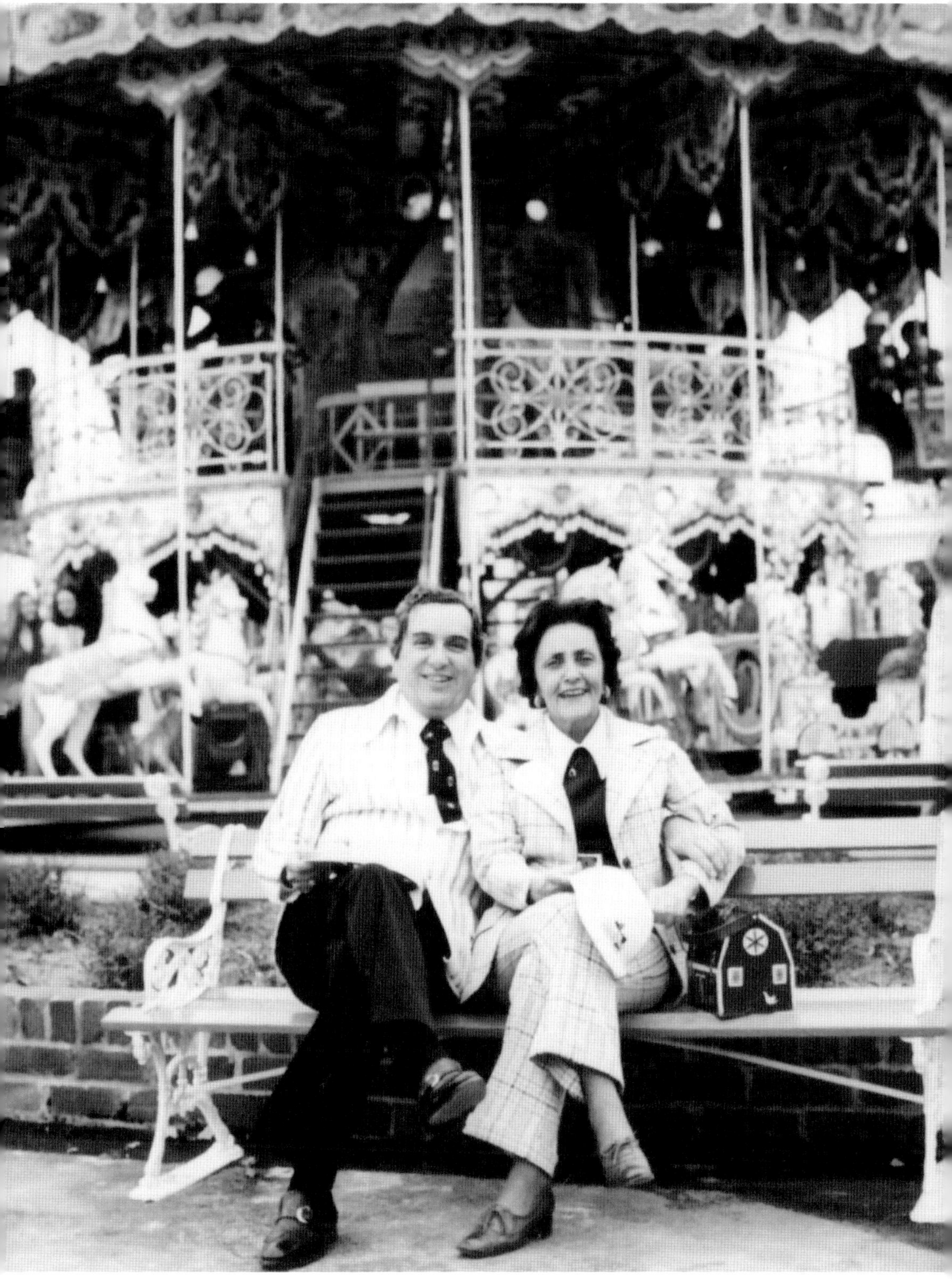

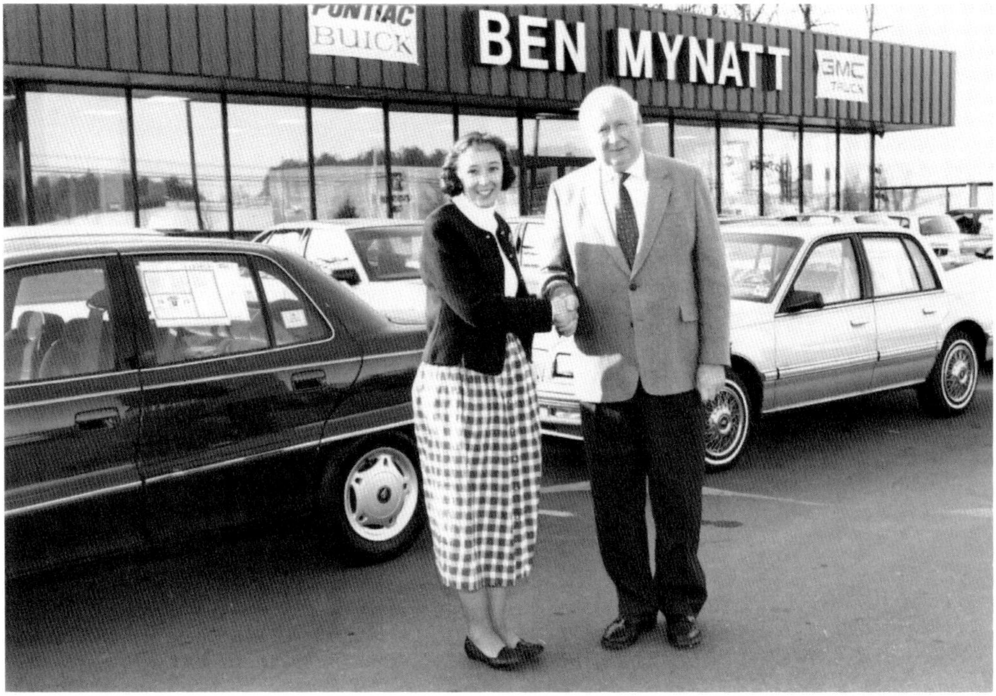

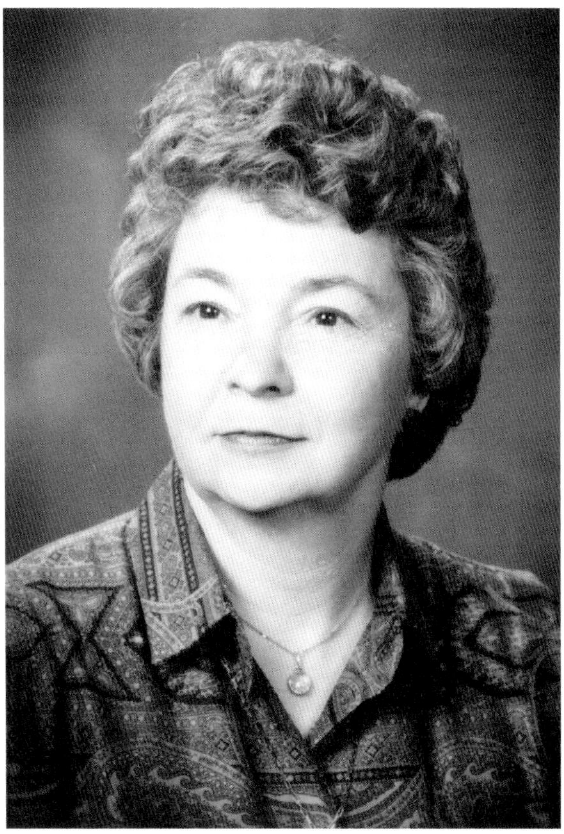

Ben Mynatt

Mynatt, originally a car salesman from Tennessee, purchased the Chevrolet dealership owned by the late Art Thomas in 1976. A board member of a number of organizations, including the Boys and Girls Club and the Salvation Army, Mynatt's contributions of over $1 million to area charities helped earn him the chamber of commerce Citizen of the Year Award in 2000. His wife, Grace, seen at left, has also served the community on the school board and as a county commissioner. Mynatt's daughter Cyndie, shown here with her father, has managed the business since Mynatt's 2001 death. Today, the Ben Mynatt "family" of dealerships comprises a number of automobile manufacturers. (Courtesy of Concord Public Library.)

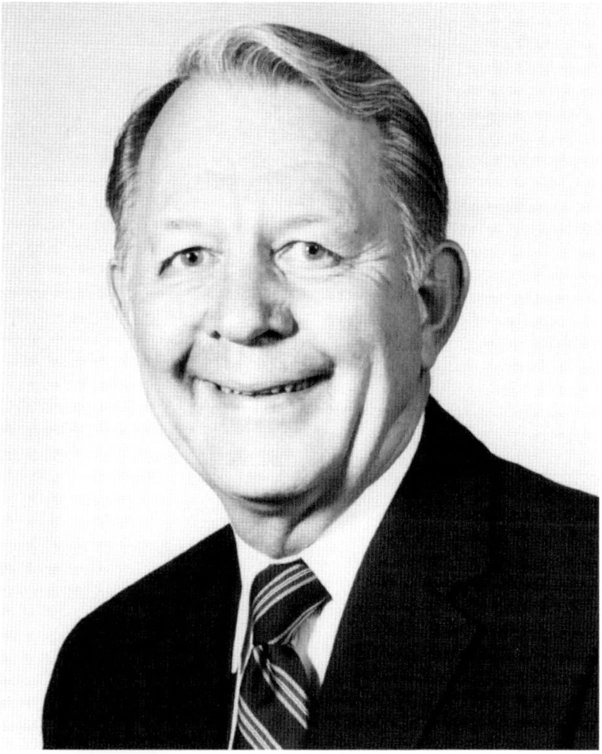

Buddy Hilbish
"Hilbish Motor Company has been a dealer for over half the time Ford has been in business," chuckled this optimistic car seller after receiving a 2012 Cabarrus County Chamber of Commerce Lifetime Achievement Award. He started moving vehicles in 1954 and by 1968 had merged two dealerships into his current location. Hilbish was fundamental in the 1969 founding of Cabarrus Academy, now known as the Cannon School. (Courtesy of Concord Public Library.)

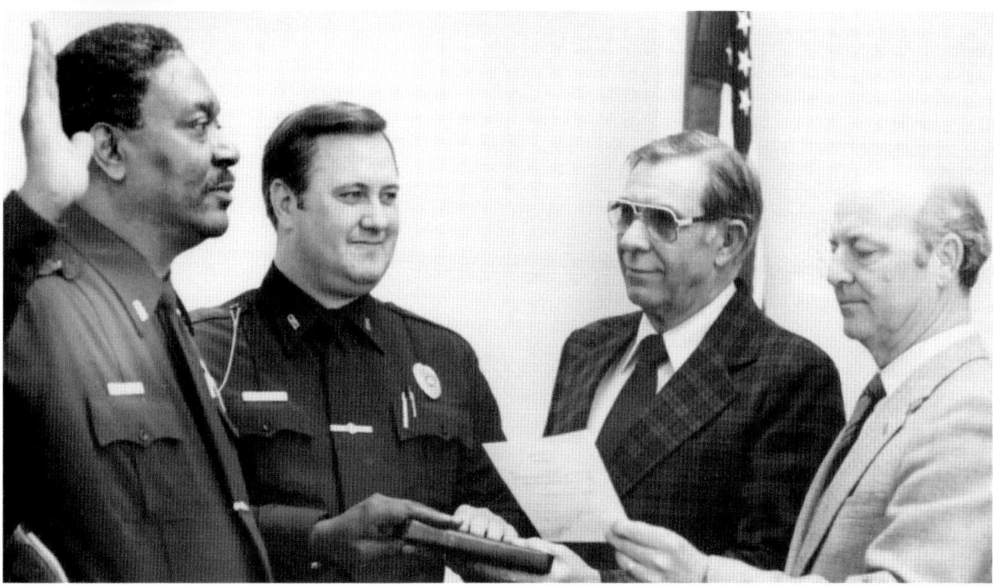

Julius Franklin
Educated locally at Logan High School and Barber-Scotia College, Franklin was encouraged by African American policemen Lawrence Evans and David Steele Sr. to join the Concord Police Department. He ultimately became the city's first black officer to reach the rank of lieutenant. In this 1981 photograph, Franklin (left) and Bucky Simpson are being promoted to sergeant by Chief Jack Moore and Mayor Harold B. McEachern (right).

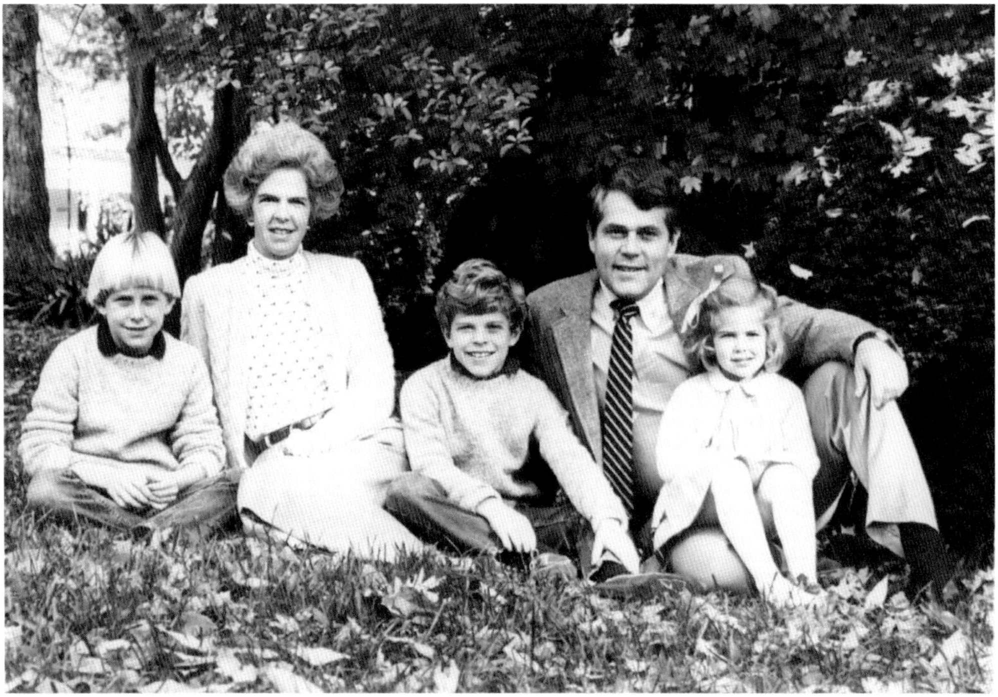

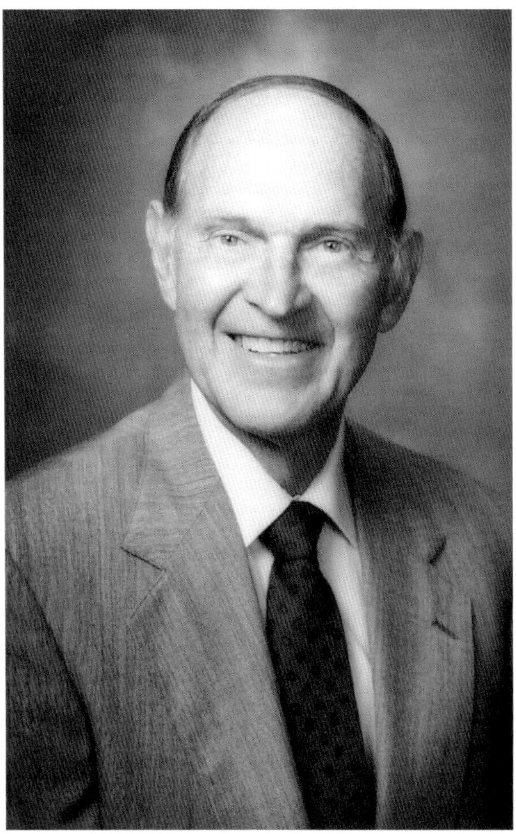

John H. Morrison Jr. Family

Morrison's grandfather, E.L. Morrison, established his lumber company in 1922, and today, John's sons are the fourth generation to manage the family business, now known as Morrison Brothers Building Center. From left to right in this 1983 photograph are Knox, Peg, Harris, John, and Margaret Morrison. Mrs. Morrison, also hailing from a lumber family, serves as a board member on several Concord nonprofits. (Photograph by Frankie Furr.)

Franklin C. Niblock Jr.

A 1953 graduate of Duke University School of Medicine, Dr. Niblock's pediatric practice cared for countless baby boomer and Generation X children. His stately Colonial Revival residence, designed in 1929 by Louis Asbury, is one of the architectural gems of South Union Street. His family name is well known in Concord through Niblock Homes, a home-development business founded by his sons in the late 1970s. (Courtesy of Concord Public Library.)

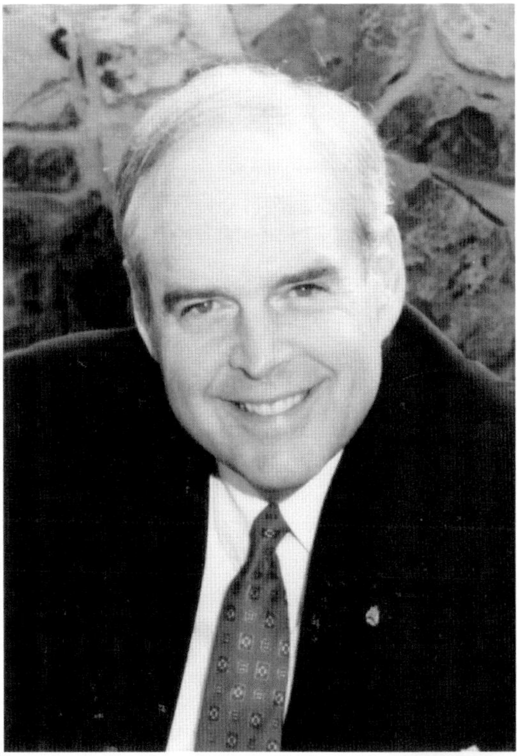

Robert Cannon "Robin" Hayes
From 1999 to 2009, Concord native Hayes served five consecutive terms in the US House of Representatives. His knowledge of North Carolina's 8th Congressional District's textile roots was literally in his blood: he is the great-grandson of Cannon Mills founder James W. Cannon. Hayes is now the chairman of the North Carolina Republican Party. (Courtesy of Concord Public Library.)

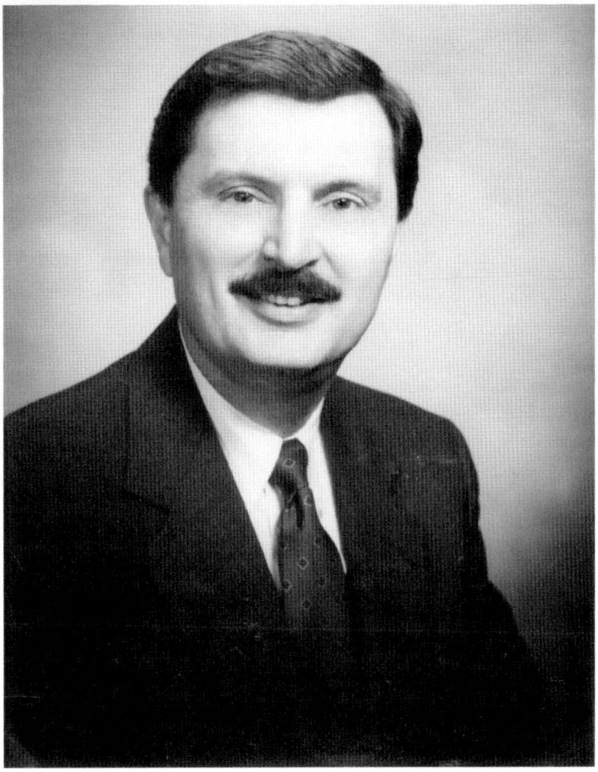

Fletcher L. Hartsell Jr.
Concord native Hartsell, a Republican, has represented the 36th District in the North Carolina Senate since 1991. A US Army veteran, since the early 1970s he has worked with the law firm Hartsell, Hartsell, and White. Hartsell is the corporate secretary of the board of directors for the conservative political group RightChange.com. (Courtesy of Concord Public Library.)

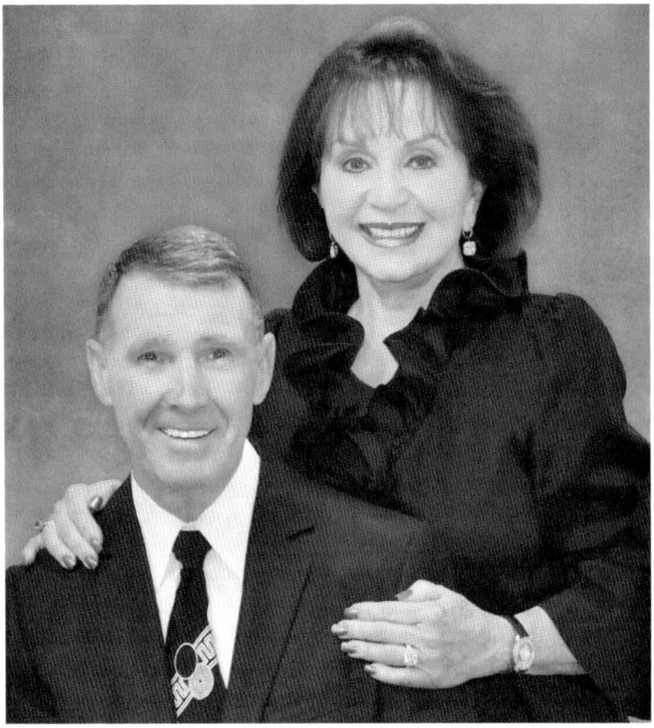

Robert and Carolyn Tucker
The Concord-headquartered Shoe Show, Inc., started in 1960 when Tucker opened a single storefront with homemade racks in Kannapolis. As detailed in his biography *Under the Radar*, Tucker expanded into often-overlooked small towns and today owns more than 1,100 stores, making his company America's biggest independently owned shoe retailer. Tucker and wife, Carolyn, generously share their good fortune by contributing to a range of local charities. (Courtesy of Carolyn Tucker.)

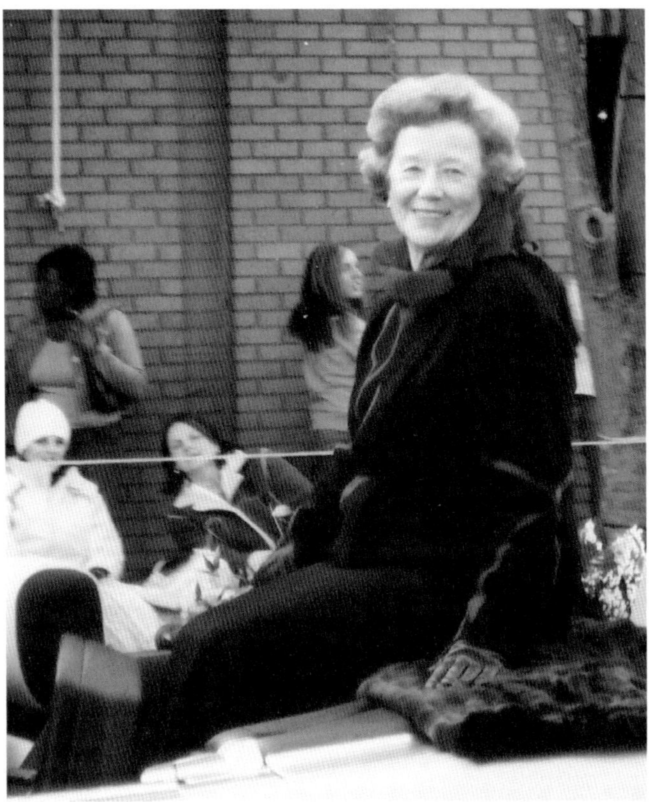

Neta Helms
When downtown Concord businesses defected to Carolina Mall in 1973, Helms, proprietor of a children's and women's clothing shop, resisted the exodus. Today, Neta's remains ensconced in its same location since the 1960s—with the same window mannequins. Yet that time warp is deceptive: a customer boasts that clothing she purchases at Neta's earns her compliments in Manhattan. Helms is shown as the grand marshal of the 2005 Concord Christmas Parade. (Courtesy of Neta Helms.)

Bobby Overcash

Employment Security Commission manager for 39 years, Overcash pointed thousands toward new jobs. He and his staff were the exclusive career screeners for Cannon Mills and tested more than 25,000 people for 1,000 openings when Philip Morris came to Concord. Overcash has been an active Rotarian since 1975, and in 2011, Mayor Scott Padgett (left) honored his Concord Rotary service by proclaiming "Bobby Overcash Day." (Photograph by Venetia Skahen.)

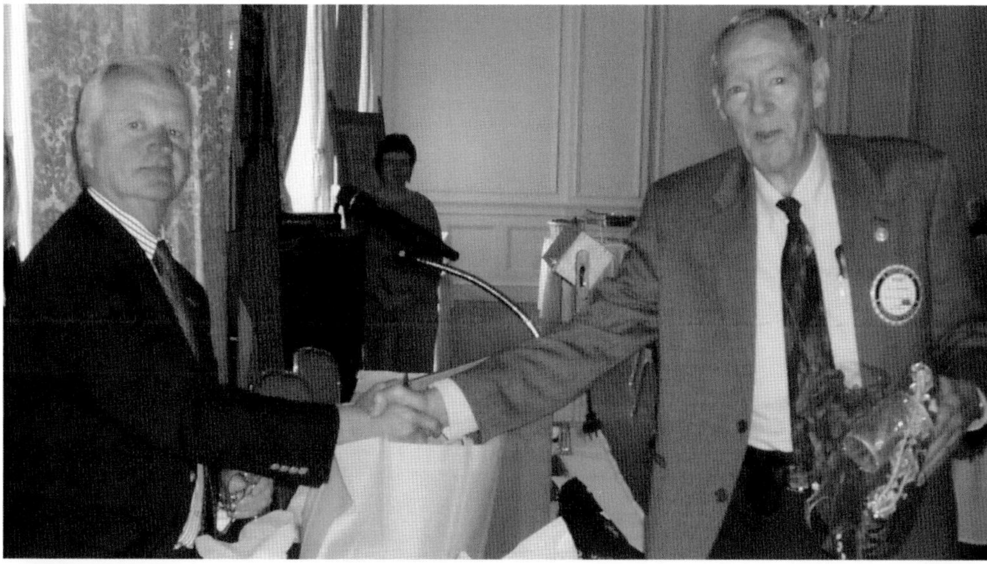

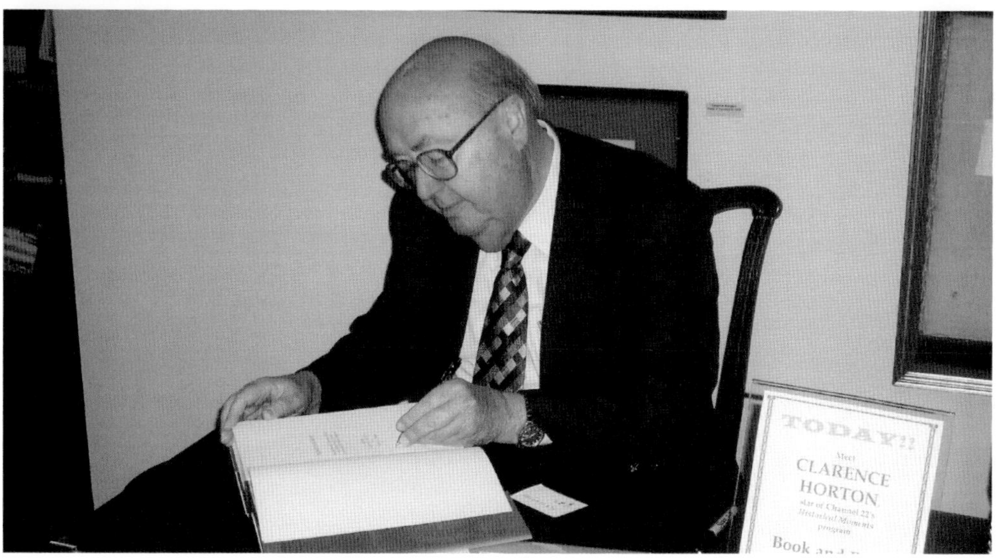

Clarence E. Horton Jr.

As a lawyer and judge, Horton, a Kannapolis resident, has observed community events from a legal perspective since 1965. But it is his knowledge of local lore for which this honorary Concordian has become legendary. Horton has produced several books about Cabarrus County heritage, and hosts the locally produced television series, the award-winning *Historical Moments*. He is shown here at a 2009 Concord Museum book signing. (Photograph by author.)

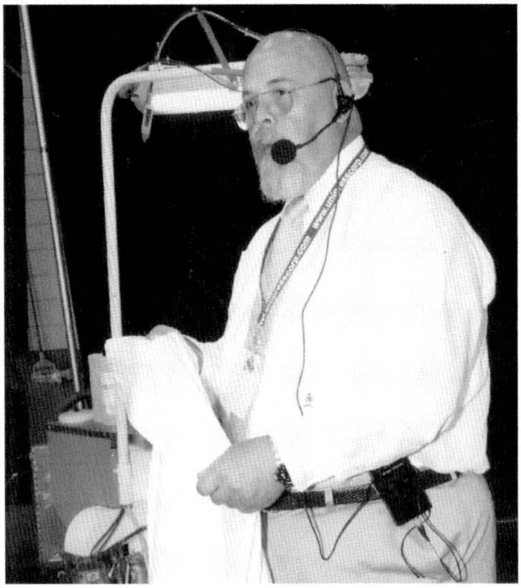

Martin Young
"One more story and I'll let you go," this chatty Church Street dry-cleaner might chuckle as you claim your freshly pressed clothes. Young's own story is worth retelling: he dabbled in other careers before finally settling down in 1980 to take over the business his stain-busting father, "Luke" Young, established in 1941. He has become a nationally known industry leader frequently in demand for seminars. (Courtesy of Martin Young.)

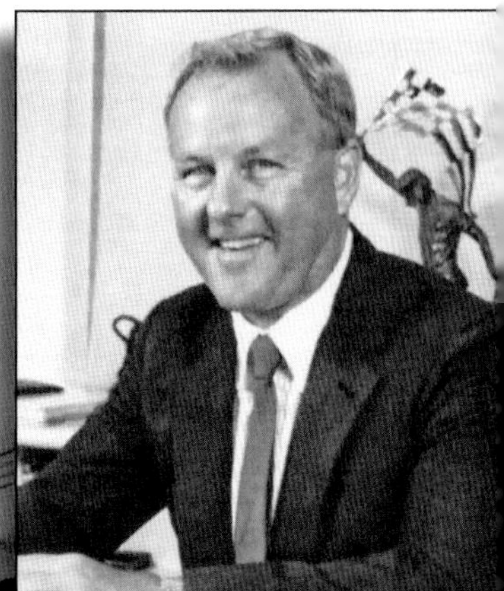

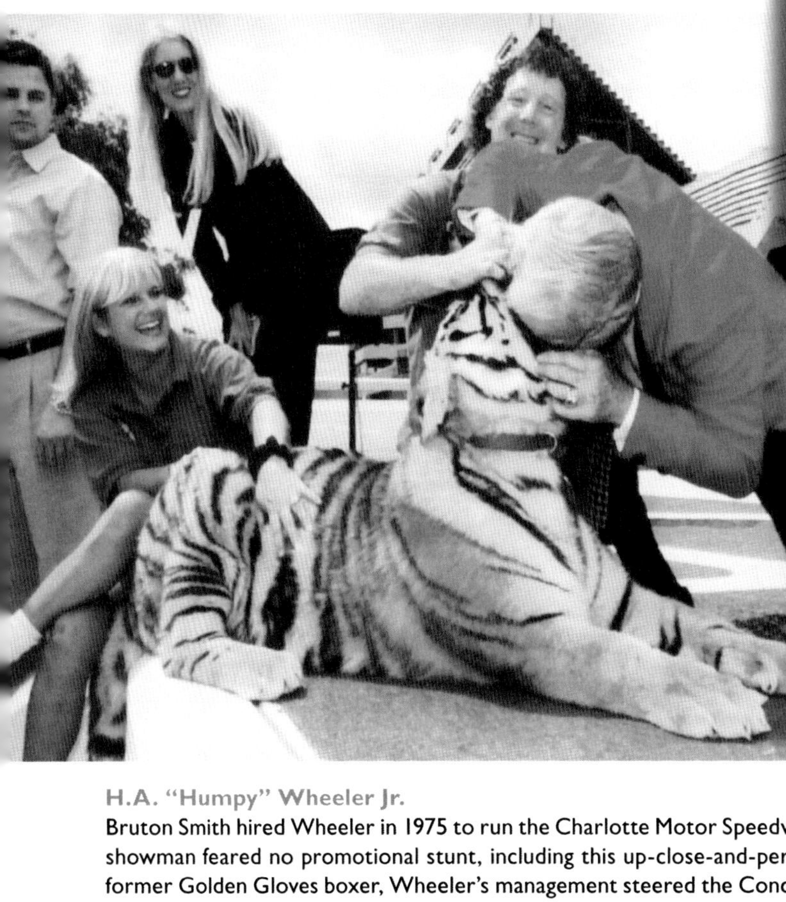

H.A. "Humpy" Wheeler Jr.
Bruton Smith hired Wheeler in 1975 to run the Charlotte Motor Speedway, and for 34 years, this super-showman feared no promotional stunt, including this up-close-and-personal encounter with a tiger. A former Golden Gloves boxer, Wheeler's management steered the Concord motorsports mecca to vast improvements including seating expansion and the installation of lights for nighttime races. He currently chairs the Wheeler Company, a management-consulting firm. (Courtesy of the Wheeler Company.)

CHAPTER FIVE

Shapers of Young Minds

Youthful nostalgia can be astonishingly diverse, but a common childhood experience links each generation: the teacher, mentor, or coach who first piqued an intellectual curiosity, imparted an unshakable life lesson, or provided guidance at an impressionable time.

Each educator who has ever etched chalk onto a blackboard is no doubt legendary in at least one student's mind. Yet some have left marks so indelible, their instructions cannot be erased from memory.

Spinsters like Clara Harris and the Stewart Sisters had little interest in marriage—teaching was their love affair, and students were their "children."

As Concord Spiders, George "Ick" Alley and E.Z. Smith III were notable as star athletes and returned to their alma mater to build new legacies as coaches and teachers.

Some Concordians profiled here earned our respect for gestures broader than classroom instruction, like Davidson College's first president Robert Hall Morrison. Some, like James Henry Alexander Sr., molded character by being impartial as the races merged during desegregation. Some hailed from different walks of life, such as John F. McInnis and Tracy N. Spencer, but cared so deeply about the well-being of children that they left behind enduring recreational institutions.

Muppets creator Jim Henson once said, "[Kids] don't remember what you try to teach them. They remember what you are." And in the cases of these shapers of young minds, what they are is unforgettable.

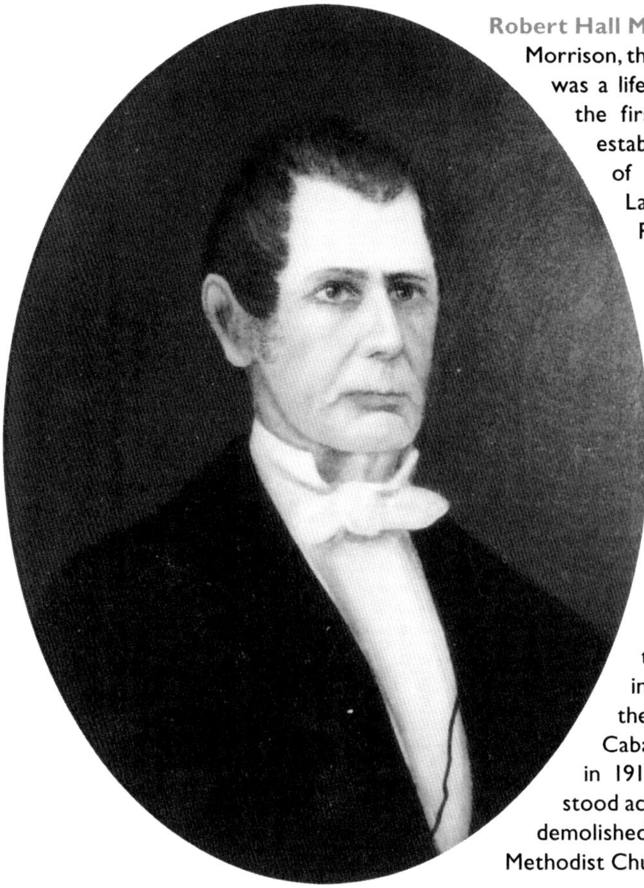

Robert Hall Morrison

Morrison, the son of a Revolutionary War soldier, was a lifelong Presbyterian minister. He was the first president of Davidson College, established in 1836 as an outgrowth of his mission to create a "Manual Labor School" within the Concord Presbytery. Of his 12 children, two daughters, Mary Anna and Eugenia Erixene, married Confederate generals Thomas J. "Stonewall" Jackson and Rufus Barringer, respectively. (Courtesy of E.H. Little Library, Davidson College.)

William R. Odell

The son of John M. Odell joined his father's mill in 1877, but as the century changed, so did his interests. "Mr. Will" was elected to the state senate in 1905 and installed as Cabarrus County school superintendent in 1913. His home, shown here in 1927, stood across from his father's estate and was demolished in 1954 to make way for Forest Hill Methodist Church's parking lot.

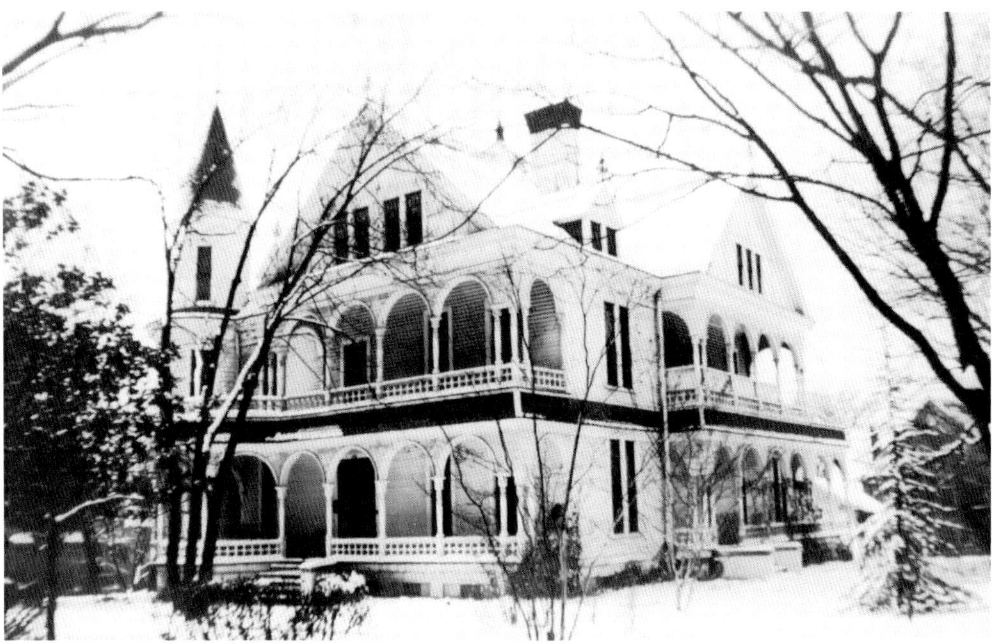

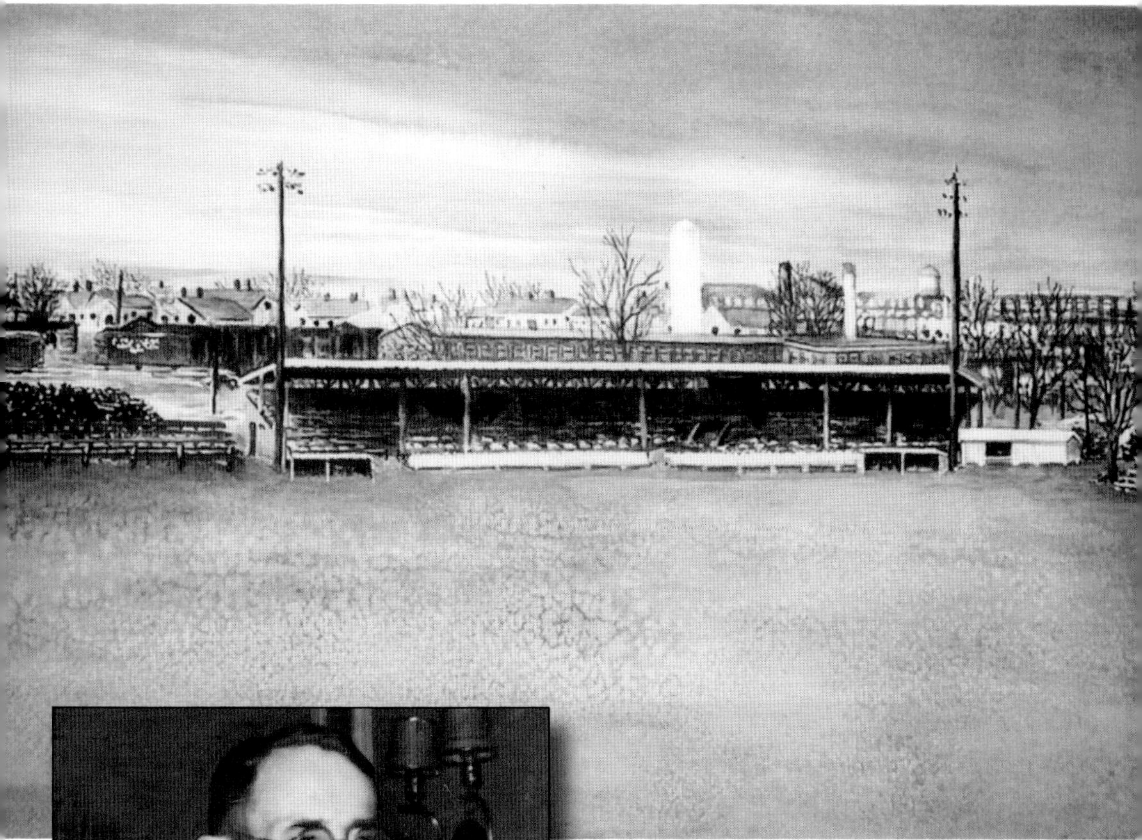

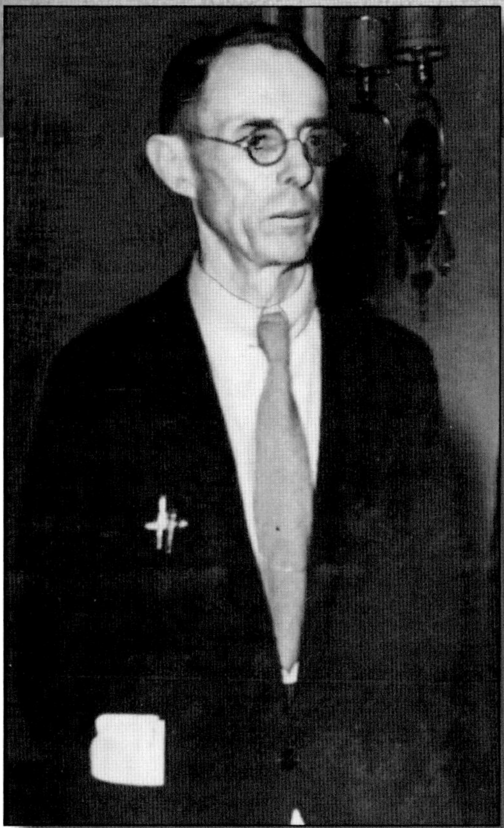

Albert Shipp Webb

This Methodist minister's son arrived in Concord in 1908 to work as the principal of the city's high school, then known as the Central School. Upon the 1910 death of superintendent J.D. Lentz, Webb was appointed his successor and held that post until retiring in 1943. His community service included the local Red Cross and the Concord Rotary Club, where he was a charter member. Coltrane-Webb Elementary School bears his name, as does Webb Field, located behind the old Concord High School. Shown above in an illustration by local artist Jennie Martin Tomlin. Webb Field originally hosted the school's various athletic teams as well as semipro baseball games. Webb's widest claim to fame was his surname's inspiration for the Concord High School mascot, the Spiders. (Left, courtesy of George M. Patterson; above, courtesy of Jennie Martin Tomlin.)

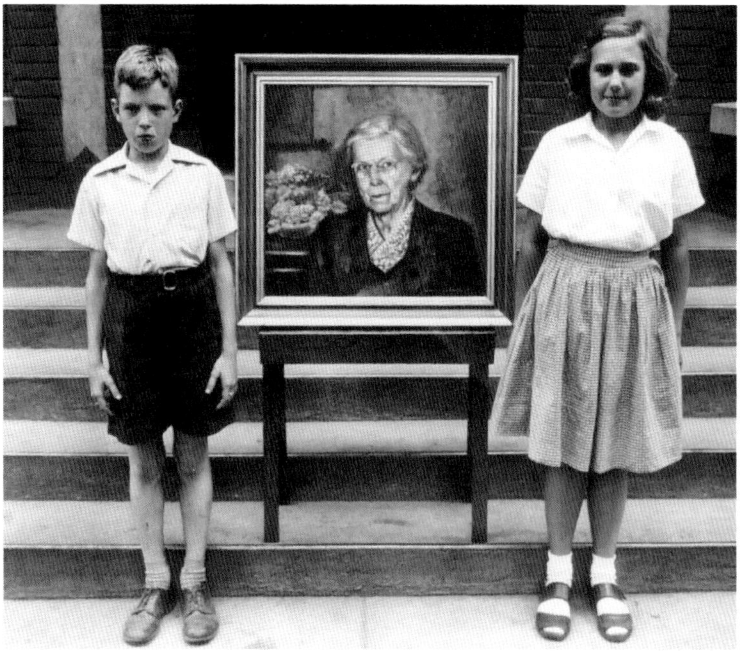

Clara Harris

In 1935, the Corban Street (now Corban Avenue) School was renamed after Harris, its beloved principal, who was described by student Mary Ann Hoover (above, right) as a "master teacher whose first interest had always been boys and girls." Hoover's mother commissioned this portrait of Harris and it was presented to the Clara Harris (Grammar) School at its 1946 commencement. James Franklin Shinn Jr. (left) was related to "Miss Clara." Clara Harris School, seen in the photograph below, opened in 1929 with Mary W. King as its first principal; Harris was a teacher there at the time. The school was located at the original site of St. James Lutheran Church, next to the current Cabarrus County jail. It later became the administrative offices for the city school system before finally being demolished. (Above, photograph by Zack L. Roberts.)

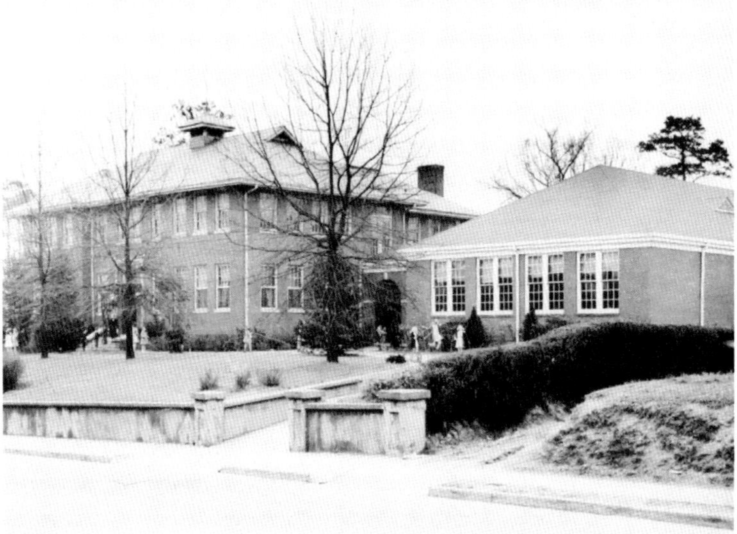

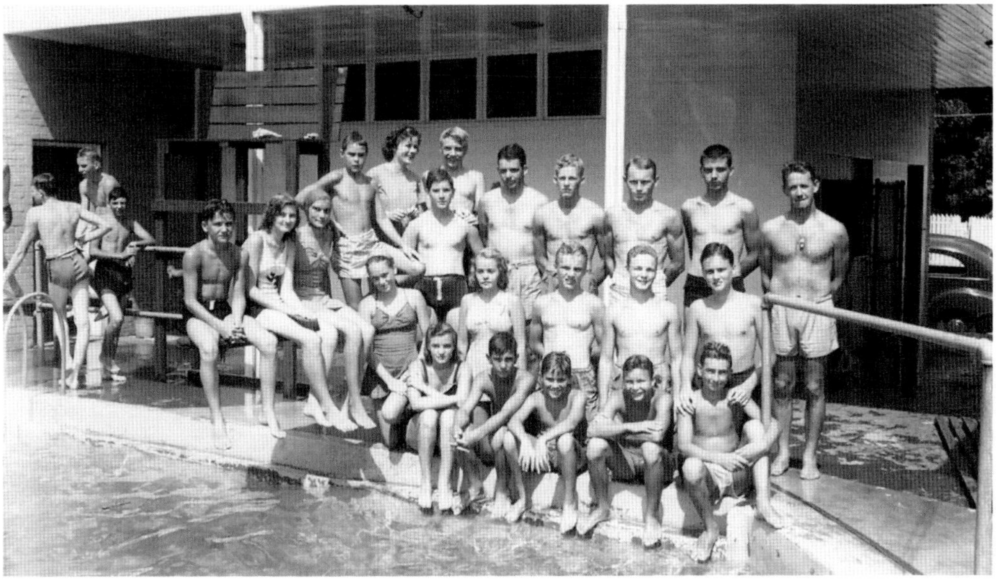

John F. McInnis

The father of Cabarrus County's sports recreation program, McInnis, shown above (back row, right) in the mid-1940s with his lifeguard staff, managed the "Rec Center," the city's community swimming pool that was built in the early 1940s as a Works Progress Administration project. He committed his entire adult life to education, working as the transportation supervisor for the school system, the principal of Coltrane-Webb Elementary, and the director of Head Start before ending his career in the 1970s as an administrator. McInnis is also remembered for spearheading a summer program to distribute baseballs and bats to youths at Concord parks. The city's aquatic center on Academy Street is named after him. In another mid-1940s image below, McInnis is conducting a life-saving training class with his staff. (Photographs by Zack L. Roberts.)

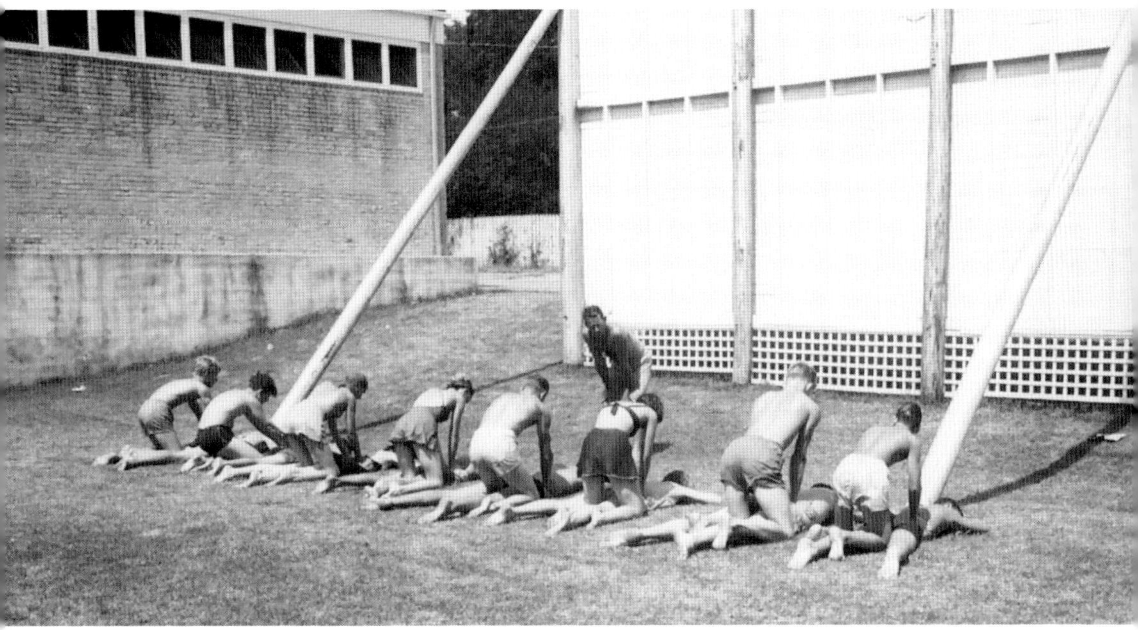

Tracy N. Spencer

Children cackling cheery refrains of the anthem "Camp Spencer is the Best Camp of All" have a Concord veterinarian to thank for their summer fun. In 1949, Doctor Spencer donated Cress Lake to become a community camp that was ultimately named after him, and orchestrated a fundraising campaign to build a new Boys Club facility, under construction in this 1950 photograph. From left to right are Jimmie Waddell, Spencer, Don Jones, unidentified, Ken Newton, unidentified, and Willy Frey. (Photograph by Jimmy Babb; courtesy of the Boys and Girls Club.)

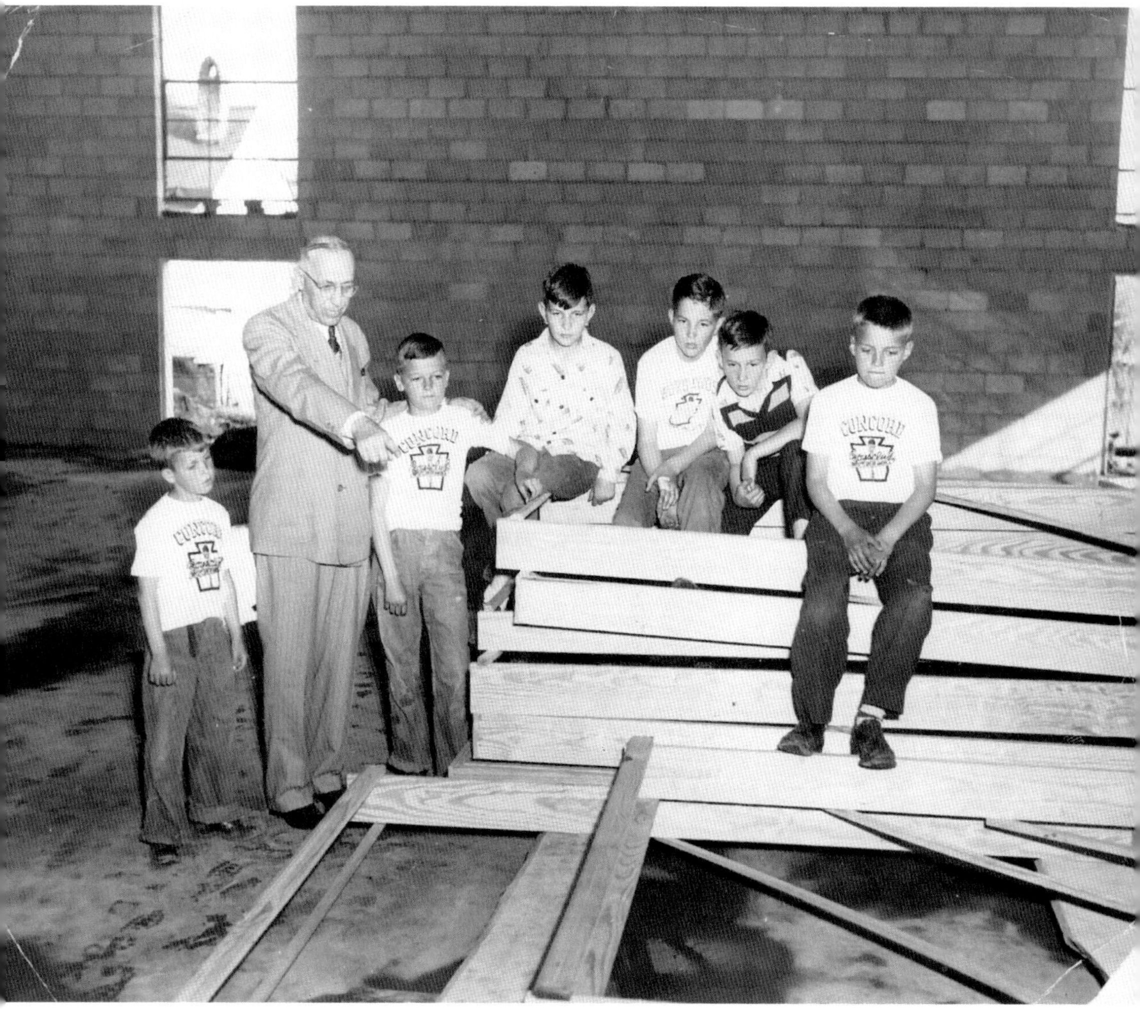

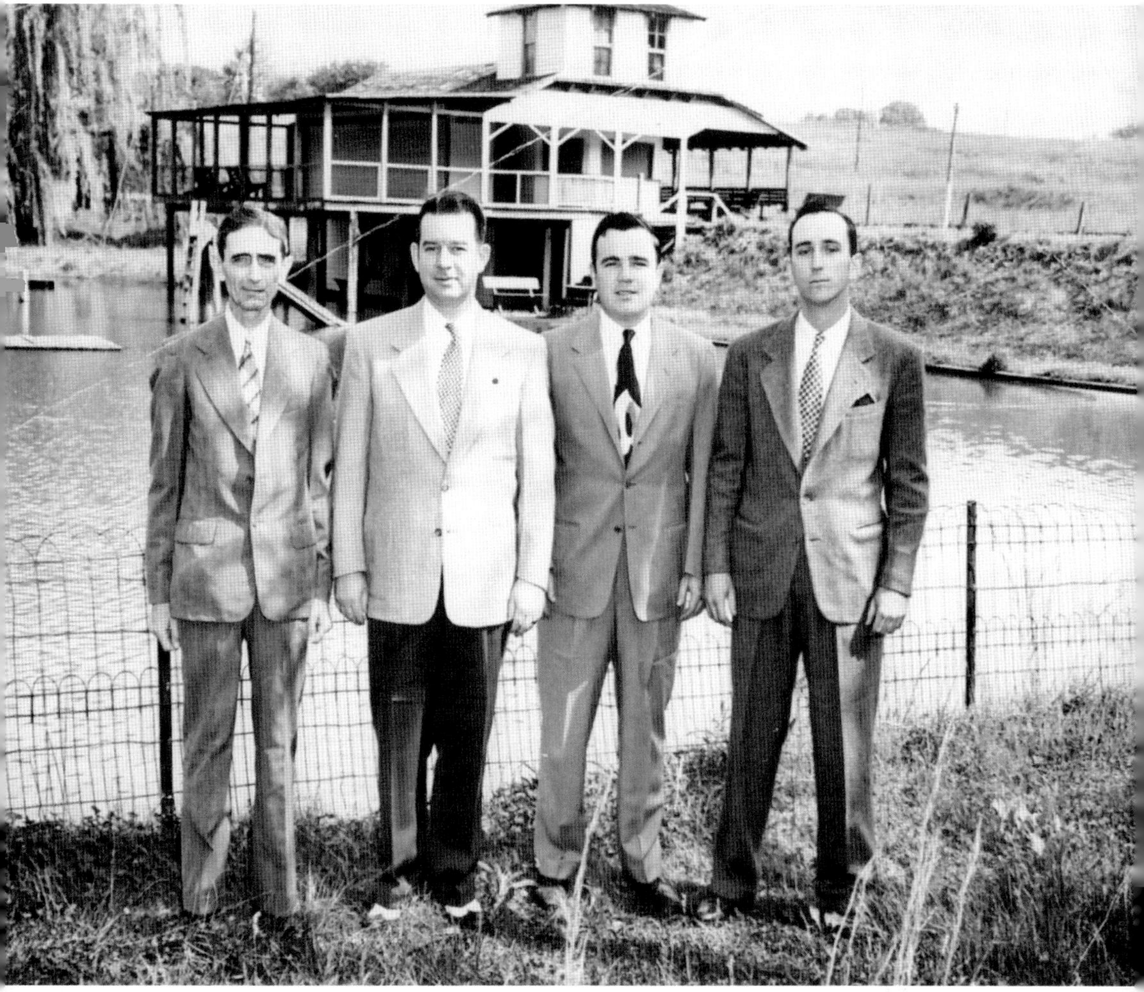

Fred Craven

Word has it that Dr. Craven (second from left) was the first person in town to use a pager. Back when the Country Club was actually on Country Club Drive and its golf course was on the grounds next door to the hospital where Carolina Mall has since been built, frantic nurses would "page" the doctor from the golf course to the delivery room by waving a sheet out the window.

Craven grew up in Raleigh, but after his residency at New York University, he was lured to Concord in 1938 to establish his medical practice. It was a homecoming of sorts, since his grandfather K.L. Craven was a Concord merchant known for two businesses established in the late 1800s, K.L. Craven and Sons Hardware and Craven's Coal Company. Temporarily leaving town to serve as an Army captain with the Medical Corps during World War II, Craven's doctor's office was on the second floor of the Cannon Building downtown; he also made house calls. Craven had a 25-year stretch of perfect attendance in the Concord Rotary Club and as that organization's president began an affiliation with the American Field Service, sponsoring exchange students.

One of the founding directors of the local Boys Club, Craven was fundamental in the fundraising campaign to build the facility in the early 1940s. He and his son Allen, currently a realtor, shared the club's "Man and Boy" Award in the 1980s for their service. Craven also provided medical care for boys at Stonewall Jackson Training School. Shown here at Camp Spencer are Ray McEachern, Craven, Tommy Craig, and Alfred M. Brown Sr. (Courtesy of the Boys and Girls Club.)

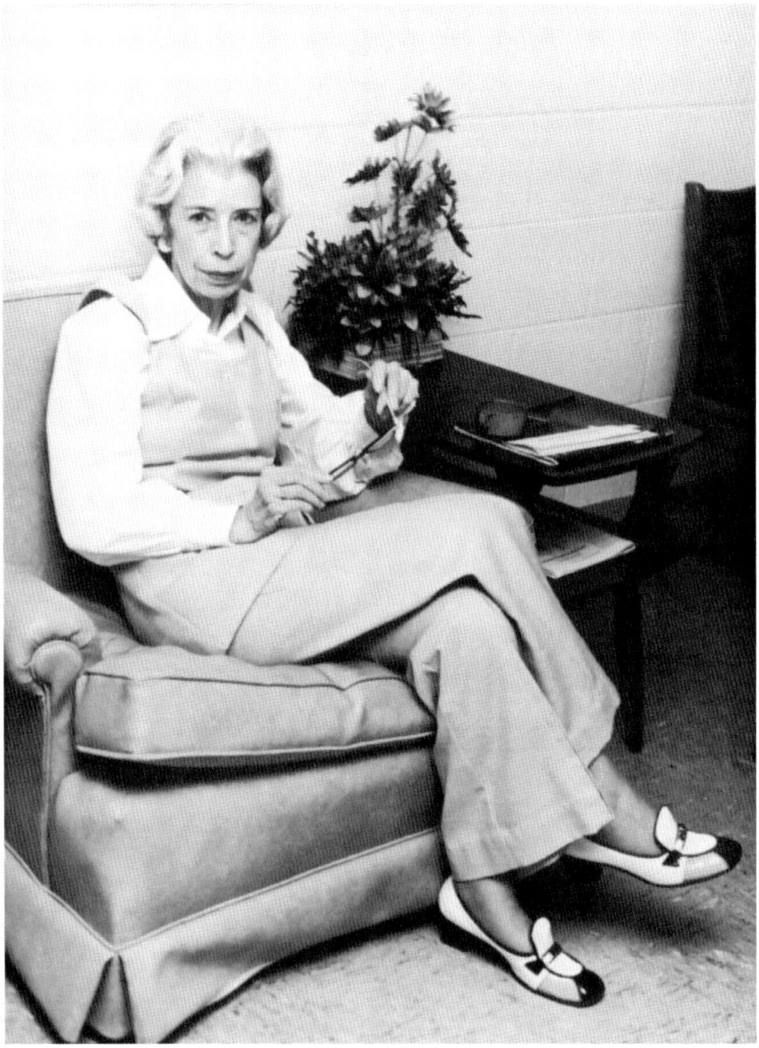

Blanche and Lillian Stewart (ABOVE AND OPPOSITE PAGE)
"She could make any historic figure come to life, and she'd enthrall you with her flamboyant descriptions of them," beamed journalist Helen C. Arthur-Cornett of her Concord High School teacher "Miss Blanche," from whom she acquired her love of history. "Miss Lillian," best known as a Latin teacher, famously remarked, "the student comes first and that never changes." Blanche, in a 1974 yearbook photograph above, directed numerous "Pan Players" stage productions, citing *Ladies of the Jury* as her personal favorite. Many students recall her humorously telling the story of how she was once stood up on a date by Barry Goldwater. Lillian, shown on page 116, was a tad less animated than her fiery older sister, but she similarly could make the long-dead culture of ancient Rome seem vibrant. The Stewart sisters dedicated their lives to teaching and retired together in 1975. They devoted their later years to traveling, and occasionally, to a spot of sherry with an adult former student who might stop by to visit.

They were the eldest daughters of William E. Stewart Sr., proprietor of Concord's first movie theater, the Pastime. While generations of Concord High School students remember the Stewarts as adult teachers, this rare 1911 photograph proves that at one time even "Miss Blanche" and "Miss Lillian" were children. From left to right on the opposite page are William, Lillian (seated on father's lap), Blanche (standing), and mother Ada. (Right, courtesy of Jimmy Babb.)

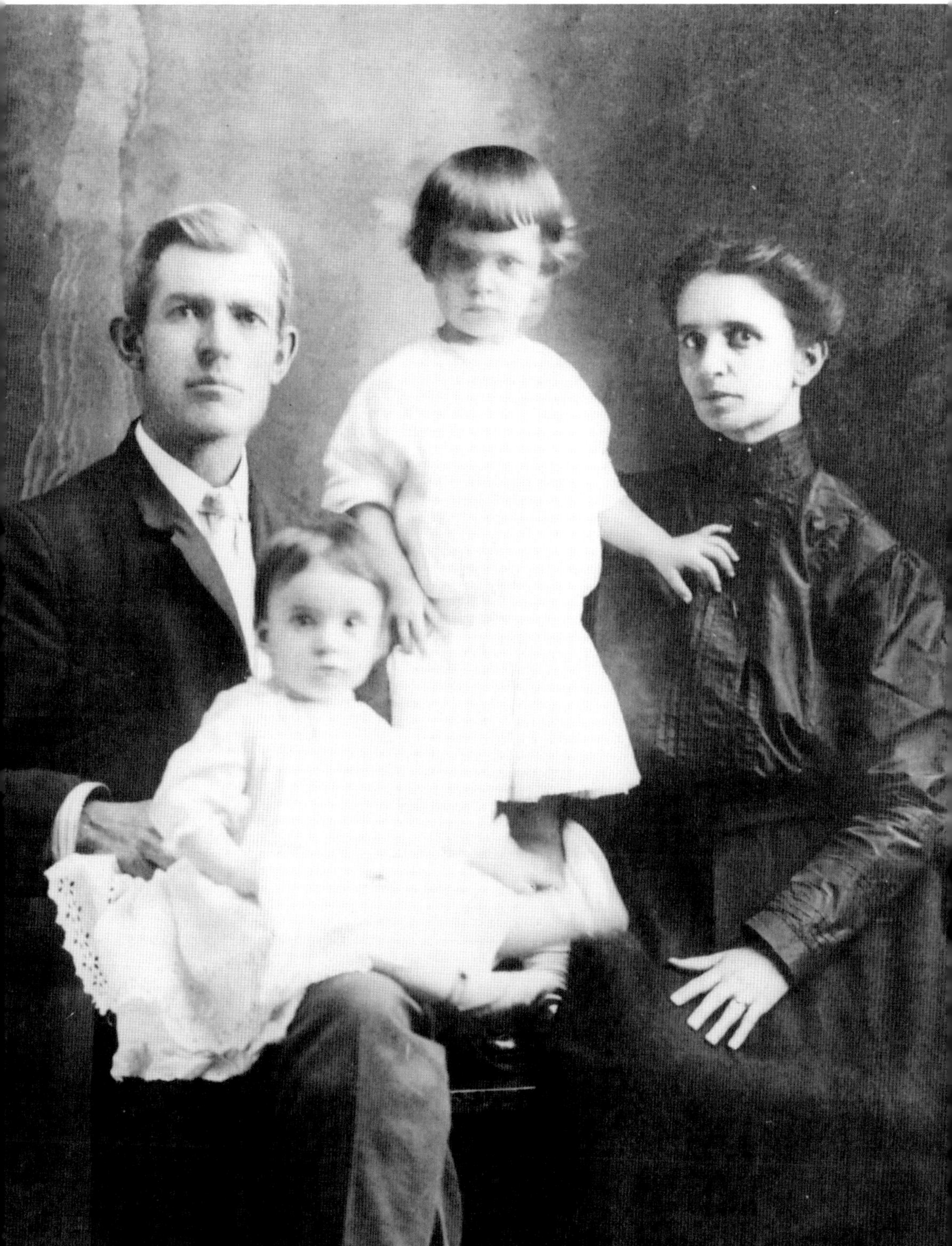

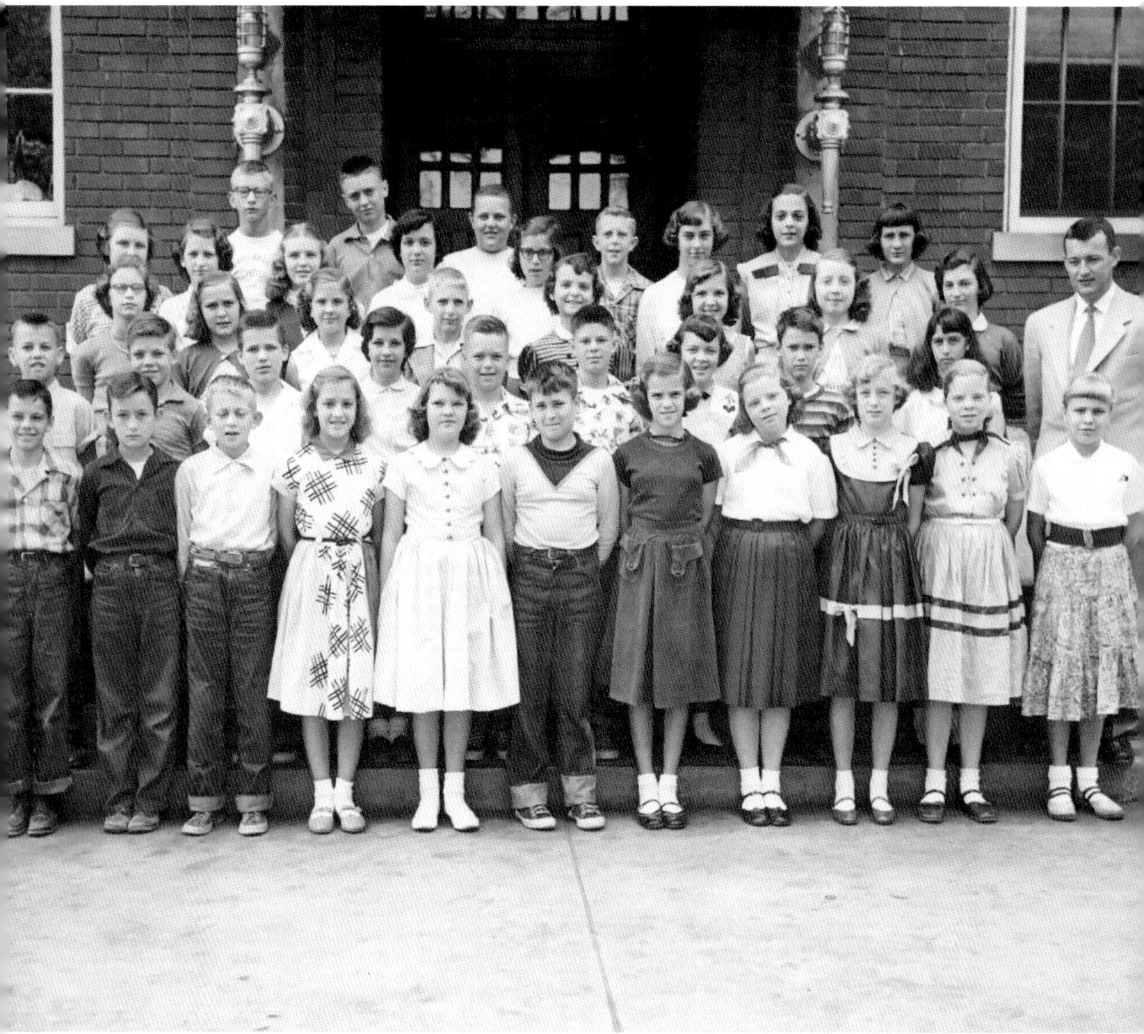

Joseph N. Fries

A convivial family man who never forgot a person's name, Fries came to Concord in the early 1950s to teach sixth grade at Clara Harris School. His wife, Betty, was also a teacher there. When Beverly Hills Elementary School opened in 1954, Fries was appointed principal and stayed in that position until 1965. He segued into administration, serving as assistant superintendent before ascending to superintendent, a post he held from 1977 through 1988. After his retirement, a local middle school was named in his honor. Fries died in 2013. From left to right in this Clara Harris class photograph are (first row) David Snyder, Ronnie Sides, Jerry Rogers, Rebecca Faggart, Donna Barbee, Jim Richie, Mary Margaret Hillman, Janice Cress, and Linda Widenhouse; (second row) Barney West, Kenneth Wilkinson, Lynn Linker, Merrillyn Eaves, Gilbert Merritt, Frank Ritzman, Beverly Joyner, Sammy Hawfield, Deloris Sutton, and Fries; (third row) Martha Ann Trexler, Rachel Smith, Nancy Towery, Donnie Fowler, Marlene Barnhardt, Frances Ann Baucom, Mary Ann Parnell, and Judy Cathey; (fourth row) Elizabeth Whitefield, Judy Moore, Rosie Killian, Sharon Howell, Alma Lou Graebe, Rebecca Linker, Gaye Holshouser, and Martha Rae Mills; and (fifth row) Kenneth Folkes, Joe Johnson, Beverly Eudy, and Glenn Fisher.

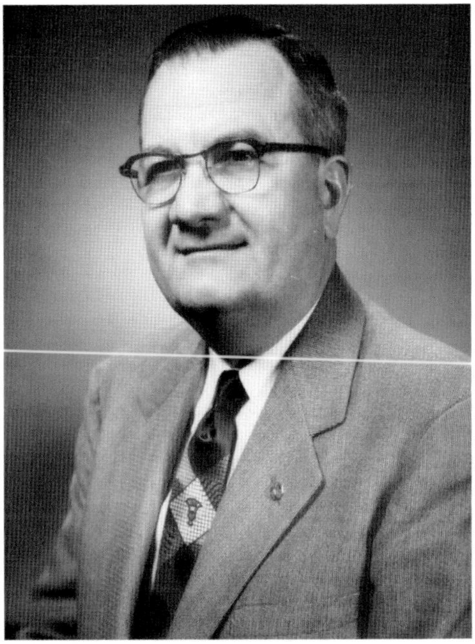

R. Brown McAllister

First gaining acclaim in 1934 as the principal of Coltrane School, McAllister succeeded Albert Shipp Webb as superintendent in 1943. Under his watch, the school system bolstered its music, arts, and Bible programs, witnessed facilities expansions, and built South Concord Elementary, a school that instead took McAllister's name. The school board resisted but reluctantly accepted his resignation in 1958, upon his retirement. (Courtesy of Concord Public Library.)

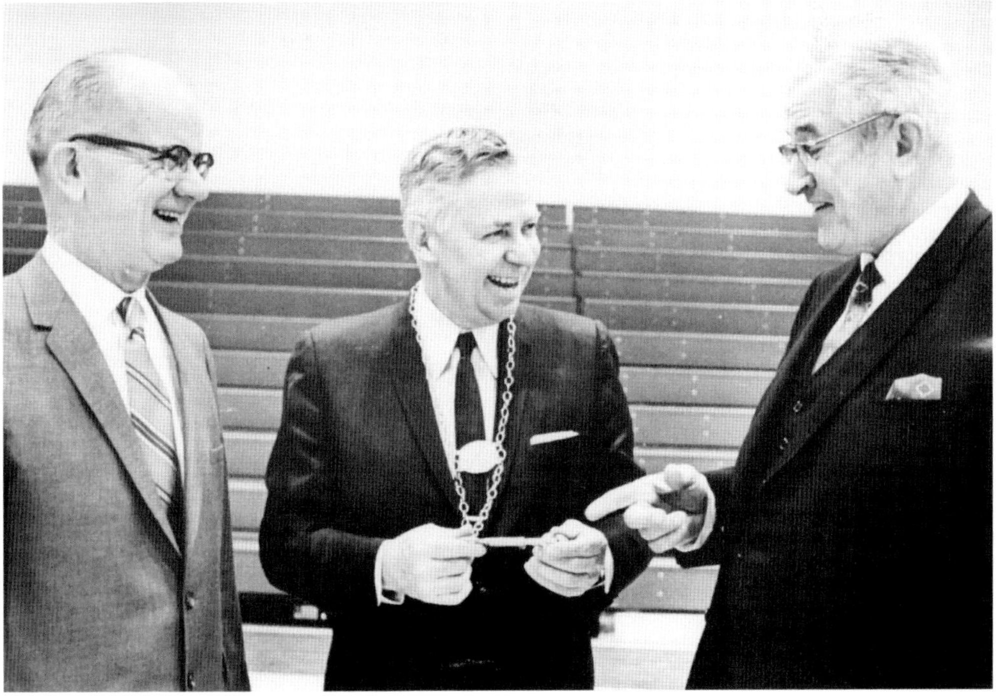

Ralph A. Glenn

Concord High's principal from 1946 to 1969, Glenn enforced former principal J. Eris Cassell's policy prohibiting student access to the Marsh Avenue building via its front steps. Glenn shepherded students through the tumultuous era of desegregation. The former high school, now a magnet school, is named after him. Glenn (left) is seen in this 1969 photograph with Jenkin Lloyd Jones and Mayor S. Les Myers. (Courtesy of Concord Public Library.)

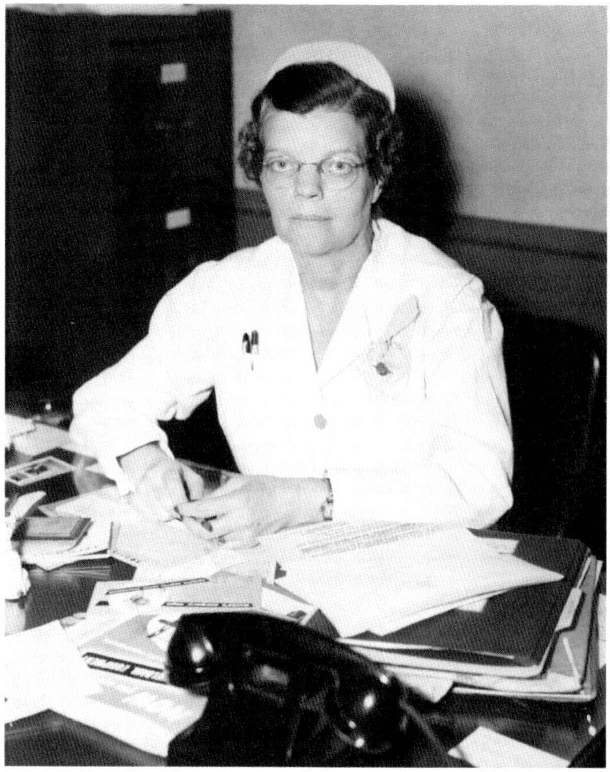

Louise Harkey

This inflexible but admired nurse was the first administrator of the Cabarrus Memorial Hospital School of Nursing. Harkey set high professional and ethical standards, insisting that students always display proper uniform (with polished shoes) and mature conduct (misbehavers would be sent to "Miss Harkey's bench" to await discipline). After her death in 1975, the nursing school was named after her and retained that name for decades. (Courtesy of Carolinas Medical Center NorthEast.)

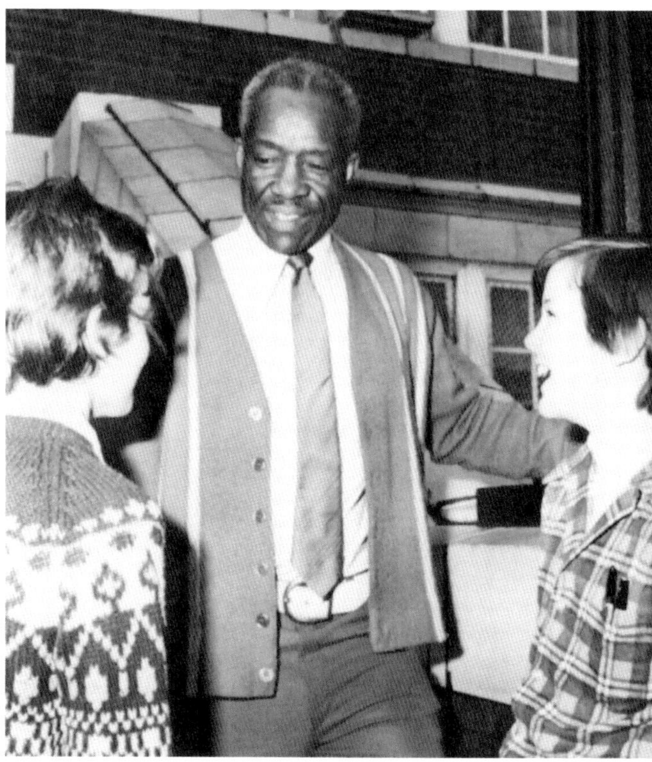

James Henry Alexander Sr.

Beginning at Logan School and then relocating to Concord Junior High (Middle) School after integration, band director "Mr. A" taught hundreds of children the fundamentals of musical instruments. A steadfast mentor, Alexander also served as assistant principal, as shown in this 1978 yearbook photograph. His father, Charles, led Alexander's Happy Pals Orchestra, an all-black ensemble founded in 1939. Alexander's oldest son, James Jr., became a speechwriter for Pres. Bill Clinton.

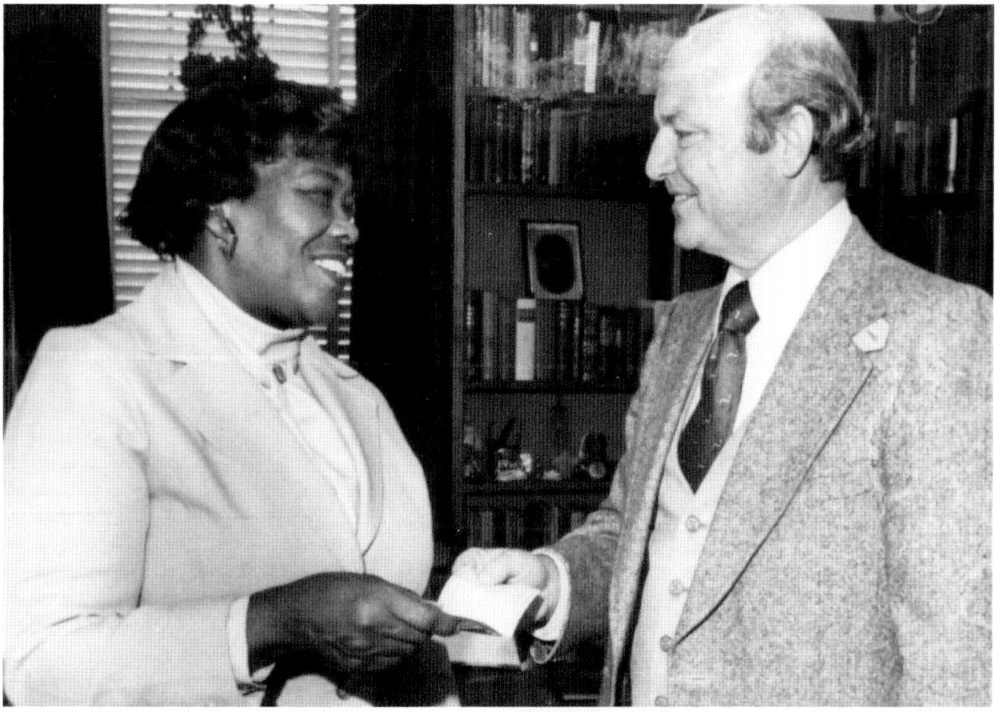

Mable Parker McLean
The first female president of Barber-Scotia College, Dr. McLean led the institution from which she graduated on three different occasions beginning in 1974. The college's student union was named after her upon her retirement. McLean was also the first woman to be elected chairperson of the United Negro College Fund's Council of Presidents. She is pictured here in the late-1970s with Concord mayor Harold B. McEachern. (Photograph by Frankie Furr.)

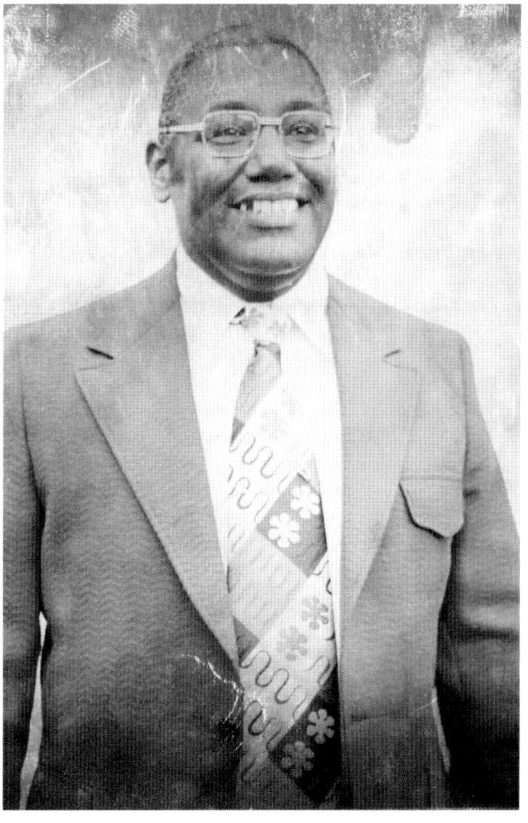

Allen T. Small
This loquacious Small stepped into the role of principal of Coltrane-Webb Elementary during desegregation; earlier, he was principal of Logan High and, later, Wolf Meadow Elementary. Small occasionally used a paddle on undisciplined Coltrane-Webb boys; he was better acquainted with some students' backsides than their faces. A city councilman, he died unexpectedly in 2006 and his seat was filled by his widow, retired teacher Ella Mae Small. (Courtesy of Concord Public Library.)

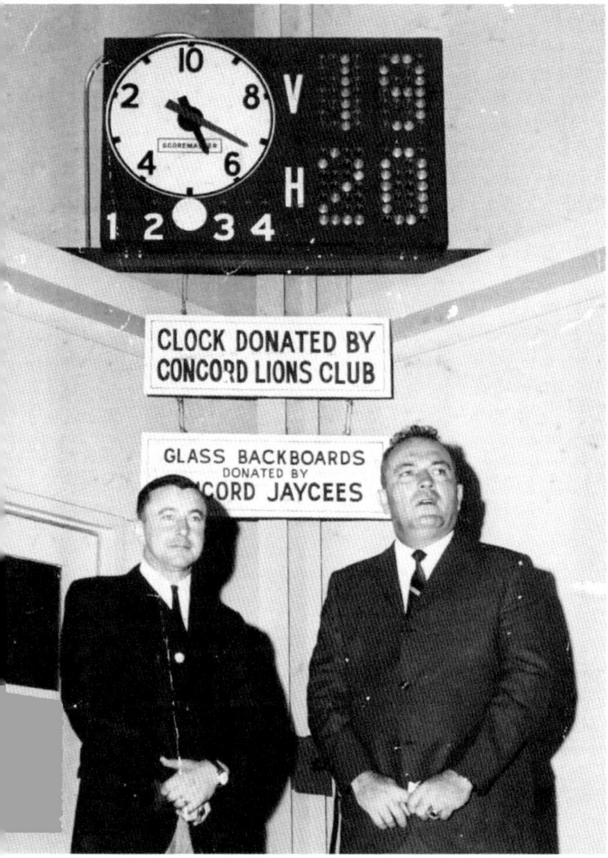

Claude "Bear" Little

His strapping size earned Little the nickname "Bear." So did his hairy chest, a forest concealing the whistle he blew when Camp Spencer swimmers ignored safety rules. But for the hundreds of children to whom he conveyed a passion for sports and sportsmanship, this bighearted coach, the Boys Club's athletic director from the mid-1950s through the 1970s, was a lovable teddy bear. Little (right) is shown with Buddy McEachern. (Courtesy of the Boys and Girls Club.)

Donnie Whittington

When the Boys Club opened in 1949, Whittington was too young for membership. But the determined athlete routinely snuck into the facility and found no other place he would rather be—he even carved his name into an oak tree on the grounds. The club's longtime athletic director, Whittington was employed there for more than 50 years. From left to right are Darrin Plott, Dane Plott, Whittington, and unidentified. (Courtesy of the Boys and Girls Club.)

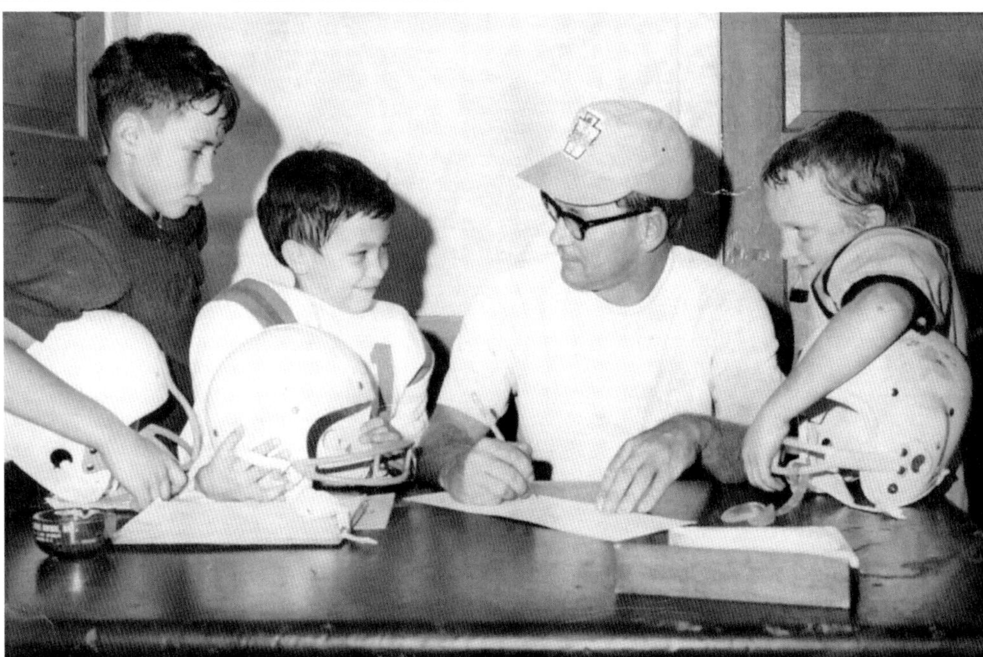

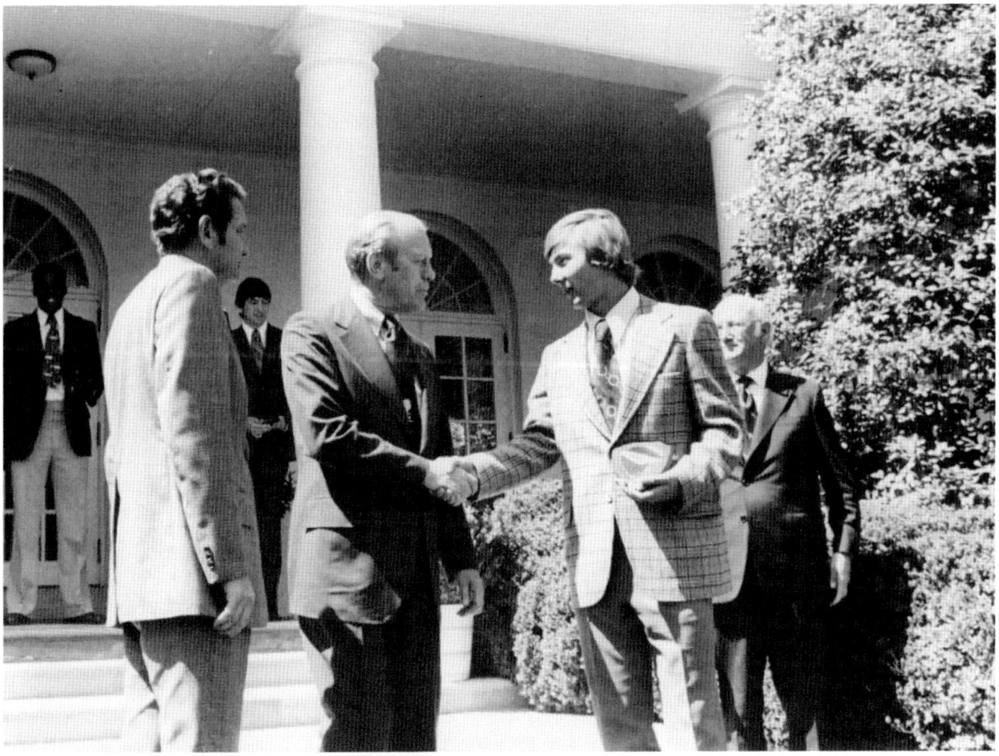

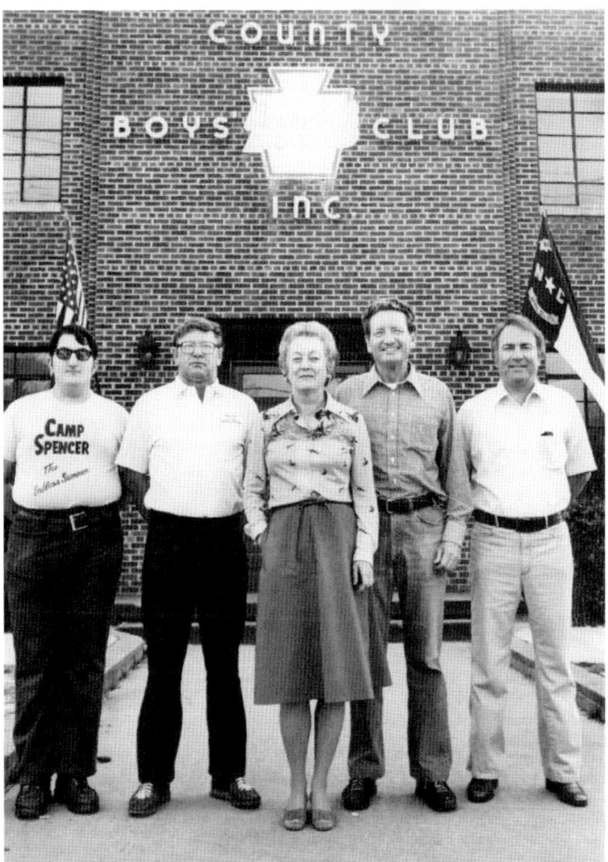

Robert G. "Hank" Utley
Executive director of the Boys and Girls Club from the mid-1970s through the mid-1980s, Utley (above, left) is at the White House's Rose Garden with Pres. Gerald Ford and Concord's Barry Cannon, the 1976 Southeast Regional Boy of the Year. The organization became the Boys and Girls Club during Utley's tenure. A baseball historian, Utley received a 1946 baseball scholarship at North Carolina State University and has coauthored books about the Independent Carolina Baseball League. This early 1980s photograph (left) shows the front of the Boys Club building on Spring Street and offers a better view of Utley, along with several of his colleagues. From left to right are Robert Williams, Donnie Whittington, Oleka Baker, Utley, and Jim Helms. (Both, courtesy of the Boys and Girls Club.)

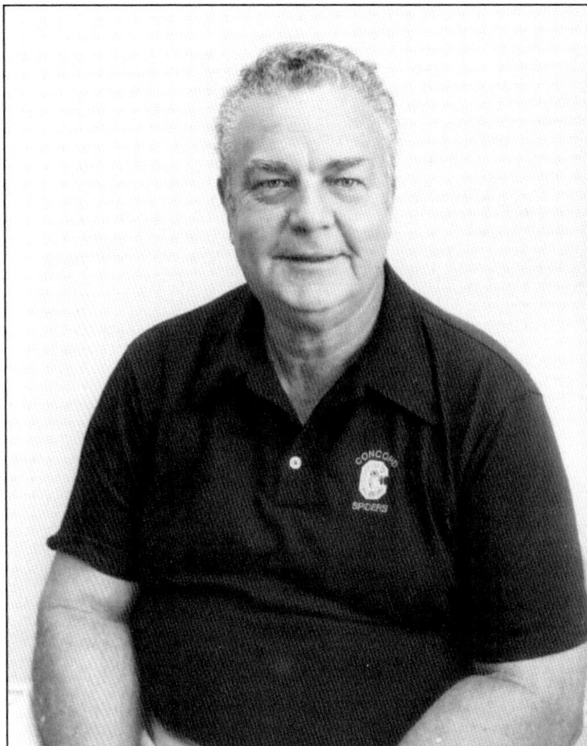

George "Ick" Alley

Thirteen was a lucky number for this 1949 Concord High graduate and star athlete: he received that many college football scholarship offers. "Ick" surprised no one when he returned to his treasured alma mater in 1955 as a faculty member. He taught US history and industrial cooperative training but is best remembered for coaching football for 24 years. Alley's gruff exterior belied his boundless paternal spirit. (Courtesy of Laura Young Alley.)

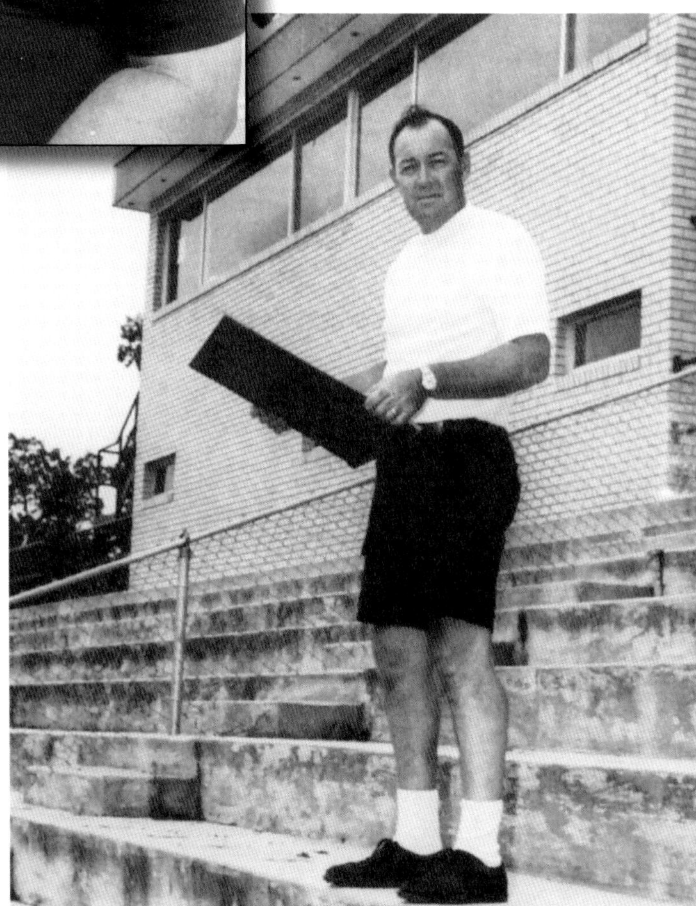

Bill Ford

If Ford's 11 years with the Reds' and Phillies' farm clubs had earned him a spot with the majors, then Concord High School would have been deprived one of its most accomplished baseball coaches. A Hartsell High School graduate and Korean War veteran, Ford returned to Concord in 1960 and spent nearly 30 years coaching and teaching. Concord High School's baseball field was named in his honor in 2013.

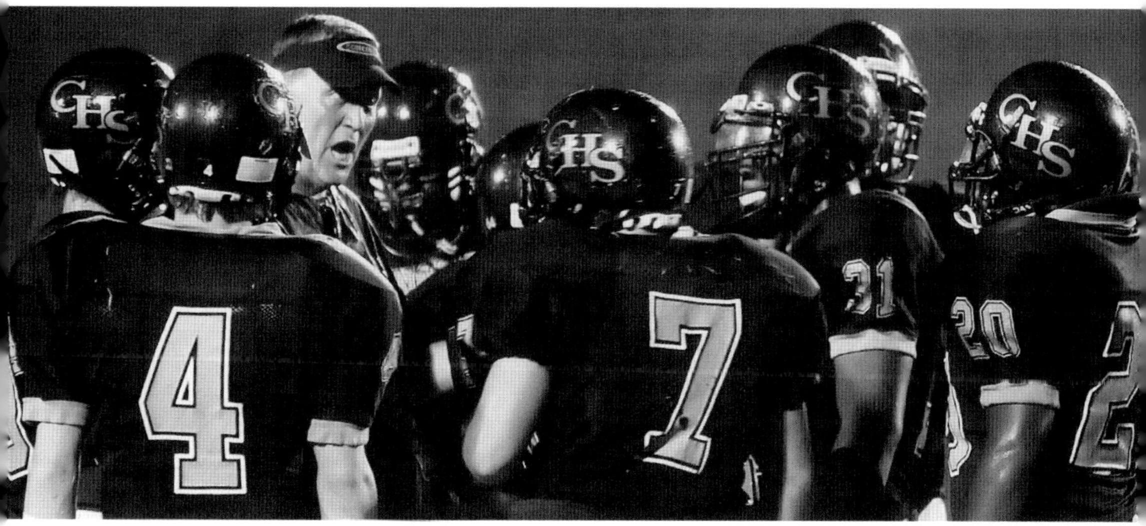

E.Z. Smith III

Earning nine varsity letters in three different sports, this 1972 Concord High graduate earned a football scholarship from the University of South Carolina. Smith returned to CHS in 1980 to coach his alma mater's football team for a remarkable 29 years, leading the Spiders to numerous division and conference wins. He is also known for his spectacular vocal talents. (Photograph by James Nix; courtesy of the *Independent Tribune*.)

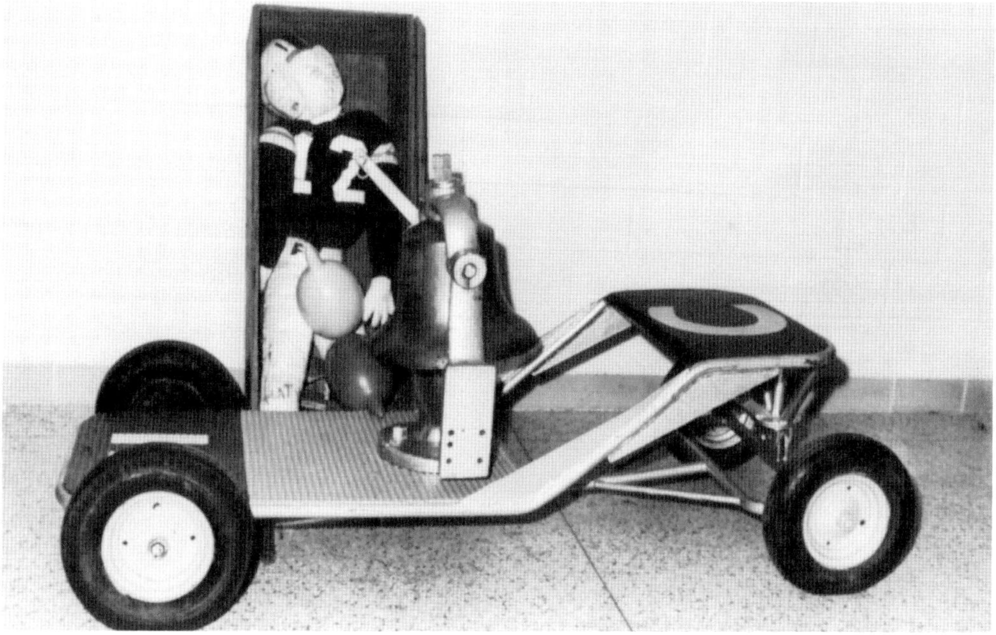

The Bell

If the Concord Spiders had their way, this part-time "resident" would settle in town permanently. The winner of each year's long-running Concord/Kannapolis football matchup—a fierce competition known as the Battle for the Bell—claims this coveted railroad bell and paints it in their school's colors. Shown with the bell in this 1972 *Spider Web* photograph is a Kannapolis effigy, the "Little Wonder."

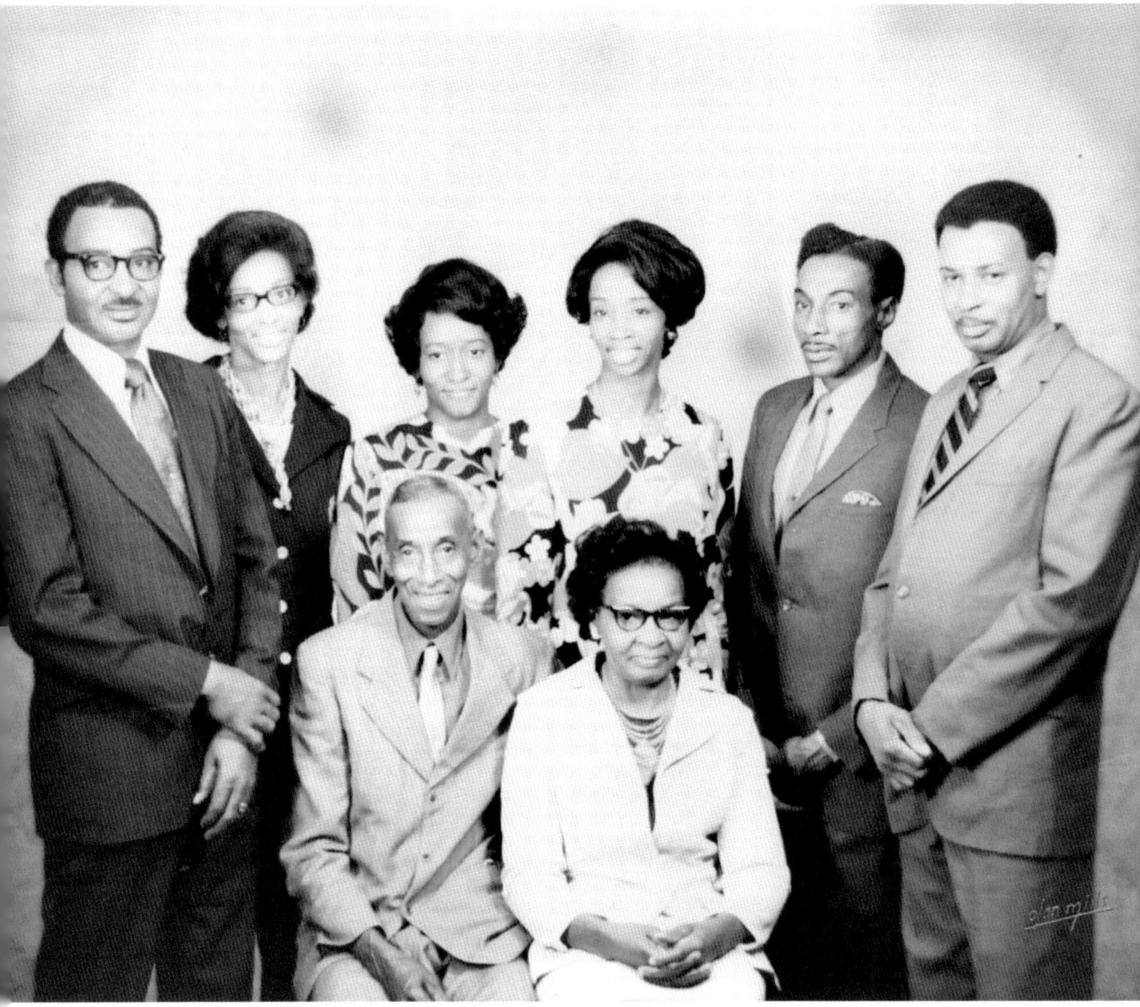

Alice Steele-Robinson

A 1961 graduate of Logan High School, Steele-Robinson (back row, fourth from left) has dedicated her entire life to educating young people. After desegregation of Concord's public schools in the late 1960s, she became the first African American to be appointed director of elementary education for the school system. Her current focus is the Academic Learning Center, a private organization established in 1995 that tutors children in the county's lowest-income schools. Shown in this undated Steele family portrait, from left to right are (front row, seated) Andrew A. Steele Sr. and Neomia Pharr Steele; and (second row, standing) Sylvester Steele, Joyce Ann Steele Caldwell, Carolyn "Peggy" Steele Gorham, Steele-Robinson, Andrew A. Steele Jr., and Ivalee Steele. (Courtesy of Concord Public Library.)

CHAPTER SIX

The Famous, the Familiar, and the Infamous

They are the headline makers and the recognizable faces of Concord.

Some of them might be remembered around town as the hustling infielder from Webb Field we knew would go far, or the pretty teen who played French horn in the Concord High School Marching Spiders, or the kids in that folk-rock band who packed 'em in at the George Washington Tavern. We beamed with pride when we later spied them on baseball cards, magazine covers, and *Conan O'Brien*.

Some we may not know personally, but we feel as if we do. We have seen them on television or in the movies. They afford us bragging rights since we hail from the same city. And occasionally, we might catch a glimpse of them sipping a drink at the Union Street Bistro or waiting in line at the Harris Teeter grocery checkout.

Some of them are our personal friends, and our hearts swell with the successes they have achieved. Some are the eccentrics that have promenaded and pedaled the streets of town, noticed by many but known by few.

And in a couple of cases, these Concordians-behaving-badly became notorious and offered us juicy gossip we find as irresistible as a Cherry Lemon Sun-drop.

This chapter examines the famous, the familiar, and the infamous of Concord.

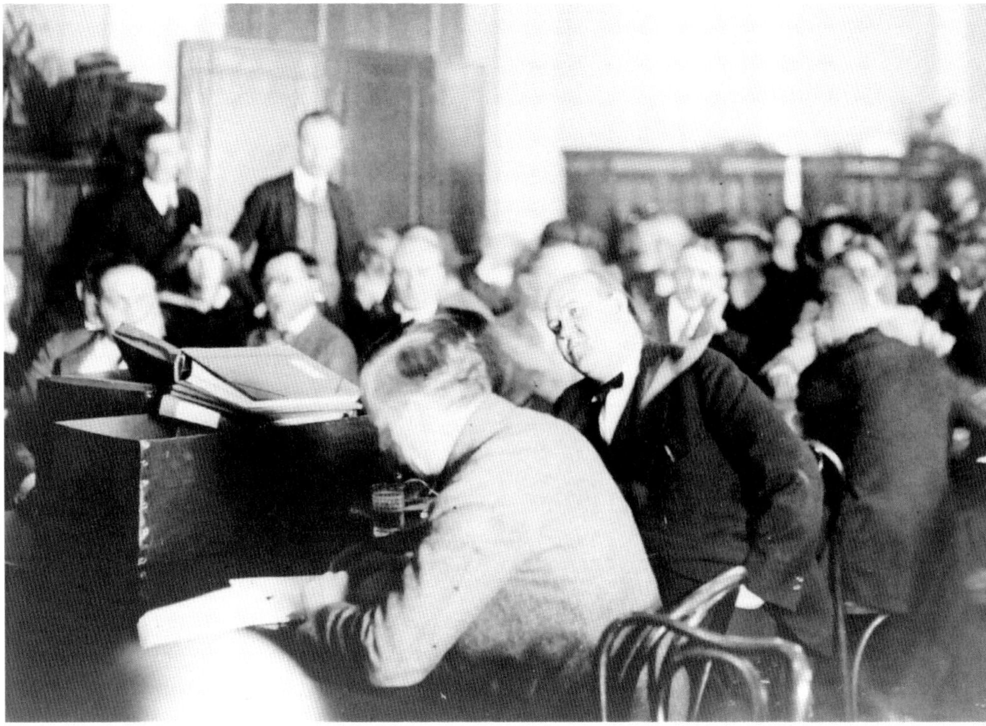

Gaston B. Means

Concord may have been a cotton town during his day, but no one could spin a yarn like Means. FBI chief J. Edgar Hoover once called Concord's most disreputable citizen "the greatest faker of all time," and this knavish smooth-talker has been interpreted on screen by three different actors, most recently in 2012 in the HBO drama *Boardwalk Empire*.

A child of privilege, Means was born in 1879 and reared in Concord's most enviable neighborhood, North Union Street. According to Edwin P. Hoyt's 1963 biography *Spectacular Rogue*, Means's grandfather William C. "the General" Means was a querulous plantation owner alternately feared and respected by neighbors. Means's iron-fisted father, William G. "the Colonel" Means, was an eminent attorney elected to four intermittent terms as Concord's mayor and one term as a North Carolina state senator.

While hubris was a family trait, Means perfected it into an art form. He never outgrew his cherubic childhood face, employing his dimpled grin as backup for his adroitly controlled Southern accent in effecting any story he could imagine. Legend has it that he told his first fib at age seven by denying that he stole a few dollars his mother had earmarked for charity. The lies became braver and bolder as he matured.

Means strutted through jobs that allowed his tongue to do his work: as an educator, a traveling salesman, and a detective. It was in the latter capacity that he, in New York City and Washington, DC, was able to "discover" conspiracies that required his investigation—for a fee. From estate matters to international plots, his frauds plundered hundreds of thousands of dollars from gullible victims. Means once blamed the death of a client, from whom he bilked a fortune via a will forgery, on an accidental gunshot wound—to the back of her head. This led to the sensational trial shown in this photograph, held back home in Concord; Means was acquitted.

Strangely, he was hired by the US Department of Justice, where his cons continued. In 1930, he hit the bestseller list with the tell-all *The Strange Death of President Harding*, sizzling with brazen allegations. Two years later, he pilfered a $100,000 ransom by claiming to know the whereabouts of the kidnapped Lindbergh baby, a con that ultimately landed him behind bars. Means died in a federal penitentiary in 1938. (Courtesy of the Library of Congress, Prints and Photographs Division, LC-USZ62-102198.)

Robert Pitts

It must have seemed like a good idea at the time, this Concord habitual heister's "brainstorm" to remove his fingerprints. Pitts endured the painful process of skinning his fingerprints; he then had his hands taped to his sides, allowing his raw, butchered digits to graft onto the flesh there. Once his fingers were cut free, his fingertips had no prints—but instead left uniquely identifiable smears that pointed Concord Police to his 1964 arrest. In Pitts's shirtless mug shot, the scars from his self-inflicted ordeal are visible. (All courtesy of the Concord Police Department.)

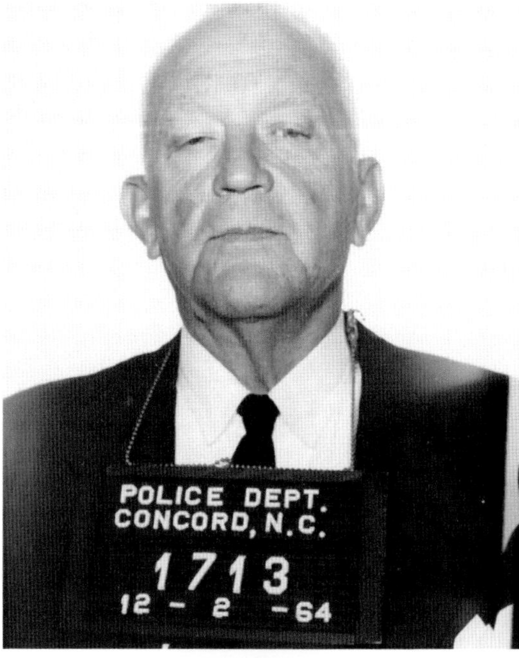

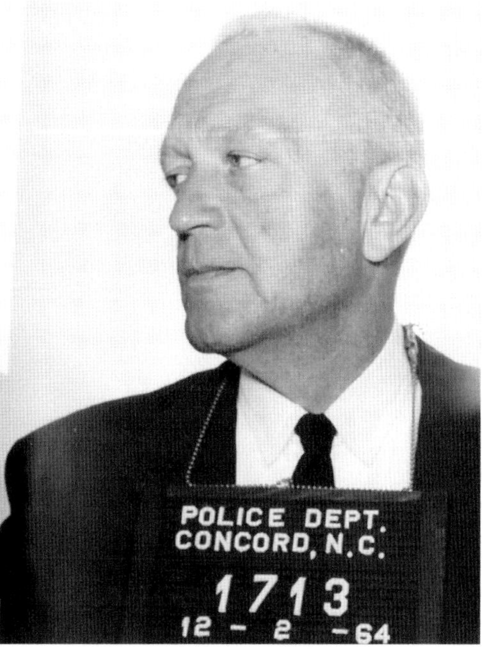

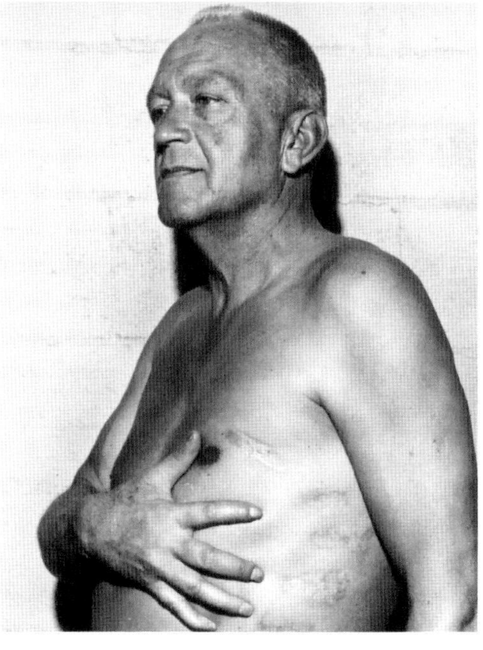

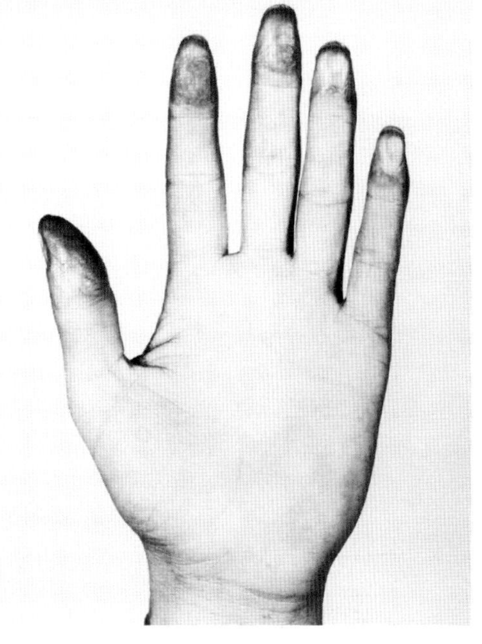

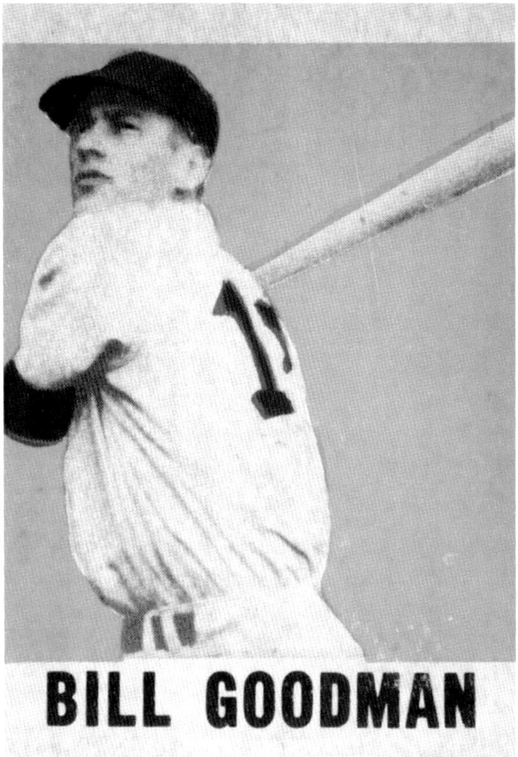

William "Billy" Goodman
Concord-born Goodman escaped the hardships of the Great Depression by playing baseball, hopping from the textile leagues to Atlanta's farm club in 1944. After service in World War II he returned to the sport, enjoying a long career with the Boston Red Sox and batting near or over .300 for most of his time in the majors. Throughout his career, this switch-off master played almost every position with the exception of catcher and pitcher. Goodman has been inducted into the North Carolina Sports Hall of Fame, the Boston Red Sox Hall of Fame, and the Cabarrus County Sports Hall of Fame. He died in 1984. Shown here are both sides of Goodman's 1949 Leaf Gum Company trading card. (Leaf copyright and courtesy of Cloetta.)

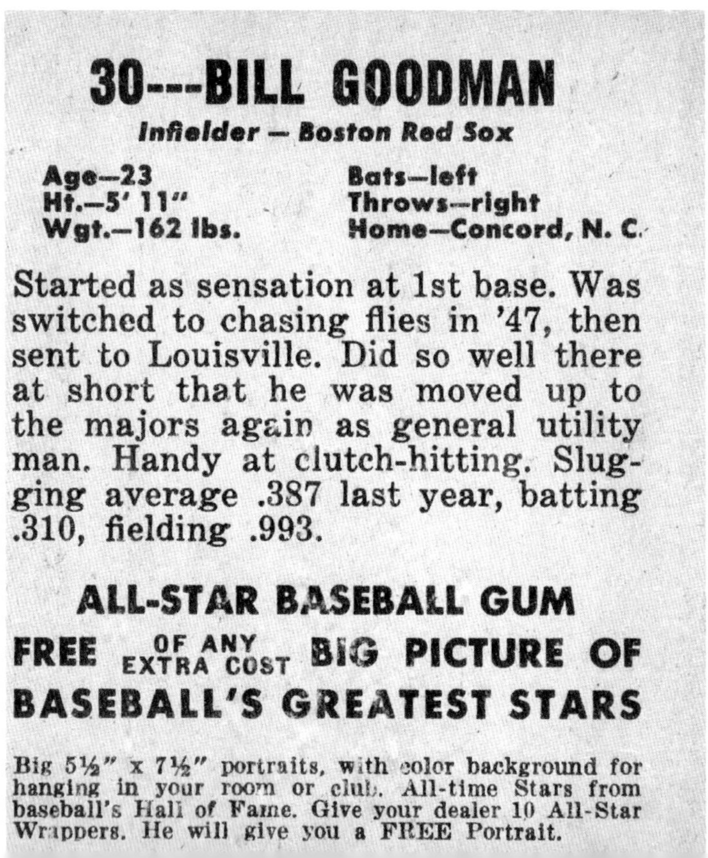
30---BILL GOODMAN

Infielder — Boston Red Sox

Age—23	**Bats—left**
Ht.—5' 11"	**Throws—right**
Wgt.—162 lbs.	**Home—Concord, N. C.**

Started as sensation at 1st base. Was switched to chasing flies in '47, then sent to Louisville. Did so well there at short that he was moved up to the majors again as general utility man. Handy at clutch-hitting. Slugging average .387 last year, batting .310, fielding .993.

ALL-STAR BASEBALL GUM

FREE OF ANY EXTRA COST **BIG PICTURE OF BASEBALL'S GREATEST STARS**

Big 5½" x 7½" portraits, with color background for hanging in your room or club. All-time Stars from baseball's Hall of Fame. Give your dealer 10 All-Star Wrappers. He will give you a FREE Portrait.

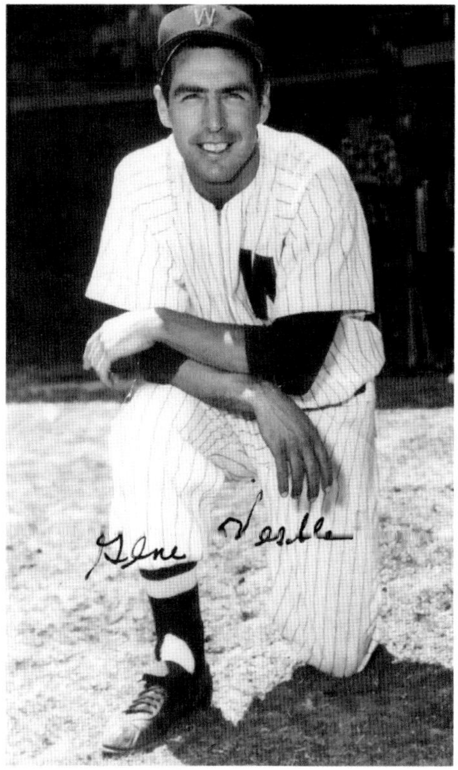

Gene Verble

This shortstop/second baseman and Hartsell High School graduate had a professional baseball career as a player and manager from 1945 through 1962, including nearly two seasons in the majors with the Washington Senators. During his stint managing the Charlotte Hornets, he led the club to a 1957 Class A Sally League championship. Post-baseball, Verble owned a local gas station, and he is now retired in his hometown of Concord. An inductee of the Cabarrus County Sports Hall of Fame, he was honored at the Concord Museum in 2013 with a "Gene Verble Day" event hosted by Historic Cabarrus Association, Inc. (Both, courtesy of Gene Verble.)

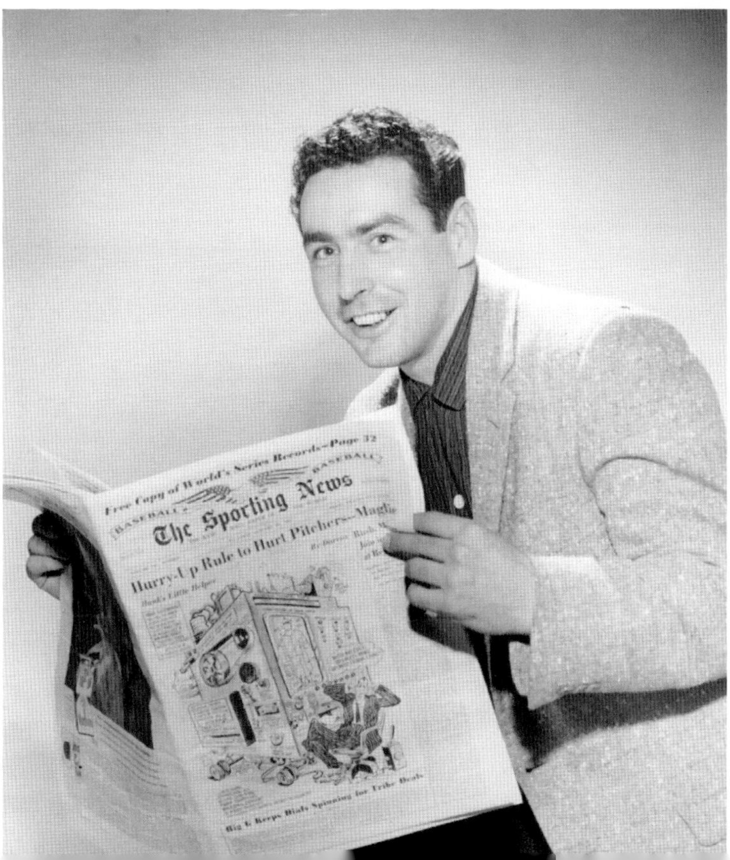

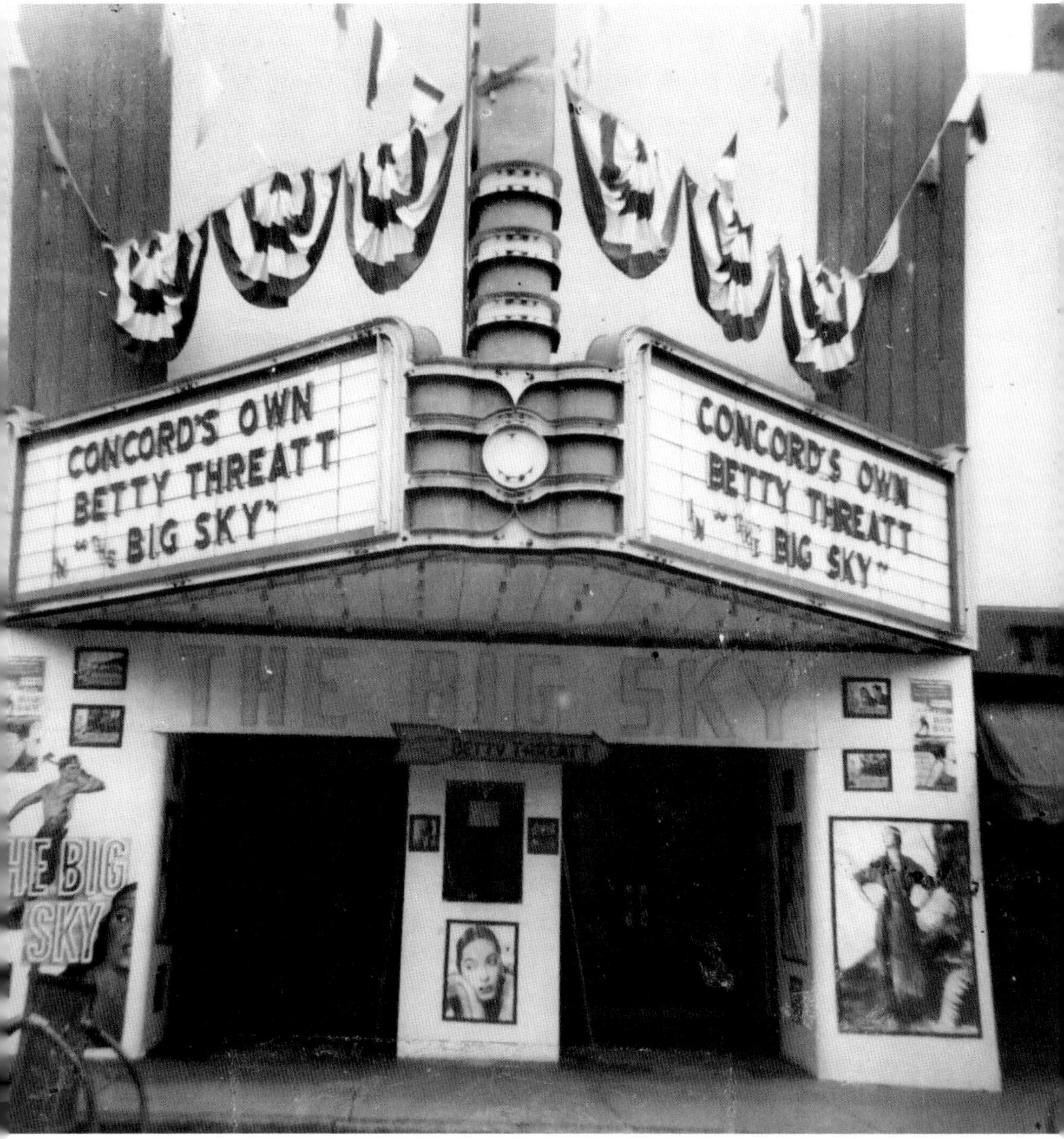

Elizabeth Threatt (ABOVE AND OPPOSITE PAGE)

This South Carolina–born beauty, the daughter of a white father and Cherokee mother, turned heads as a successful New York fashion model and stopped hearts in 1952's *The Big Sky*, a frontier film directed by Hollywood icon Howard Hawks and starring Kirk Douglas. Her performance as a fetching Blackfoot named Teal Eye tantalized reviewers and fans. With a future of fame and fortune at her feet, Threatt inexplicably performed an about-face, moving to Concord, marrying Count Antoine DeContades, becoming the mother of two children, and working in the local textile mills. Outside of a showing of her sole movie at the Cabarrus Theatre, few locals were aware that the woman they knew as "Betty" once had an enviable career she chose to forsake. She died in 1993 and is buried at Oakwood Cemetery. (Opposite, author's collection.)

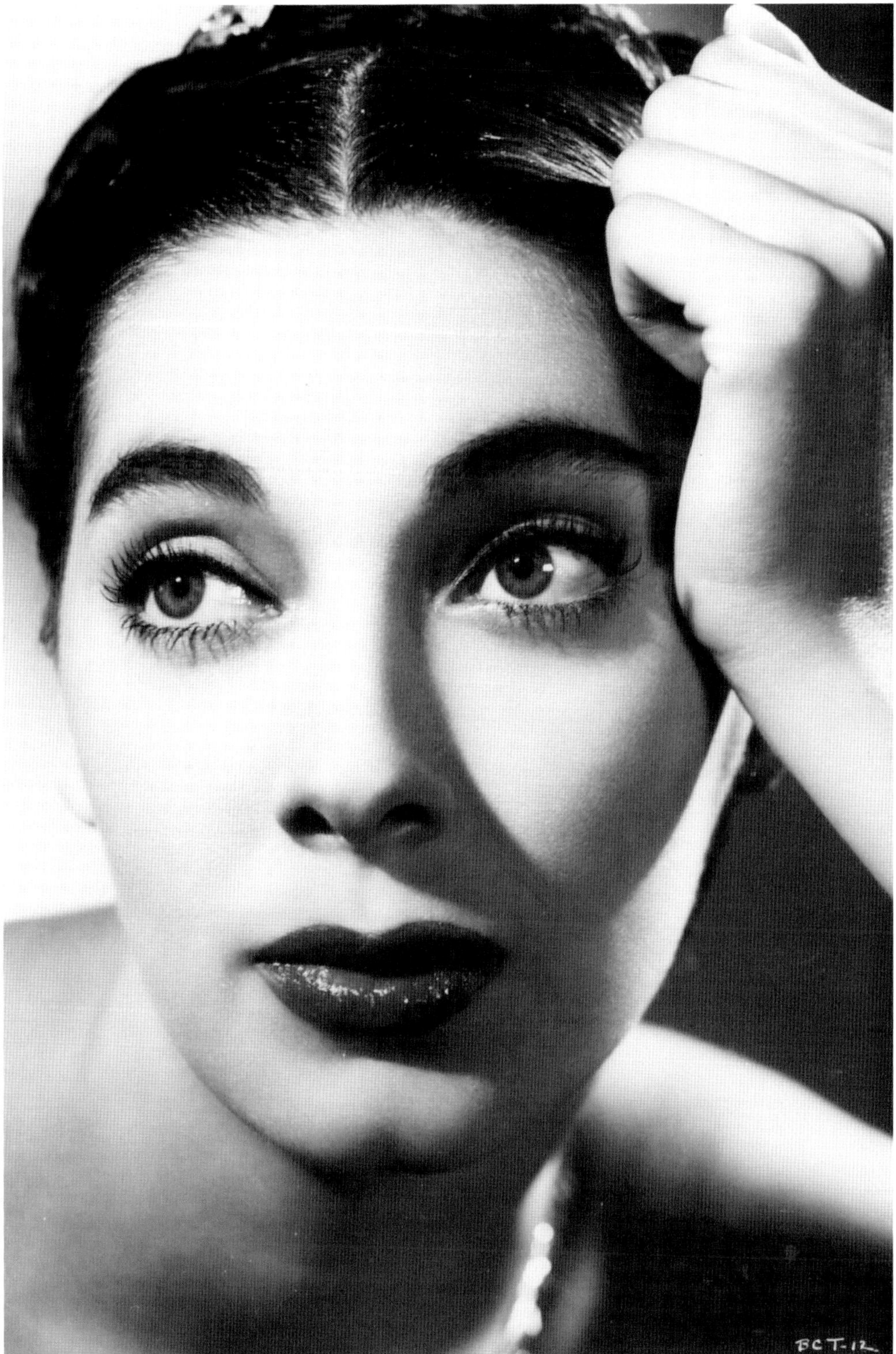
BCT-12

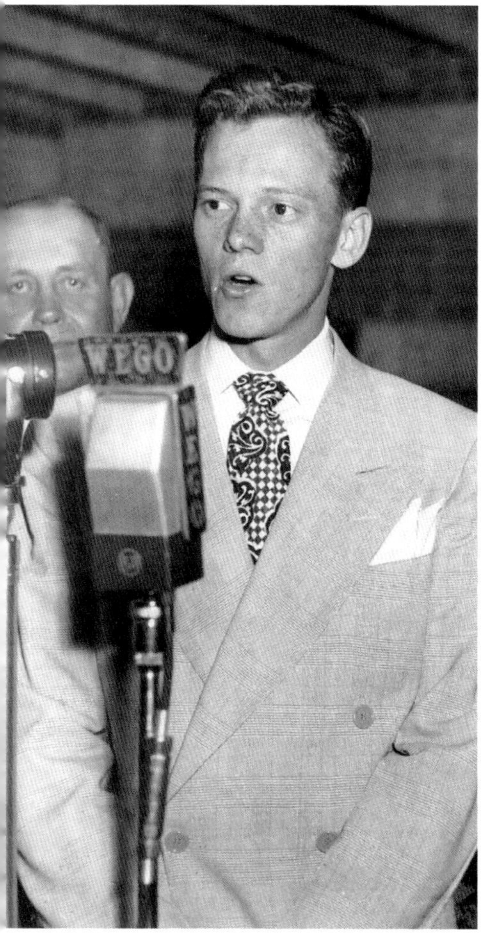

Robert D. Raiford

Raiford was a freckle-faced 20-year-old in this 1947 photograph, but by then, he had logged two years behind the mike calling Concord Weavers minor league games for WEGO-AM. His broadcasting career in radio and television whisked him away from his hometown to markets in Charlotte, Washington, New York, Philadelphia, and Charleston, but he eventually circled his way home to Concord and occasionally can be spotted zipping around town on his motorcycle.

One of Raiford's favorite haunts is the What-A-Burger on Church Street, where he relishes his encounters with locals from every walk of life. Some of these folks are friends or acquaintances; others' eyes light up with recognition when they spy him nursing a coffee at a window booth. Chances are, they know him from his Charlotte news anchor days, where he was seen nightly in the late 1970s and through much of the 1980s. Or perhaps they recognize him from one of his supporting roles in 28 movies and several televisions series, in which he often played a judge or an authority figure. His credits include *The Handmaid's Tale*, *Billy Bathgate*, *Super Mario Bros.*, *Radioland Murders*, and episodes of the courtroom drama *Matlock*.

Today, Raiford's radio voice still richly resonates, and he uses it in his role as a self-proclaimed "curmudgeon" on the nationally syndicated *John Boy and Billy* morning show. (Left by Jimmy Babb; both, courtesy of Robert D. Raiford.)

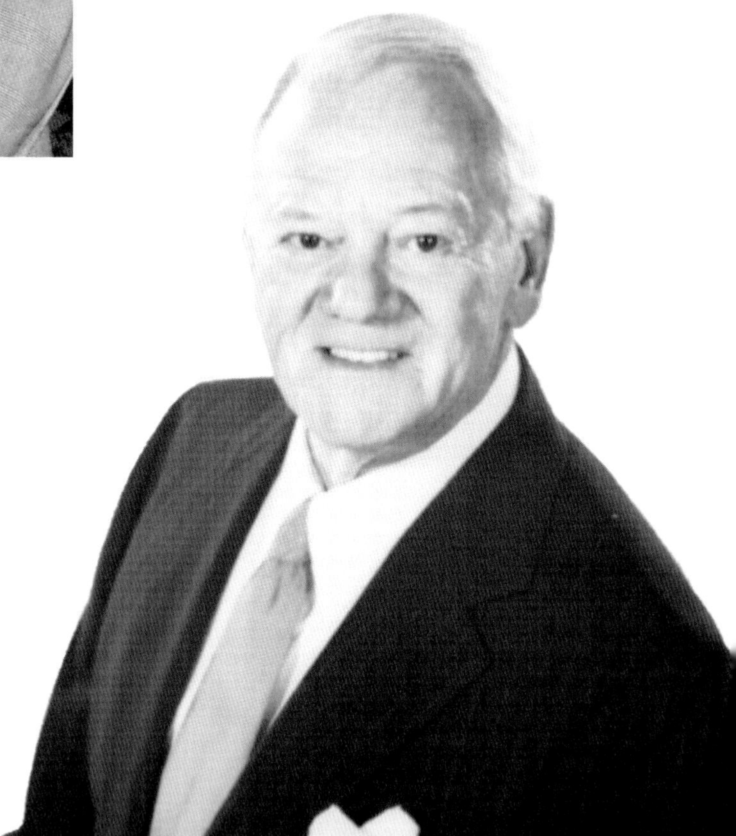

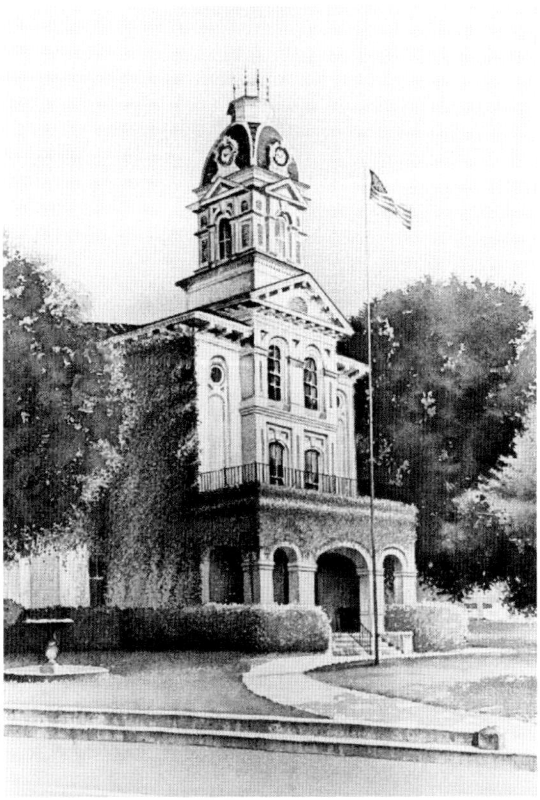

Mel Kester
Concord artist Kester was to pastoral scenery what Norman Rockwell was to Americana—from noble landmarks to quaint hideaways, his paintings of yesteryear radiated with warmth and photorealism. On occasion, Kester generously allowed signed prints of his portraits to be marketed as charity fundraisers, including this rendition of the 1876 Historic Courthouse, which the first 488 sustaining or patron members of Historic Cabarrus, Inc., received when that group was formed in 1973. Also shown is Kester's recreation of a vintage postcard depicting downtown Concord in the early 1900s, issued as part of Concord's bicentennial celebration in 1996. An avid horseman, Kester died in 2004.

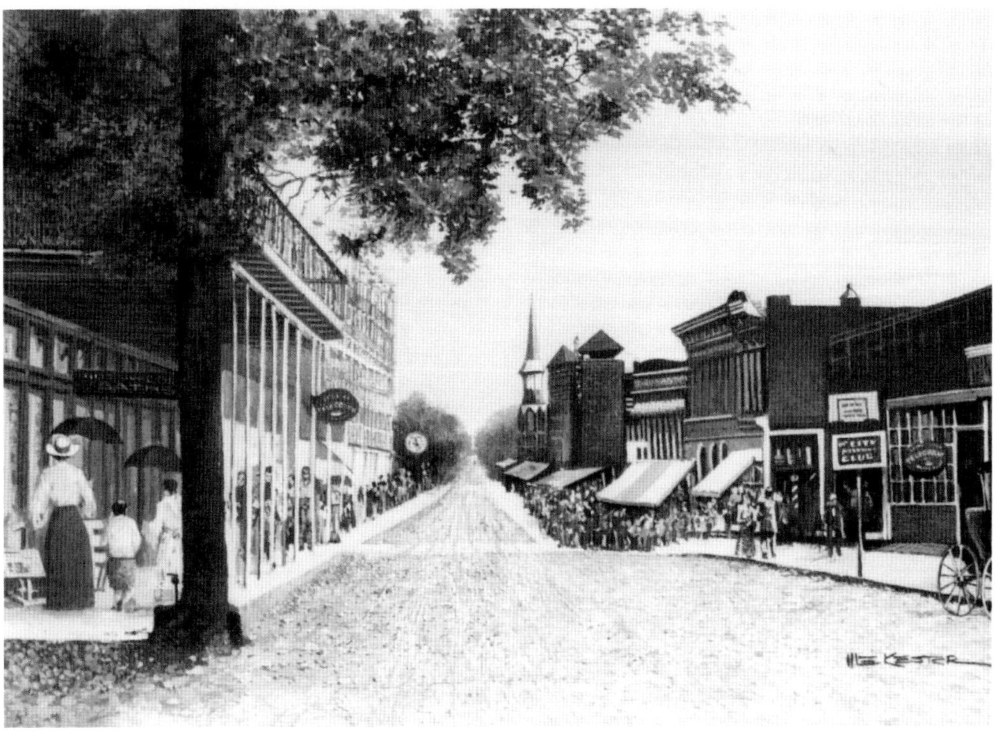

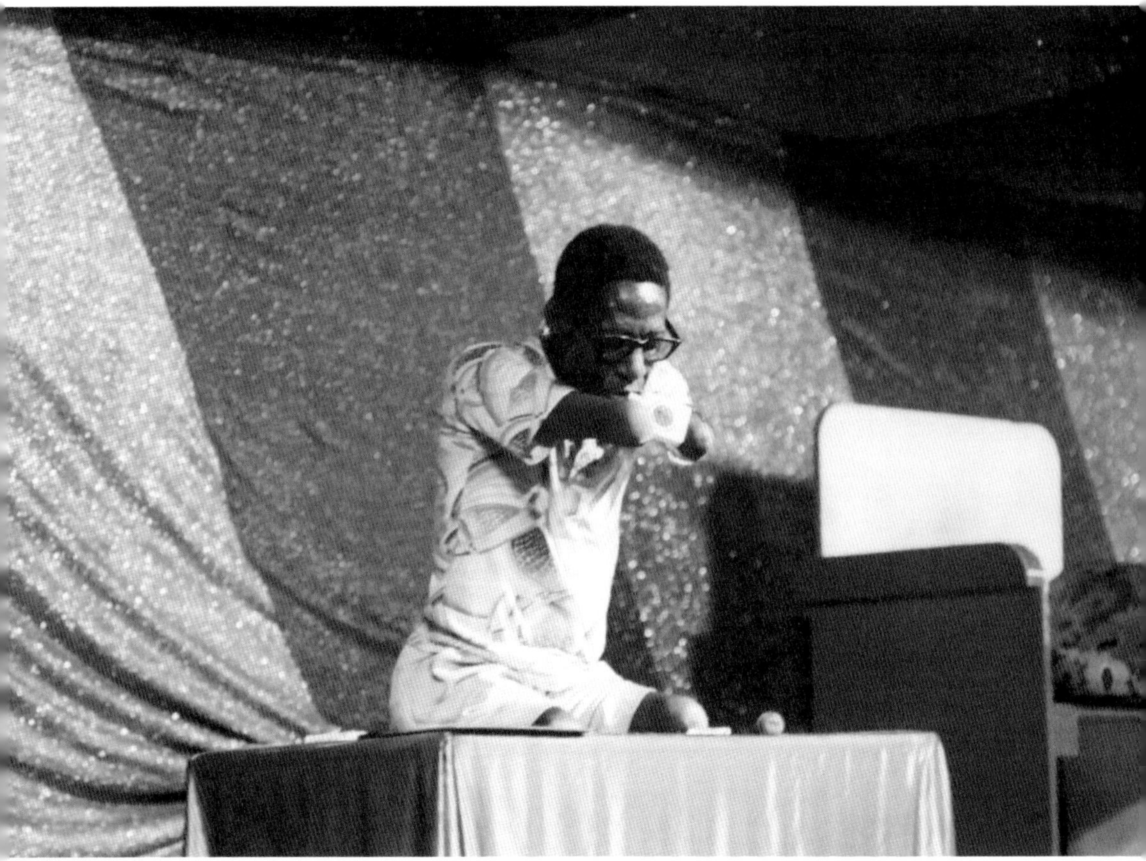

Emmett Blackwelder

Some might have accused Blackwelder's father of cruelty because he refused to help his young son (born with partial limbs) with routine endeavors including dressing. Yet that fostered an autonomy that the Concord native parlayed into a sideshow career as a juggler known as "the Turtle Man." Blackwelder retired from the road in 1978 and returned to Concord, marrying his hometown sweetheart. He died in 1996. (Photograph by Nick DeWolf; courtesy of Steve Lundeen.)

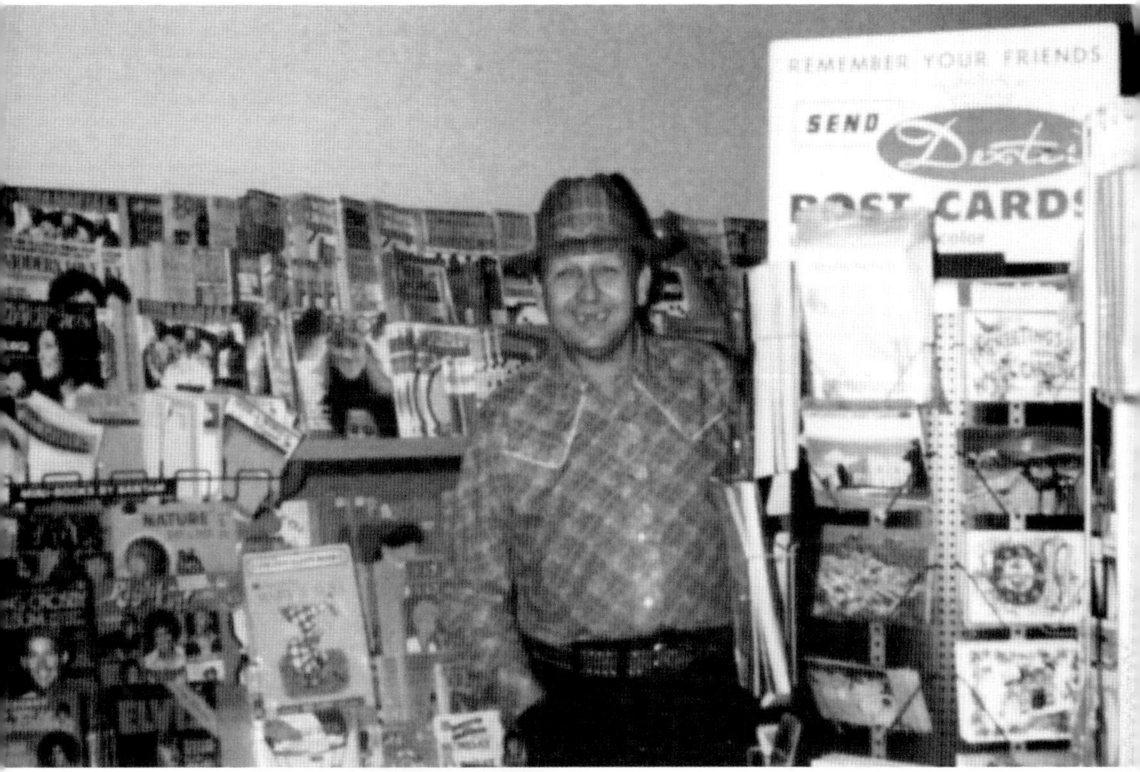

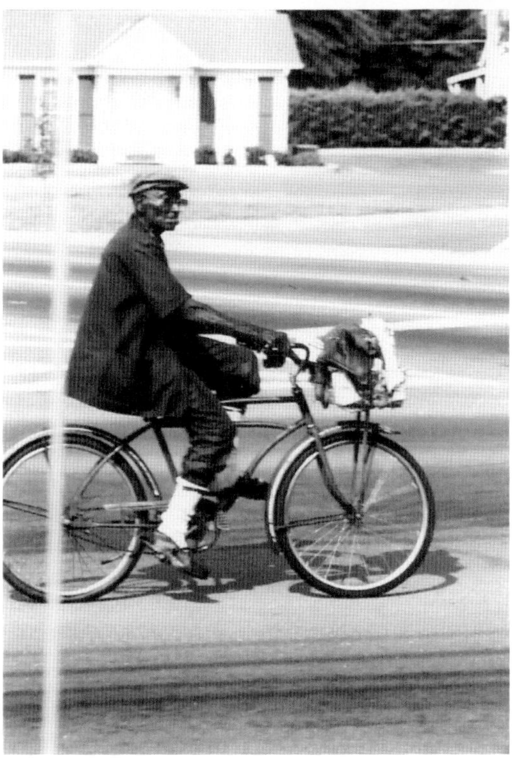

Robie Wright

This cantankerous but likeable character was a downtown Concord fixture from the 1960s through the early 1990s. Locals enjoyed good-natured ribbing with Wright, but his huffy "Shut up, by God!" would signal that your conversation had reached an abrupt end. Rarely seen without his cigar and transistor radio, he earned his living mowing lawns. This 1977 photograph shows Wright inside his hangout, Williams Candy Kitchen. (Photograph by author.)

Walter Rainey

You could never predict where you might spot this bicycling tatterdemalion, collecting refundable bottles or salvageable junk. Legend has it that Rainey led a normal life until a jilted girlfriend persuaded a "root doctor" to place a spell on him, making him undesirable to women. At various times, he called a cardboard box and dilapidated car his home. Rainey died in 1997 at age 88. (Courtesy of Bernard Davis Jr.)

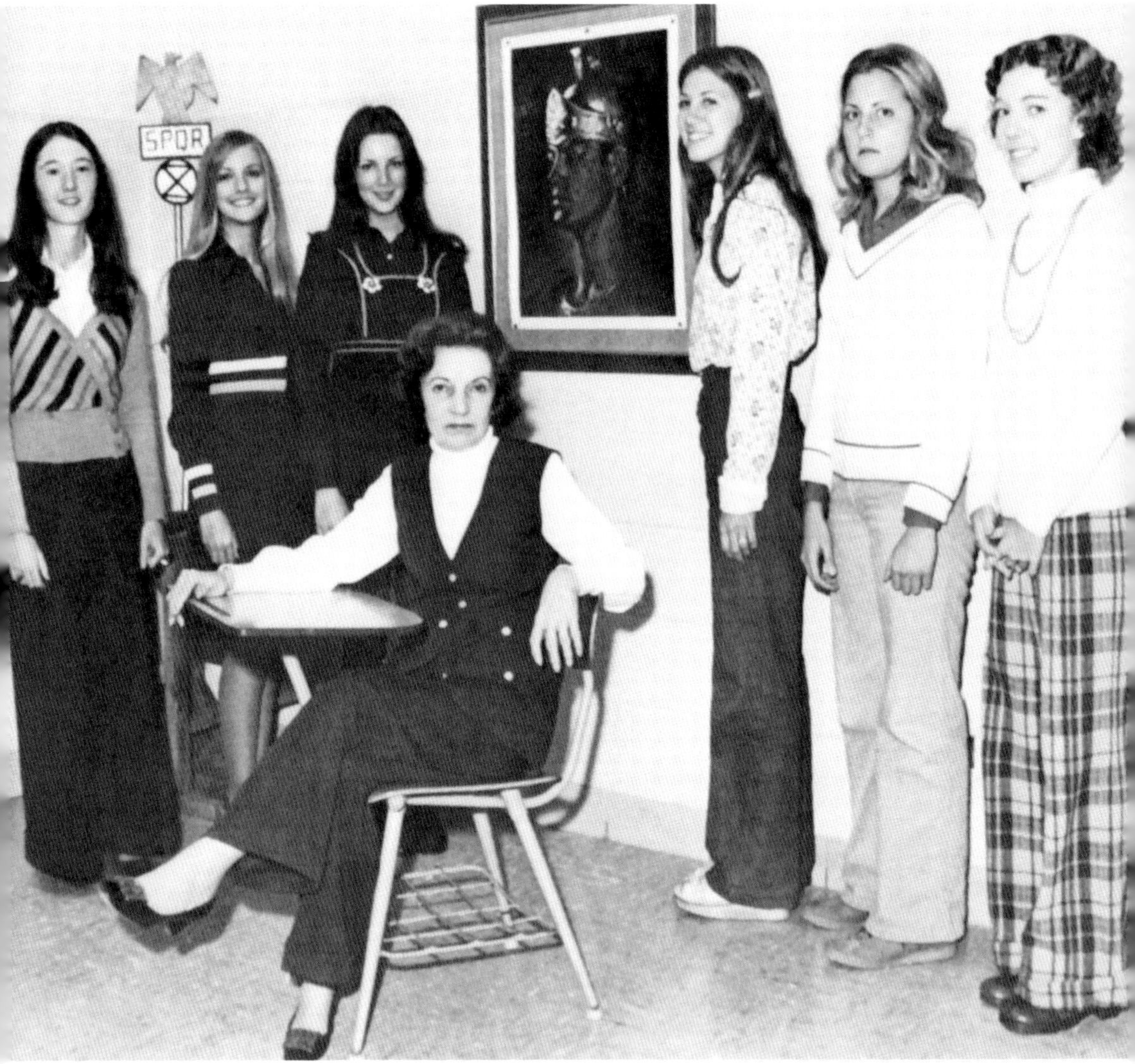

Silda Wall Spitzer

The daughter of Robert Wall, one-time administrator of Cabarrus Memorial Hospital, this member of Concord High School's Class of 1976 graduated with honors from Meredith College and Harvard Law School before becoming a successful Manhattan corporate attorney. She entered the national spotlight in early 2007 as the first lady of New York State. In March of the following year, a scandal forced her husband, Gov. Eliot Spitzer, to resign from office. During this difficult time, the folks back home, particularly CHS alumni who remembered Wall as a friendly, scholarly, and talented classmate, offered her an outpouring of support, their sentiments shared in an *Independent Tribune* newspaper article. She has also dedicated herself to raising three daughters and the development of nonprofit organizations, including Children for Children.

This photograph from the 1975 CHS *Spider Web* yearbook depicts Wall, then a high school junior, with the Junior Classical League. From left to right are Sara Cagle, Janet Ward Black, Patti Eller, adviser Lillian Stewart (seated), Wall, Elizabeth Moose, and Brenda Swan.

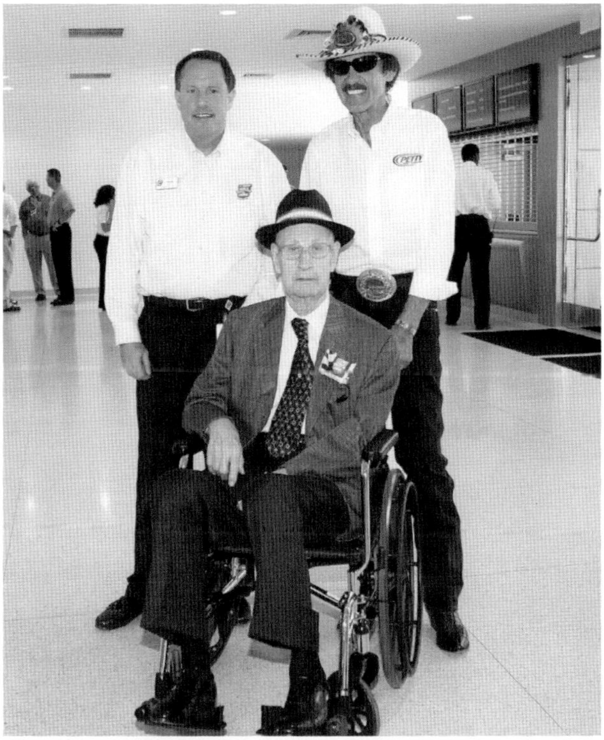

Winston Kelley
Concord native Kelley grew up in the fast lane. His father, Earl Kelley, was an acclaimed sports announcer and promoter. The younger Kelley began a motorsports-broadcasting career in 1988, detouring into an executive position with Duke Energy before being appointed executive director of Charlotte's NASCAR Hall of Fame. Kelley (left) is shown with NASCAR cofounder Raymond Parks and racing legend Richard Petty. (Courtesy of the NASCAR Hall of Fame.)

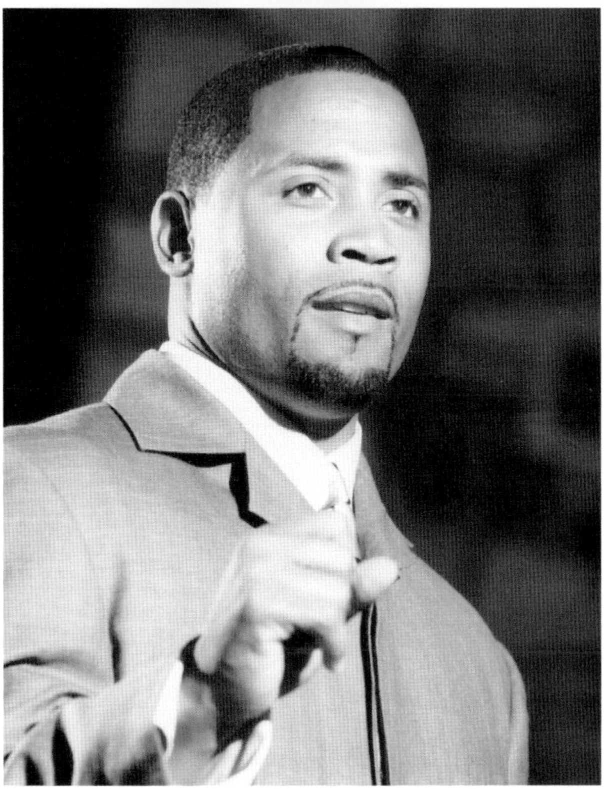

Mike Minter
From an exhilarating Super Bowl appearance to a crushing 1-15 losing season, this former Carolina Panthers star has experienced life's highs and lows firsthand. Through his Concord-based nonprofit Mike Minter Enterprises, he engages at-risk youth with motivational messages. Currently, Minter is the head football coach for Campbell University's Fighting Camels. (Courtesy of Mike Minter Enterprises.)

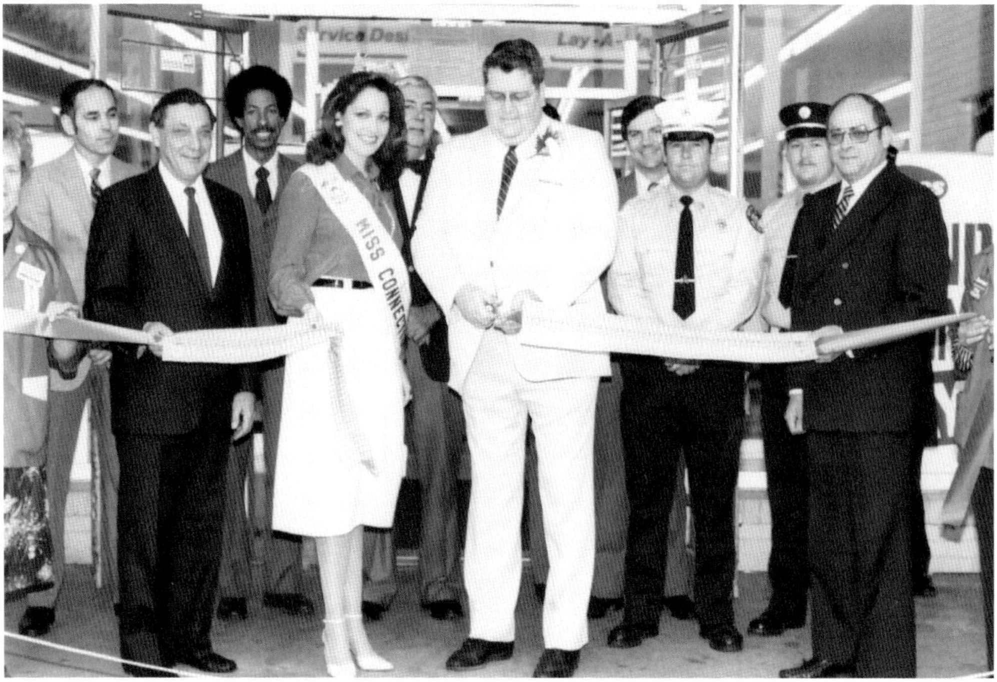

Dakeita Vanderburg Johnson

The winsome face of Southgate Masonry and Lumber, the business started in 1960 by her parents Hayden and Dot Vanderburg, Vanderburg Johnson is also recognized throughout Cabarrus County for her support of literacy and the arts. Many who know her from these capacities may be unaware of the gowns and crowns in her past. Vanderburg Johnson was Miss Mecklenburg County 1979. As Miss Connecticut 1983, she competed in the Miss America pageant. She warmly recalls the duties associated with the Miss Connecticut crown, including hospital visitations with wounded soldiers and the aged. The photograph above shows Vanderburg Johnson and Norwich, Connecticut, dignitaries at a 1983 business grand opening. The second image shows the 1983 Miss America pageant. (Courtesy of Dakeita Vanderburg Johnson.)

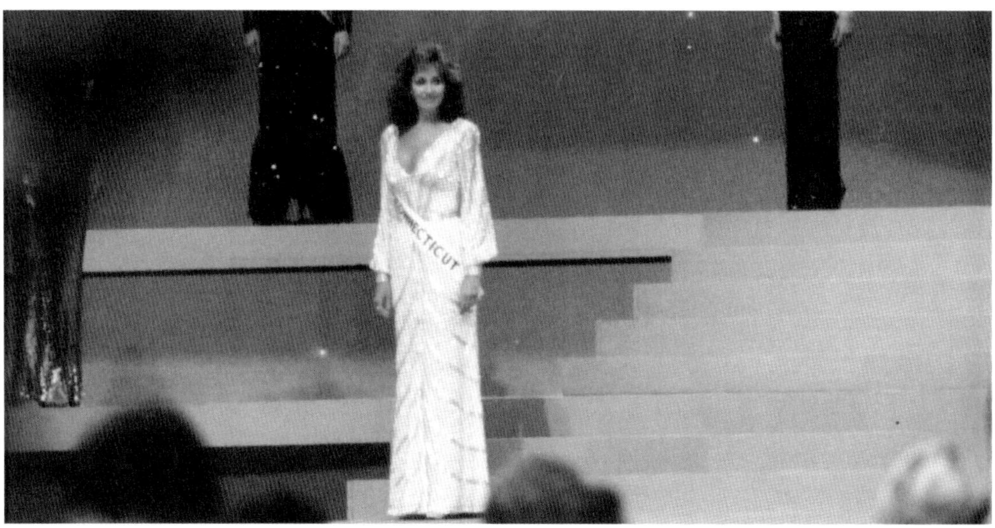

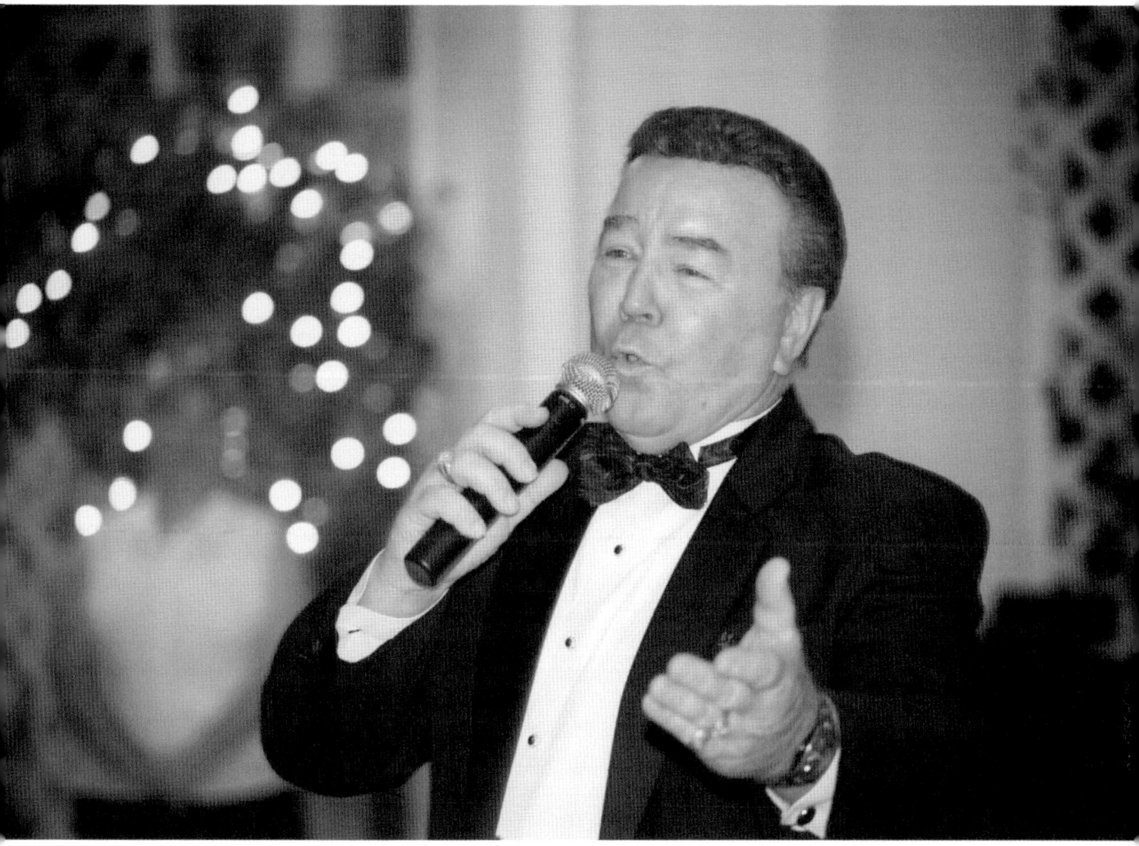

Daniel Truhitte

Amid a sartorial sea of overalls and plaid flannel shirts, Truhitte swims against the tide when having lunch at Troutman's Bar-B-Q on Church Street in Concord. In other towns, his tailored sport coat and satin pocket hankie might peg him as an outsider, but here, he is as familiar to locals as is the mound of red slaw on their chopped barbecue plate. Most know him as "the guy from *The Sound of Music*," and that he is: at age 20, Truhitte played Rolf Gruber, the messenger-turned-Nazi who, along with actress Charmian "Liesl Von Trapp" Carr, immortalized the song "Sixteen Going on Seventeen" in that 1965 film's unforgettable gazebo scene. He has an impressive stage résumé that has taken him from Las Vegas to Europe, and counts among his credits a US tour with Juliet Prowse as her lead singing and dancing partner. A California native, Truhitte has lived in Concord since 1991, making the town his home after settling down with a local gal, Tarealia "T.J." Today, he teaches young performers in the Concord area and continues to sing professionally, including the 2011 release of a catchy holiday single, "Christmas is Bustin' Out Again." Nearly half a century after the release of the movie that made him famous, Truhitte's association with *The Sound of Music* continues: in 2010, his rendition of "Sixteen Going on Seventeen" was heard in a Hyundai television commercial, and he is part of a tour to commemorate the film's golden anniversary. (Courtesy of Bella Zu Photography.)

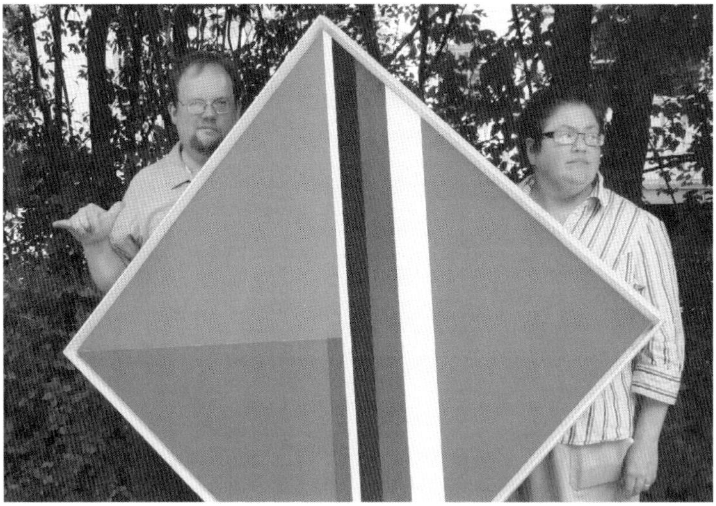

Beth Feeback

In mid-2012, Feeback was scrounging at Goodwill for framed art bargains—canvases to transform into another quirky cat portrait for which she is known around town. That day, she snagged a brightly hued, diamond-shaped painting for a mere $9.99, but a suspicious fellow artist urged her to research the painting's signature. After trolling the Internet and rifling through a paper trail, Feeback was floored to learn that she had purchased the original of "Vertical Diamond" by Russian painter Ilya Bolotowsky, one of the 20th century's leading abstractionists. As she told television personality Katie Couric in an April 2013 appearance on Couric's daytime show, Feeback's reaction to the discovery was "Ka-ching!" The episode was merely part of a blitz of national media attention Feeback received, and the Bolotowsky art netted over $34,000 (including a buyer's premium) at a Sotheby's auction. Feeback and husband, Steve, are shown here with the "Vertical Diamond," shortly after her fortunate find. (Courtesy of Beth Feeback.)

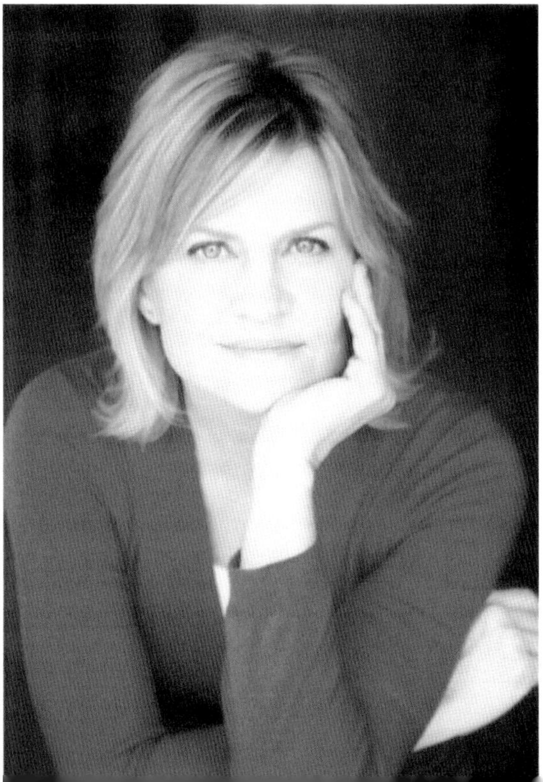

Carol Barbee

Her classmates from Central Cabarrus High School were thrilled when Barbee landed a part in a 1989 episode of NBC's *L.A. Law.* After a string of television and movie roles, Barbee transitioned into a successful career as a writer, producer, and executive producer. Among her credits are *Providence, Judging Amy, Three Rivers, Jericho, Hawaii Five-0,* and *Touch.* (Courtesy of Carol Barbee.)

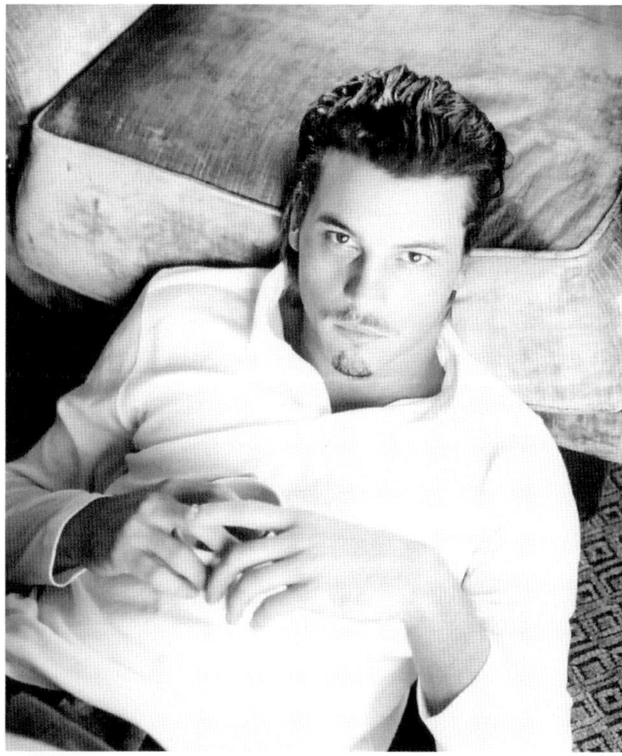

Skeet Ulrich
Born Bryan Ray Trout, Ulrich headed to Hollywood after graduating from Northwest Cabarrus High School in 1988. Garnering acclaim in the 1996 shocker *Scream*, he has since been seen theatrically in *As Good As It Gets* and on television in *CSI: NY* and *Law & Order: LA*. As Jake Green on the critically acclaimed series *Jericho*, Ulrich worked with another former Concordian, executive producer Carol Barbee. (Author's collection.)

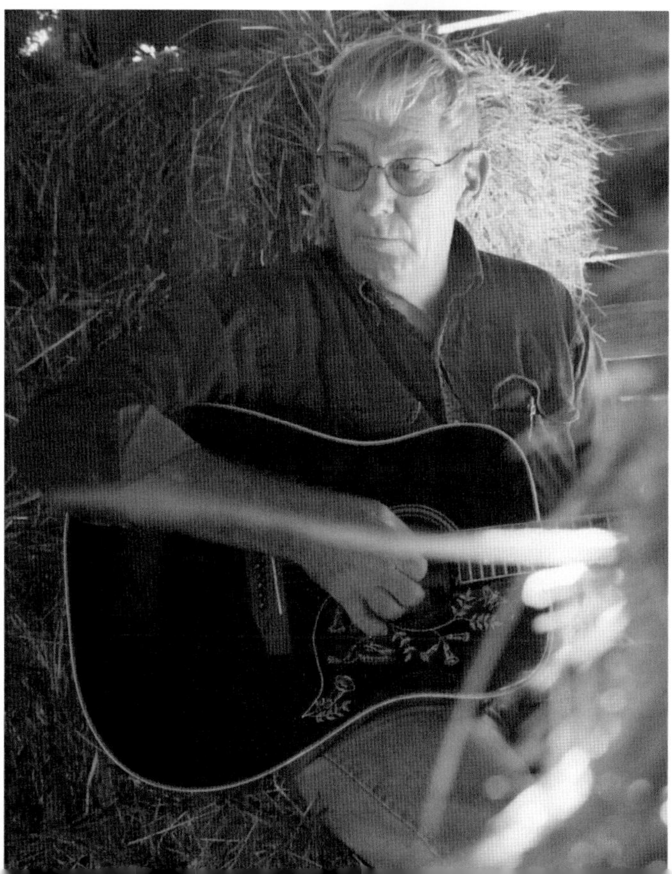

Jim Avett
Avett is a good daddy. His old man raised him right, as you might expect a preacher would, and his momma, a pianist, guaranteed he would never know a music-less moment. But love of family trumped the Muse's lure, and Avett devoted 35 years of his life as a welder to provide for his children, Bonnie, Scott, and Seth. His 2008 retirement handed him a second chance, and since then, he has been telling stories through song. Avett has released several CDs and tours regularly. (Photograph by Crackerfarm; courtesy of Ramseur Records.)

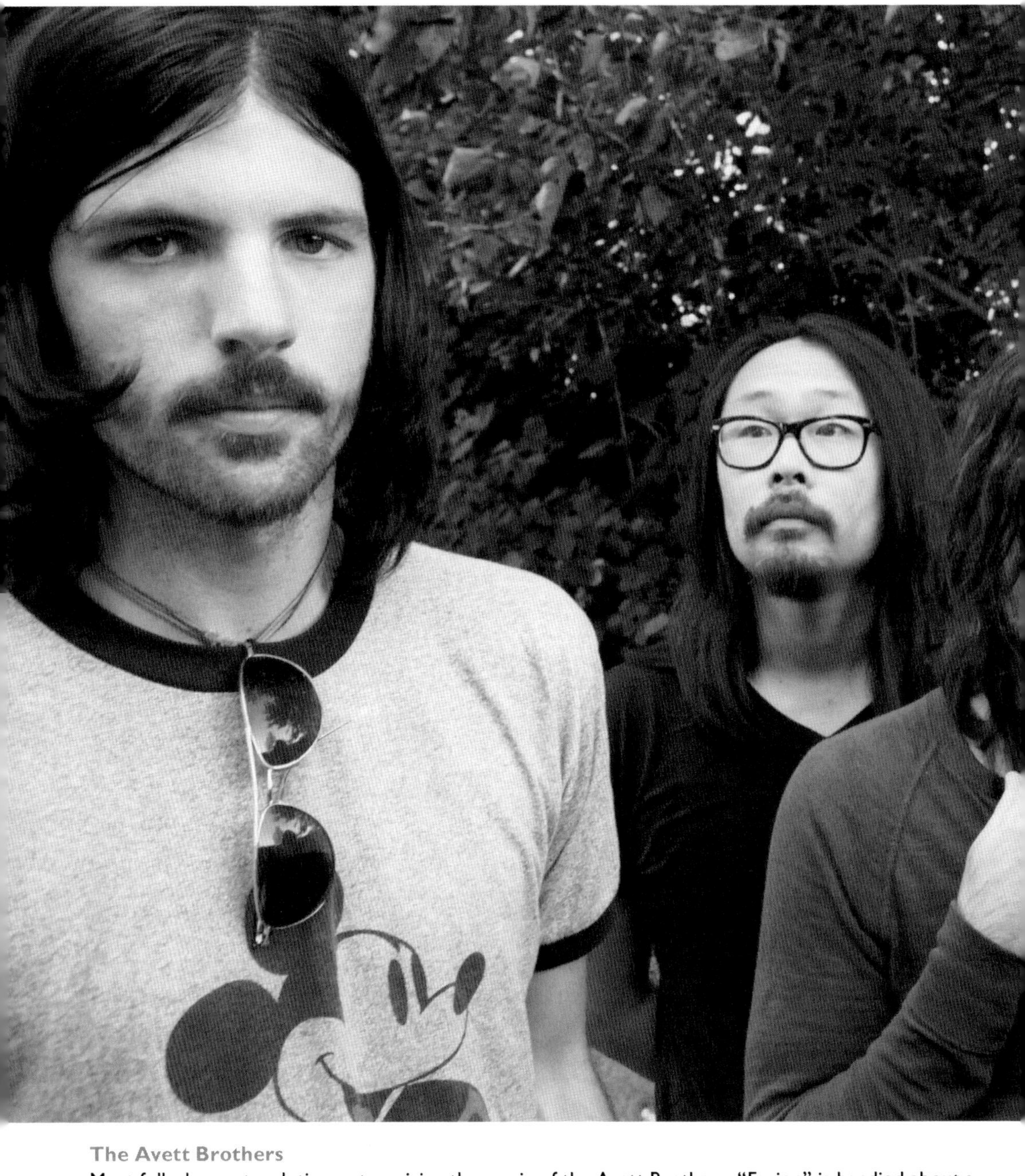

The Avett Brothers

Most folks have a tough time categorizing the music of the Avett Brothers. "Fusion" is bandied about a lot, a merger of rock, bluegrass, country, and folk, with some garage-band grunge thrown in at times. Their sound is also like Scott and Seth Avett's hometown of Concord, always in transition but never straying too far from its roots. The raw energy that the Avetts and bassist Bob Crawford displayed in their earliest gigs at dives and Dairy Queens in Concord and Charlotte is still there, but like the musicians themselves, their songs, their lyrics, and their harmonies have matured.

Scott and Seth, along with their sister Bonnie, grew up in a house filled with music, and their father, Jim, pushed the boys to take their guitar and piano lessons seriously. After playing with school-based

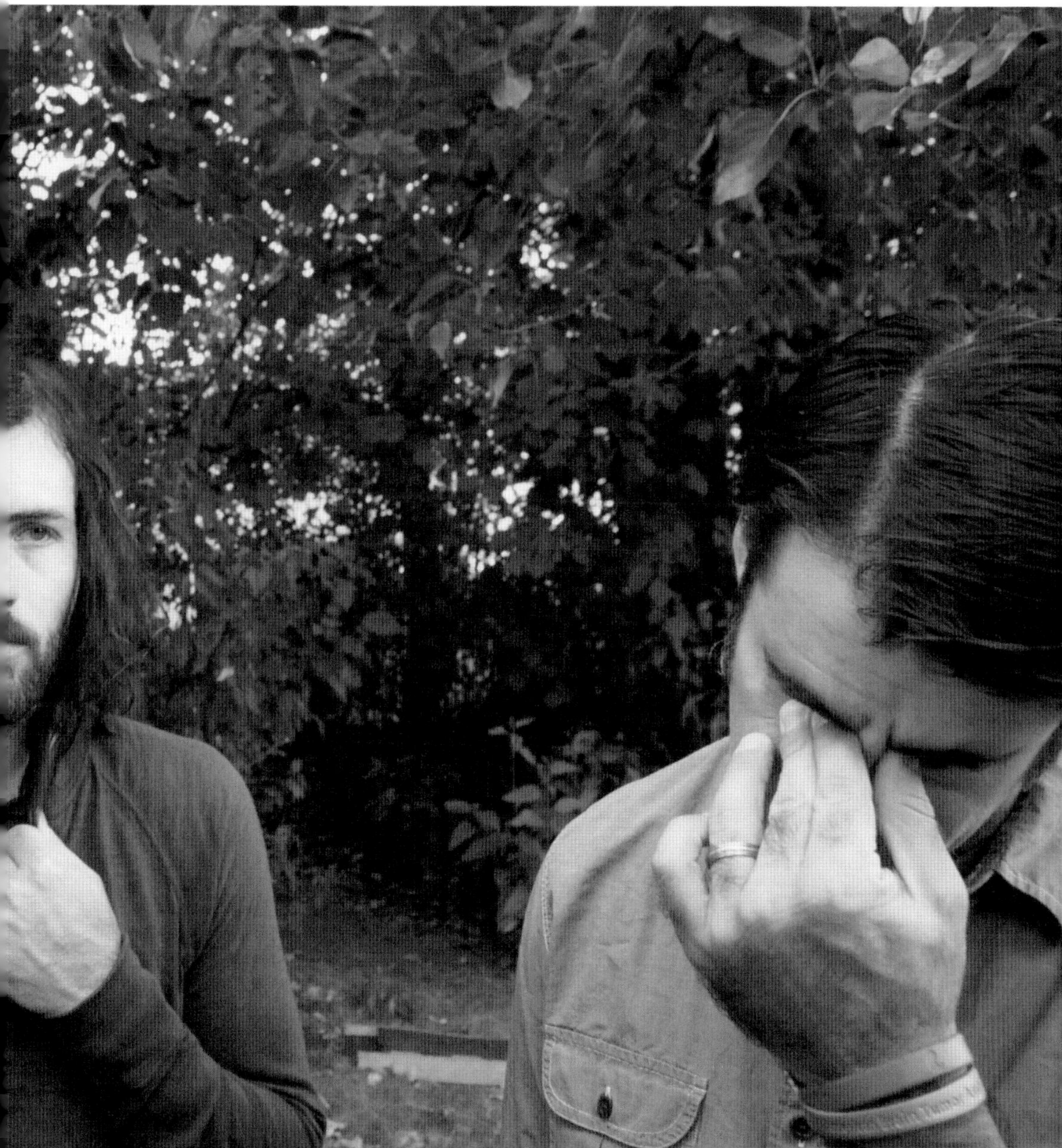

bands, the brothers and Crawford developed a local cult following in the early 2000s, attracting the eye of Concord record producer Dolphus Ramseur of Ramseur Records. With Ramseur as their manager, the Avett Brothers began an evolution that helped them build a national audience with a particularly rabid following in the indie-crazed Pacific Northwest. After scoring live performances on late-night television shows and at the 2011 Grammy Awards, their seventh studio album, *The Carpenter*, produced by Rick Rubin, was nominated for a 2013 Grammy in the "Americana" category. The Avett Brothers are now touring internationally, yet their hometown loyalties remain, with the band occasionally performing benefit concerts in the Concord area. From left to right are Seth Avett, Joe Kwon, Scott Avett, and Bob Crawford. (Photograph by Crackerfarm; courtesy of Ramseur Records.)

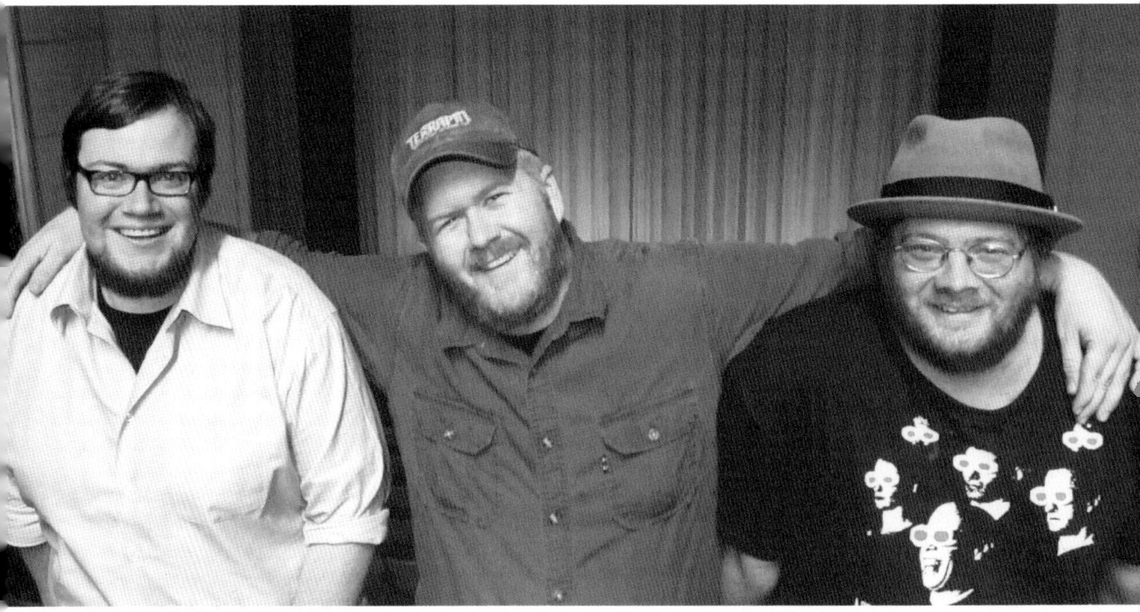

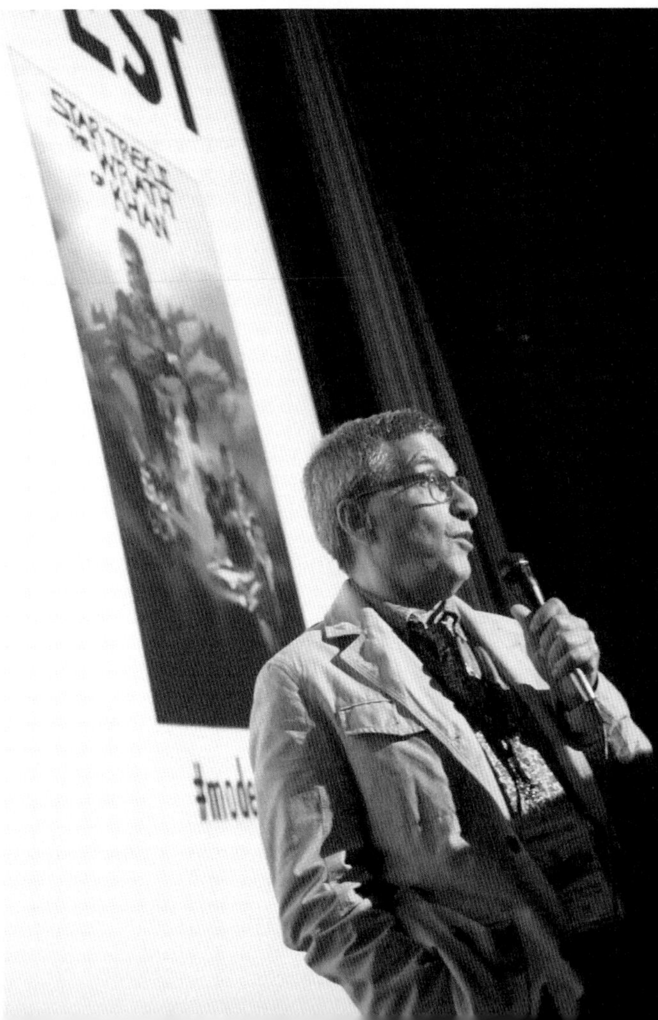

Modern Film Fest

Michael Knox's "harebrained idea" in 2009 to premiere his first movie documentary steamrolled into an annual film festival with a focus on North Carolina filmmakers, screened at the majestic Gem Theatre in Kannapolis. Knox (right) and colleagues Ben McNeely (left) and James Nix have watched their Modern Film Fest grow each year, adding monthly screenings at downtown Concord's Davis Theatre. While the festival's purview remains regional filmmakers and movies, in October 2012 the Modern Film Fest scored a coup by attracting as a guest Nicholas Meyer, the screenwriter, director, and author whose credits include *The Seven-Percent Solution*, *Time After Time*, and several *Star Trek* motion pictures. The Academy Award-nominated Meyer is shown here during a question-and-answer session that followed the festival's 30th anniversary showing of his film *Star Trek II: The Wrath of Khan*. (Both courtesy of the *Independent Tribune*.)

INDEX

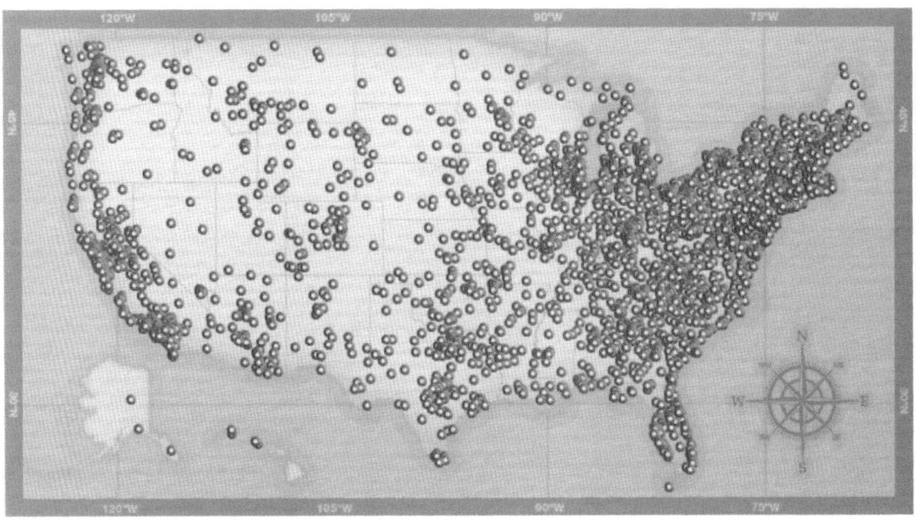

Consistent with our mission to preserve history on a local level, this book was printed in South Carolina on American-made paper and manufactured entirely in the United States. Products carrying the accredited Forest Stewardship Council (FSC) label are printed on 100 percent FSC-certified paper.